# MEMLING'S
*Portraits*

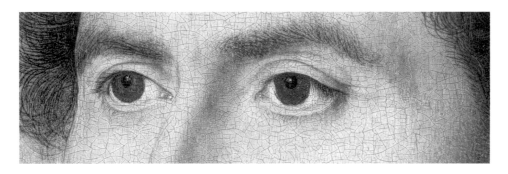

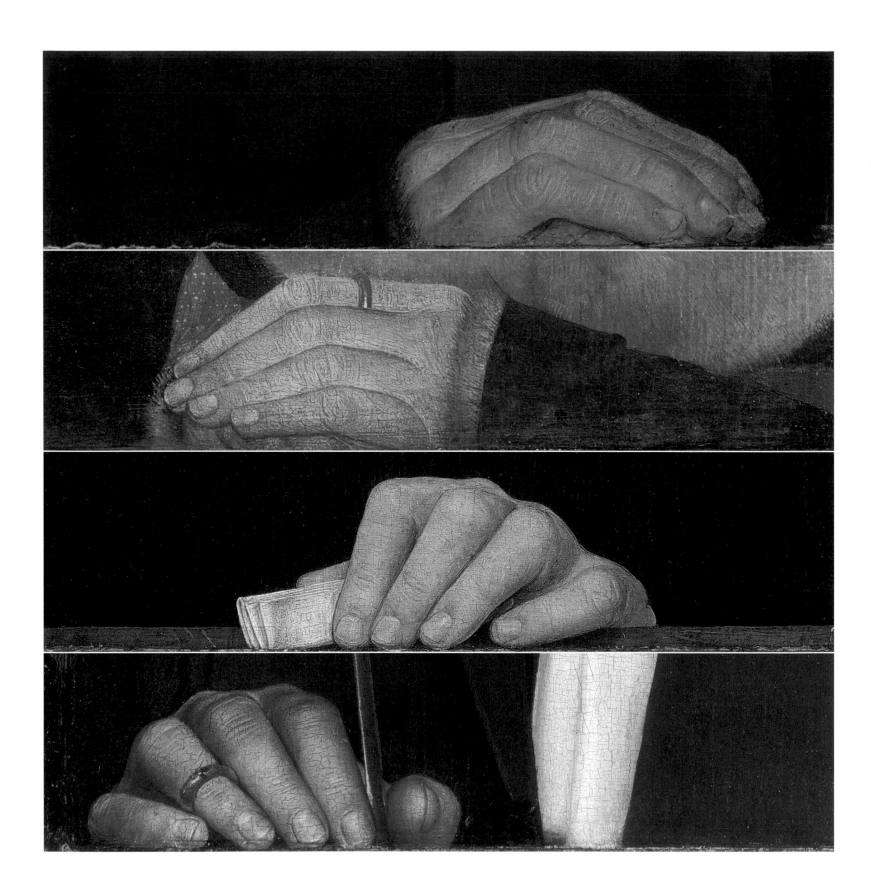

# MEMLING'S
## *Portraits*

Till-Holger Borchert

*with contributions by*
Maryan W. Ainsworth
Lorne Campbell
Paula Nuttall

*With 170 illustrations, 120 in color*

 Thames & Hudson

First published on the occasion of the exhibition
"Memling's Portraits"

Museo Thyssen-Bornemisza, Madrid
15 February – 15 May 2005

Groeningemuseum, Bruges
7 June – 4 September 2005

The Frick Collection, New York
6 October – 31 December 2005

**Curator of the Exhibition**
Till-Holger Borchert

**Organizing and Scientific Committee**
Colin B. Bailey, *Chief Curator, The Frick Collection*
Till-Holger Borchert, *Curator, Groeningemuseum*
Tomàs Llorens, *Chief Curator, Museo Thyssen-Bornemisza*
Walter Rycquart, *Managing Director, Stedelijke Musea*
Manfred Sellink, *Artistic Director, Stedelijke Musea*
Mar Borobia, *Curator of Old Master Paintings,*
   *Museo Thyssen-Bornemisza*

*Translation from the German:*
Kristin Lohse Belkin *(catalogue entries)*
Ted Alkins *(Till-Holger Borchert's essay)*
*Editor:* Paul van Calster
*Designer:* Antoon De Vylder
*Typesetting:* Anagram, Ghent
*Colour origination and printing:* Die Keure, Bruges

First published in 2005 in hardcover in the United States of America by
Thames & Hudson Inc., 500 Fifth Avenue, New York, New York 10110

thamesandhudsonusa.com

© 2005 Ludion Ghent-Amsterdam; the authors
© 2005 English edition: Thames & Hudson, Ltd

Library of Congress Catalogue Card Number 2004118016

ISBN-13: 978-0-500-09326-9

ISBN-10: 0-500-09326-1

Printed and bound in Belgium

# Contents

# Preface and Acknowledgements

Just over a decade ago, the Municipal Museums of Bruges organized a major monographic exhibition devoted to Hans Memling; in 2002, it mounted the tremendously ambitious 'Age of Van Eyck: The Mediterranean World and Early Netherlandish Painting, 1430–1530'. Given the scope of both projects and the scale of the loans (the majority on panel), it was understandable – if regrettable – that neither of these exhibitions was able to travel.

In the final stages of preparing the latter exhibition, Manfred Sellink, Artistic Director of Bruges' Stedelijke Musea, and Till-Holger Borchert, Curator of the Groeningemuseum, approached Colin B. Bailey at The Frick Collection about the possibilities of future collaboration. Portraiture as an aspect of Memling's work was considered ripe for re-examination, and the Frick's early *Portrait of a Man*, acquired in 1968, was in principle available for loan. Tomàs Llorens, Chief Curator of the Museo Thyssen-Bornemisza, Madrid, enthusiastically embraced this project, and a three-venue exhibition, with showings on both sides of the Atlantic, came into being. Given the constraints of borrowing works on panel for more than one venue, it was agreed that the presentation would be slightly different at each institution, but that the three venues would share a group of core loans and publish the same catalogue. It is with pleasure and gratitude that we acknowledge the pioneering role of the Municipal Museums of Bruges, whose collections and expertise in the field of fifteenth-century Netherlandish art are without equal.

In keeping with the earlier exhibitions noted above, it is our hope that 'Memling's Portraits' will make a significant contribution to our understanding of early Netherlandish painting and stimulate further research in the field. The introductory essays to the catalogue are exemplary in their various approaches: from stringent stylistic and visual analysis, via a consideration of Memling in a European context (notably the relationship with Italian Renaissance portraiture), to the insights and refinements that technical examination can bring to the fragile consensus on Memling's chronology. For these, we are indebted to Paula Nuttall, Lecturer, Victoria & Albert Museum, London; Lorne Campbell, Research Curator, National Gallery, London; and Maryan W. Ainsworth, Curator, European Paintings Department, The Metropolitan Museum of Art, New York. The introductory essay and the catalogue itself, written by Till-Holger Borchert, provide complete entries on all of Memling's portraits and felicitously summarize the current state of research on this issue, while not infrequently challenging it and suggesting avenues for future enquiry.

Above all, we are most grateful to the museums that have generously agreed to participate in this exhibition. At the Groeningemuseum, we thank Till-Holger Borchert – the exhibition's principal impresario, who selected the loans and lobbied tirelessly on the project's behalf. We are also grateful to Walter Rycquart, Managing Director, Stedelijke Musea, and Véronique De Schepper, Acting Loan Registrar. We appreciate the support of Brugge Plus, organizers of Bruges' Corpus 05 festival for the arts, wherein this exhibition will occupy a prominent place. For their generous support of this exhibition, it is a pleasure to acknowledge the Openbaar Centrum voor Maatschappelijk Welzijn, Bruges, and its chairman, Frank Vandevoorde. At the Museo Thyssen-Bornemisza, we are grateful to Mar Borobia, Curator of Old Master Paintings, and Lucia Cassol, Head Registrar, who have handled flawlessly and with consummate professionalism the practical arrangements for this exhibition. The presentation of the exhibition in Madrid has been generously supported by the Banco Urquijo. Peter Ruyffelaere, Director of Ludion Press, and Paul van Calster, who edited the catalogue, were most helpful coordinators of the production of the catalogue.

At The Frick Collection, we thank Chief Curator Colin B. Bailey, who has been a tireless advocate for the project and who is responsible for the selection in New York; Diane Farynyk, Registrar and Head of Exhibitions, who has coordinated the shipping for all three venues, with the assistance of Joanna Sheers and Allison Galea; and Elaine Koss, who supervised the production of the English-language edition of the catalogue with the help of Margaret Iacono and Mary Lydecker. In New York, major funding for 'Memling's Portraits' has been provided by The Peter Jay Sharp Foundation, with generous support from Melvin R. Seiden in honour of Joseph Koerner, Meg Koster, and Leo Anselm Koerner; The Samuel H. Kress Foundation; and The Helen Clay Frick Foundation. Additional support has been provided by the Fellows of The Frick Collection.

We also wish to acknowledge the following individuals:
Lut Autloos, Maria Elisa Avagnina, Julie Bakke, Stephanie Belt, Edgar Peters Bowron, Douglas Brine, Helena Bussers, Véronique Bückens, Jos Casier, Alessandro Cecchi, Guy Cogeval, Minora Collins, Michael Conforti, Hilde De Bruyne, Yolande Deckers, Jan de Maere, Livia Depuydt, Elisabeth Derveaux, Antoon De Vylder, Simon Dickinson, Frits Duparc, Rhoda Eitel-Porter, Carlos Fernández de Henestrosa y Argüelles, Susan Foister, Katherine M. Gerlough, John Oliver Hand, Astrid Huth, Paul Huvenne, Laurence B. Kanter, Jan Kelch, Peter Klein, Cécile Krings, Alistair Laing, Barbara G. Lane, Frederik Leen, Bernd W. Lindemann, Christopher Lloyd, Hilde Lobelle, Mauro Lucco, Alexandru Lungu, Anne Luyckx, Mireille Madou, Peter C. Marzio, Philippe de Montebello, Susi Nash, Giovanna Nepi Scirè, Annamaria Petrioli Tofani, Charles E. Pierce Jr., Peter van der Ploeg, Kadi Polli, Timothy Potts, Earl A. Powell III, Richard Rand, Jochen Sander, Karl Schütz, Jennifer Scott, Cécile Scaillerez, Myriam Serck, Ron Spronk, Eva Tahon, Griet Teetaert, Pierre Théberge, Roxana Theodorescu, Dominique Thiébaut, Laurence van Kerkhoven, Robert van Nevel, Muriel Vervat, Giovanni Villa, Malcolm Warner and Martha Wolff.

Manfred Sellink, *Artistic Director, Stedelijke Musea, Bruges*
Tomàs Llorens, *Chief Curator, Museo Thyssen-Bornemisza, Madrid*
Anne L. Poulet, *Director, The Frick Collection, New York*

# Lenders to the Exhibition

**Belgium**

Antwerp, Koninklijk Museum voor Schone Kunsten [cat. 10]

Bruges, Stedelijke Musea, Groeningemuseum [cat. 22]

Bruges, Stedelijke Musea, Memlingmuseum – Sint-Janshospitaal (OCMW) [cat. 17 and 23]

Brussels, Musées Royaux des Beaux-Arts de Belgique [cat. 7 and 18]

**Canada**

Montreal Museum of Fine Arts [cat. 19]

Ottawa, National Gallery of Canada [cat. 4]

**Germany**

Berlin, Staatliche Museen, Gemäldegalerie [cat. 5]

Frankfurt, Städelsches Kunstinstitut und Städtische Galerie [cat. 1]

**Italy**

Florence, Galleria degli Uffizi [cat. 8, 11 and 24]

Venice, Galleria dell'Accademia [cat. 16]

Vicenza, Museo Civico, Pinacoteca [cat. 27]

**The Netherlands**

The Hague, The Royal Cabinet of Paintings Mauritshuis [cat. 21]

**Romania**

Sibiu, Museum Sammlung Samuel Brukenthal [cat. 14]

**Spain**

Madrid, Museo Thyssen-Bornemisza [cat. 25]

**United Kingdom**

Banbury, Bearsted Collection, National Trust, Upton House [cat. 26]

The Royal Collection, H. M. Queen Elizabeth II [cat. 12]

**United States of America**

Fort Worth, The Kimbell Art Museum [cat. 28]

Houston, The Museum of Fine Arts [cat. 9]

New York, The Frick Collection [cat. 2]

New York, The Metropolitan Museum of Art, Robert Lehman Collection [cat. 15]

New York, The Pierpont Morgan Library [cat. 20]

Washington, National Gallery of Art, Andrew W. Mellon Collection [cat. 13]

Williamstown, Sterling and Francine Clark Art Institute [cat. 3]

**Private collection** [cat. 6]

Till-Holger Borchert

# Memling – Life and Work

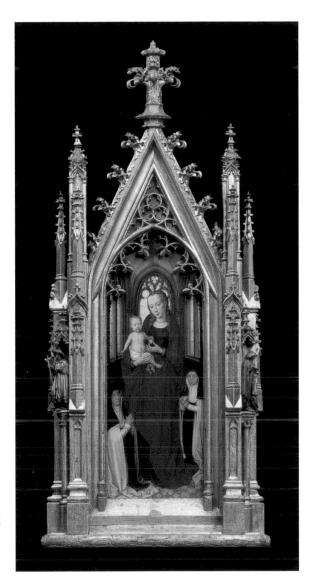

fig. 2
Memling
St Ursula Casket, detail
Bruges, Stedelijke Musea,
Memlingmuseum –
Sint-Janshospitaal

fig. 1
Memling
*Portrait of a Man with a Coin of the
Emperor Nero (Bernardo Bembo?)*
[cat. 10], detail of pl. 11
Antwerp, Koninklijk Museum voor
Schone Kunsten

In addition to being one of the key painters of fifteenth-century Bruges – alongside Jan van Eyck, Petrus Christus and Gerard David – Hans Memling has long been numbered among the most important exponents of early Netherlandish art as a whole. With almost a hundred surviving paintings traditionally ascribed to Memling or his workshop, the scale of his oeuvre lends it a prominent position among Netherlandish painters before 1500, while also identifying him as one of the most productive and versatile masters of his era.[1]

The extant oeuvre allows a relatively firm reconstruction of Memling's activities as a painter – there is a series of works for which we have been able to identify the patron, while other paintings can be securely dated by means of inscriptions or other sources. But when it comes to the artist's biography, whole swathes remain entirely obscure. What information we *can* glean from contemporary documents referring to Hans Memling does not exactly paint a detailed picture of the artist's life and circumstances. What is more, those sources are predominantly legal or administrative in character and so focus primarily on property, money and legal matters. The information they provide is limited to certain highly specific details of Memling's life, as is the case with most of the painters active in Flanders in the period in question. Only through painstaking detective work – combining snippets of information from different archives and comparing them with contemporary sources – has it been possible to reach certain conclusions regarding the reality of Memling's life in Bruges in the latter part of the fifteenth century.[2]

In addition to the archival material, art-historical texts from the sixteenth, seventeenth and eighteenth centuries contain some interesting remarks about Memling. Taken together with the biographical details and the painter's firmly ascribed oeuvre, these enable us to formulate plausible hypotheses regarding the artist's career.[3]

The earliest archive reference to Memling dates from 1465: on 30 January of that year, the painter paid 24 Flemish shillings – equivalent to one month's wages for a craftsman – to acquire citizenship of Bruges. Foreigners settling in the Flemish town had to register as citizens before being permitted to engage in business or to pursue their profession there. Citizenship could be acquired through marriage, by spending 'a year and a day' in the city or by paying a fee. The fact that Memling opted for the latter tells us two things. Firstly, he had the financial resources to purchase citizenship immediately on arriving in Bruges and to become professionally active in the prosperous Flemish trading metropolis without delay. It also suggests that it was as an independent master that Memling arrived in Bruges early in 1465 and hence that he had already put in his years as apprentice and journeyman.

We can now safely say that before moving to Bruges, Memling was employed in Rogier van der Weyden's workshop in Brussels and that he did not seek to set up an atelier of his own until immediately after Rogier's death in 1464. The master–apprentice relationship between the two painters was cited by Giorgio Vasari and is supported by clear stylistic parallels including – especially in Memling's early works – the general character of the underdrawing and the way the painted layers are structured. Moreover, Memling continued throughout his career to borrow motifs and compositions from the repertoire of the Brussels city painter.[4] As time went by, however, he increasingly adapted them, throwing in models from early Bruges painting – Van Eyck and Petrus Christus – to achieve a highly personal style of expression that came to function as an exemplar for local contemporaries like the Master of the Legend of St Ursula.

The relevant entry in Bruges' *Poorterboek* (citizens register) for the years 1454–78 fails to tell us from which town Memling came to Bruges. It does, however, provide some important details regarding the painter's origins and parentage: the birthplace of *Jan van Mimnelinghe* is given as the German town of Seligenstadt, while his father's name is recorded as *Hamman*.[5] Seligenstadt's *Anniversarienbuch* lists two annual commemorations for Memling's parents in 1451 and 1454. *Hamman Mommeling* and *Luca Styrne* came from Kleinkrotzenburg, a village to the north of Seligenstadt and probably succumbed to the plague outbreak that struck the Middle Rhine and Cologne area in 1450, as recorded in the *Koehlhof'sche Chronik*.[6] Memling had most likely left his parental home by that time in order to start his training as an artist; he appears to have been about thirty years old when he took Bruges citizenship, which would place his birth not much later than 1435.

Interestingly, there were evidently people in both Bruges and Seligenstadt who remembered Memling's origins in subsequent years. Bruges chronicler Rombout de Doppere's record of the painter's death on 11 August 1494 gives Memling's birthplace as Mainz ('*oriundus erat Magunciaco*'),

although this probably does not refer to the city itself but to the territory ruled by the powerful Archdiocese of Mainz, to which Seligenstadt had belonged since 1309.[7] The painter's memory also persisted in his native town; four memorial masses for '*Henn Mommelings, burger zu Pruck in Flandern*' (... citizen at Bruges in Flanders) were paid for in 1540/41 and 1543/4 – half a century after the artist's death.[8]

While by no means exerting a significant influence on his work, Memling's Middle Rhenish origins were less unusual than might appear at first sight. Fifteenth-century Bruges was an international financial and trading metropolis that attracted many business and tradespeople from Italy, Spain, France, England and Germany; many of them settled there semi-permanently. The citizens registers of the period form an impressive record of the many foreigners who adopted Bruges citizenship each year to enable them to carry out a highly varied range of occupations. Bruges' international character and the relative prosperity of its inhabitants made it particularly attractive to people involved in the production of luxury goods; in addition to panel paintings, these included illuminated manuscripts and goldsmith's work. There was ample demand in the city for products of this kind, holding out the promise of a secure livelihood.

As far as his origins were concerned, therefore, Memling was by no means exceptional among the city's painters. On the contrary, virtually all the artists we think of today as typical exponents of Bruges painting and whom we know by name were actually 'foreigners' – they did not come from Bruges or even from the County of Flanders: Jan van Eyck was born in the Prince-Bishopric of Liège and had previously worked in Holland before settling in Bruges in 1432 as court painter to the Duke of Burgundy; Petrus Christus, who was registered as a Bruges citizen in 1444, originally came from Baerle in Holland; Gerard David came to the Flemish city in 1484 from Ouwater near Haarlem; and Jan Provost, who obtained citizenship in 1494, was born in the town of Mons in Hainaut and had previously worked in Valenciennes (in present-day France). The register of the Bruges corporation to which panel painters, canvas painters, saddlers, stained-glass artists and mirror-makers all belonged, includes numerous painters from Germany: Hugo Noben from Aachen, Jan van Heppendorp and Nikolaas van Keersbeck from Cologne, Willem van Varwere from Wesel, Konrad de Valckenaere from Uden and Maarten van Keinsele, whose

birthplace cannot be identified any more specifically.[9] All together, the foreign panel painters who registered with the Bruges corporation in the fifteenth century accounted for more than half of the total.[10]

Memling's own status raises further questions; for one thing, it is surprising that he never held any official position within the organization during the almost thirty years that he was active in Bruges: he neither represented the interests of the craft in court cases, which Petrus Christus is recorded as doing on several occasions, nor did he occupy any administrative posts in the board as, for instance, Gerard David and Jan Provost did.[11] It seems likely that Memling received a sufficient supply of private commissions right from the outset and would thus not have had to rely on the craft network for public commissions. This view is supported by the fact that, unlike Christus, David and Provost, Memling never received any commissions from Bruges' civic authorities, despite working for politically influential local families like the Moreels and Van Nieuwenhoves.[12]

Another feature of Memling's professional life is even more striking: although he obtained the required citizenship in 1465, the register of the painters' corporation shows no trace of any initial enrolment on the artist's part; this in spite of the fact that painters had to register with the craft if they wanted to work in the city. The only exceptions to the rule – which also entailed payment of membership dues – were artists attached to the court, which was demonstrably not the case with Memling.[13] The most plausible explanation for this is a slip on the part of the corporation's record-keeper, who simply forgot to note Memling's name in the register as required. He is certainly recorded in later years as the master of two apprentices (1480 and 1483), and his name also features in the obituary list of the Bruges Guild of St Luke – the religious confraternity to which painters belonged. Other than Memling, only seven out of a total of 245 members of the painters' corporation (all of them, oddly enough, panel painters) were not registered properly on joining it between 1453 and 1525.[14]

Memling's personal circumstances remain largely obscure, too. There are virtually no precise details regarding his financial situation, for example, and what few secure facts are available are open to interpretation. The artist evidently lived in 1466–7 in a complex comprising two brick buildings on Vlamingdam and Jan Miraelstraat

– the likely owner of which at the time was a certain Johannes Goddier. Memling himself acquired the larger of the two houses – on which the painter Lodewijk Boels, who also probably came from Brussels, paid the property tax in 1470 – no later than 1479/80; it remains to be ascertained, however, when the second building was purchased.

Although the fact that Memling became a property owner is by no means evidence of exceptional prosperity, it nevertheless suggests a solid financial situation and the savings to go with it. Nor was property ownership unusual for other panel painters, sculptors, goldsmiths or members of privileged crafts in general. Calculations suggest that an average craftsman had to work for about 25 years to save the money to buy a house; in Memling's case, just under fifteen years elapsed between his registration as a Bruges citizen and the purchase of his home. Judging from the tax returns of the district in which his houses were located, he did not live in one of the more prestigious parts of Bruges but in an area that was chiefly home to artisans and their families.[15] Memling's house – and most likely his workshop, too – had the homes of other artists as direct neighbours: one example is the Utrecht-born illuminator Willem Vrelant, but Gerard David, Jan Provost, Lancelot Blondeel, Antoon Claeissens and Pieter Pourbus all subsequently lived in the district as well. It was near the Augustinian abbey, which was a favoured institution for the endowment of altars and other foundations by the foreign merchant communities in Bruges – particularly those from Spain, Italy and Nuremberg.[16]

Significantly, Memling took on his first apprentice, Hannekin Verhanneman, in 1480 – shortly after buying his own house in Bruges. The second, Passchier van der Meersch, followed in 1483.[17] We may infer from this that the artist's personal and professional situation was in sufficiently good shape at that time to afford him the money and space he needed to start training apprentices. We may also safely assume that he was already married by then to Tanne, who died no later than 1487 leaving the painter with three under-age children – Hannekin, Neelkin and Claykin. The inventory of the family's possessions drawn up on the death of his wife offers important testimony to the true state of the artist's finances and his social relationships.[18] The orphans' board in Bruges traditionally awarded guardianship of non-adult offspring to relatives of the deceased parent. In the case of Memling's children, it was the guardians' duty to oversee the children's

*figs. 4–5*
Robert Campin
*Portrait of a Man*; *Portrait of a Woman*
London, National Gallery

maternal inheritance, which was estimated at the time at 12 *livres tournois* and probably comprised the wife's dowry. They came from the higher reaches of the artisan class and included a goldsmith, which tells us something about the painter's social status and his involvement with the community.

There is, after all, no evidence that Memling enjoyed any particular social prestige in Bruges that would have enabled him to rise beyond the station of his better-placed colleagues.[19] Late-medieval society was certainly not so dynamic that his professional relationship with patrons drawn from the urban élite will have had any lasting impact on his own status. The extent of his possessions – of which we gain a broad impression from the municipal orphans' records – places him firmly among the more prosperous of the city's craftsmen. However, people like this by no means enjoyed the same opportunities for social advancement as members of established patrician families, high-ranking Burgundian court officials or international financiers – all of whom tended to model their lifestyle on that of the aristocracy.

The painter's financial situation was certainly not static; like those of Bruges' other residents, Memling's wealth was hard hit by the economic crisis of the 1480s and the accompanying inflation. He had probably earned a certain amount of money before coming to Bruges, and having arrived there, he continued to save in the ensuing years so that by 1480 he had the funds he needed to buy a house of his own. He seems to have reached the financial zenith of his career at this point, as that same summer he was one of a total of 875 individuals assessed as the richest 10% of Bruges' citizens, who were obliged to finance a loan to the municipal authorities in support of Archduke Maximilian's military campaign against France. Memling's contribution to the compulsory loan was one Flemish pound – an amount extracted from 300 other citizens, too. The other 574 were required to lend larger amounts, with two paying as much as 20 Flemish pounds each.[20] Much has been made of this source in the literature, where it has been taken as evidence of Memling's wealth and social standing.[21] What is overlooked, however, is the fact that the painter's name does not crop up again in connection with subsequent loans (this method of raising money was applied at regular intervals from 1487 onwards); nor is there any trace of the artist's name in connection with the purchase of annuities or lotteries. It may be concluded from this that Memling's financial situation – like that of most of his fellow craftsmen – was adversely affected by the economic crisis that struck Bruges in the 1480s. Although he was probably able to maintain his standard of living – he was not obliged, for instance, to sell off any of his property – he would never again be numbered amongst the city's wealthiest inhabitants.[22]

Memling's membership from 1473 of the renowned Confraternity of Our Lady of the Snow is a similarly ambiguous piece of evidence.[23] The organization owed its name to the commemoration all over Flanders every 5 August of the foundation of Santa Maria Maggiore in Rome. Judging by the social prestige it enjoyed, it was one of Bruges' most prominent religious brotherhoods. It was originally founded by the tailors' guild, but membership was opened up in the second half of the fifteenth century to all the city's professions and crafts. The tailors enjoyed particular esteem within the Bruges crafts hierarchy, and membership of the confraternity was increasingly extended to representatives of prominent local families and senior Burgundian court officials. They were joined by wealthy merchants and diplomats like the Scottish envoy Alexander Bonkil and Giovanni and Michele Arnolfini, and by Bruges 'proto-humanists' such as Antonius de Roovere and Aliamus de Groote. Even more important, however, was the involvement of high-ranking Burgundian-Netherlandish nobles, among them Isabel of Portugal, Charles the Bold, Philip of Cleves and Louis of Bruges, Lord of Gruuthuse, which further enhanced the confraternity's prestige.[24] Charles the Bold was especially attached to the organization, which in 1472 was given its own chapel in the collegiate church of Our Lady, of which the duke was the most prominent patron. Unsurprisingly, members of the ducal chapel also belonged to the confraternity and probably played an active part in its religious services. Charles's court painter Pierre Coustain was a member as well; for some reason, he paid his membership dues for nineteen years in advance.[25]

In addition to Hans Memling himself, the confraternity's membership included his neighbour Willem Vrelant and Petrus Christus and his wife. A distinguished religious organization, its principal aim was to care for the souls of its almost one thousand members, many of whom were undoubtedly drawn from the same circles in which Memling and Christus customarily sought their patrons. It is reasonable to assume, therefore, that it was

*fig. 6*
Rogier van der Weyden
*Portrait of a Woman*
Staatliche Museen zu Berlin, Preussischer
Kulturbesitz, Gemäldegalerie

*fig. 7*
Jan van Eyck
*Portrait of a Man ('Leal Souvenir')*, 1432
London, National Gallery

*fig. 8*
Memling
*Portrait of Gilles Joye* [cat. 3], 1472
Williamstown (Mass.), Sterling and
Francine Clark Art Institute

*Memling – Life and Work*  ■

not only religious motives that drew the painters to join – the decision must also have reflected the potential for contact with prospective customers. However, when the confraternity commissioned a new painted banner in 1480, they turned to another member – the painter Jan Fabyaen – rather than to Hans Memling.[26]

The fact that Memling was able to join such a prestigious organization in 1473 – barely eight years after moving to Bruges – shows that, within the bounds of the well-to-do craft community in which he operated, he was socially well established in his new home. We ought not, however, to draw any more far-reaching conclusions; on the contrary, the evidence suggests that Memling only belonged to one of Bruges' exclusive confraternities, whereas members of the city's true social élite tended to be members of several. Petrus Christus, for instance, also joined the Confraternity of Our Lady of the Dry Tree, which was based at the Franciscan abbey.[27]

The reality of Memling's life can, as we have seen, only be ascertained in fragmentary fashion from surviving legal and administrative documents; that it did not differ substantially from that of other established colleagues is, however, apparent even at the moment of his death. Writing in the fourth book of his Bruges chronicle (which survives only in a sixteenth-century Latin translation), Rombout de Doppere, secretary of the collegiate church of St Donatian's, recorded that Memling died on 11 August 1494. As noted above, De Doppere stated that the artist had been born in Mainz and also recorded his burial in the cemetery of the church of St Giles in Bruges ('*sepultus Brugis ad Aegidii*') – the parish in which the artist's house was located.[28] The painter's finances did not stretch to a burial place inside the church, as was customary for members of Bruges' social élite. Of all the artists active in the city in the fifteenth century, Jan van Eyck seems to have been the only one to have enjoyed the privilege of being interred inside a church – and St Donatian's at that. Even in Van Eyck's case, however, this was not until after his brother succeeded in having the body transferred to the church, which also functioned as the ducal chapel.[29]

Memling's resting place, by contrast, is entirely in keeping with his social status and profession. It is intriguing, none the less, that the artist did not make arrangements for a requiem mass to be celebrated for him in Bruges, unlike several of his fellow painters we know to have done so. The only archival evidence of a memorial service held

for him in Bruges appears in the records of the Confraternity of Our Lady of the Snow; and, curiously, another memorial mass is recorded half a century after his death in his Middle Rhine birthplace.[30] All this bolsters the conclusion to be drawn from a critical reading of contemporary documents touching on the circumstances of Memling's life, namely that he was a prosperous but by no means especially wealthy member of his profession and that, unlike the case of Van Eyck, his artistic talents did not lead to any special privileges.

Another aspect deserves our attention in this context: as noted earlier, Memling was the only one of the Bruges painters we have been able to identify in the fifteenth and early sixteenth centuries who appears never to have received official commissions from either the city or the Franc of Bruges (the surrounding jurisdiction). He is equally invisible when it comes to the large-scale decorative commissions handed out by the civic authorities and the Burgundian court in 1468 in connection with Charles the Bold's ceremonial entry into Bruges, the subsequent chapter meeting of the Order of the Golden Fleece and, finally, the celebrations marking the duke's marriage to Margaret of York.[31] To ensure that the huge decorative paintings would be ready on time, the court was obliged to bring painters to Bruges from all over the duke's territories – Jacques Daret and Hugo van der Goes among them.[32] Locally based artists appear to have been entirely engaged on the city's behalf with decorations for processions and the organization of a large number of *tableaux vivants*; Petrus Christus, for instance, was paid to restore a *Tree of Jesse* for the traditional Holy Blood Procession, which coincided with the chapter meeting of the Golden Fleece.[33]

Memling's name, by contrast, is nowhere to be found in the civic accounts covering the festivities in question. It is entirely feasible, of course, that not every painter who contributed to the decorative works was specifically named in the accounts – some of them might, after all, have subcontracted some of the work to other artists whom they paid directly. However, unlike Petrus Christus, Memling did not receive official commissions from the Bruges civic authorities at any time in his career; this, allied with the fact that he began to work for highly positioned patrons immediately after arriving in the city, suggests that there were other factors behind the artist's failure to participate in the decorative commissions that arose in 1468.

fig. 9
Master of the St Ursula Legend
*Portrait of Ludovico Portinari*
Philadelphia Museum of Art,
John G. Johnson Collection

One plausible explanation is that Memling was able to specialize in panel painting from the outset and that the commissions he received removed any financial imperative to bother with restoration work, ephemeral decorations or paintings on canvas. In 1478/9, Memling was commissioned to paint wings for a carved wooden shrine for the book illuminators' (*librariërs*) guild, based at Eekhout Abbey in Bruges. Unlike his contemporaries in the city, whom the records show to have carried out similar work on a regular basis, this is the only commission of its kind that Memling is known to have accepted. Willem Vrelant, himself a book illuminator and member of the guild, appears to have acted as intermediary and financier; later descriptions of the now-lost altarpiece reveal that the painter included portraits of Vrelant and his wife in the wings.[34]

The lost donor wings of the illuminators' altarpiece are the only Memling commission, moreover, to be mentioned in contemporary sources. He had already been living in Bruges for almost fifteen years when he received it in 1478/9; he was an established painter in the city and, as far as we can tell, was at the financial peak of his career. He could also look back on an impressive sequence of important commissions carried out during the stable political and economic climate of the late 1460s and 1470s.

The fact that some of those commissions were received immediately after his arrival in Bruges suggests that he must already have built up a solid reputation by that time, probably thanks to the period he spent working in Van der Weyden's atelier. Memling seems to have collaborated – most likely in Brussels – on a large altarpiece for Ferry de Clugny (died 1483) which remained unfinished on Van der Weyden's death but was subsequently completed in his workshop. All that now remains of that work is a monumental Annunciation scene (New York, Metropolitan Museum).[35] Clugny was a senior Burgundian official who was appointed chancellor of the Order of the Golden Fleece in 1473 and Bishop of Tournai a year later; Memling might have made his acquaintance through the aforementioned commission. A courtier of such prominence could undoubtedly have recommended Memling to influential patrons in Bruges, although the painter's earlier collaboration with Rogier might have been sufficient recommendation in itself.

Whatever the case, shortly after settling in Bruges, Memling was commissioned to paint a triptych, the component parts of which are now to be found in several

different collecti[...]
however, thanks [...]
or eighteenth cen[...]
tic grounds, the p[...]
likely to have bee[...]
or oratory. The [...]
surrounded by t[...]
Mary Magdalene, John the Baptist, Bernard of Clairvaux
and a Cistercian abbot kneeling in prayer. Two other wor-
shippers – an elderly woman and a younger man – appear
in the wings, each under the protection of their respective patron saints, Anne and William of Maleval (fig. 13);
the closed wings have an Annunciation scene. The donor,
who is accompanied by his patron saint, John the Baptist,
and by the founder of his Order, St Bernard, is no less a
figure than Jan Crabbe, abbot (1457–88) of the powerful
Cistercian abbey of Ter Duinen near Koksijde. Crabbe
instructed the artist to include his 80-year-old mother,
Anne Willemszoon, and his nephew, Willem de Winter.[37]
The condition of the individual panels – especially that of
the central Crucifixion – is far from perfect, substantially
affecting our ability to judge their appearance. Because
of its heavily abraded surface, from which the fine layers
of glaze that provided the modelling have entirely disappeared, the central panel now creates an oddly clumsy
impression and contrasts, at least partially, with donor
wings that are more characteristic of Memling.

For the composition of this Crucifixion scene – which, if
only for the prominent and exacting patron,[38] must have
been an important commission – Memling resorted to the
example of his recently deceased teacher, Rogier van der
Weyden, and hence to Brussels painting in general, offer-
ing persuasive evidence in the process of his artistic background. Rogier's influence is immediately apparent in early
works such as the Brussels *Virgin and Child* (fig. 12), which
no doubt formed part of a small portrait diptych or triptych (fig. 33). The repertoire of motifs and styles on which
Memling drew in the 'Triptych of Jan Crabbe' is set out
in Van der Weyden's *Crucifixion* triptych for Oberto Villa
(Riggisberg), and above all in his Vienna *Crucifixion* and in
the triptych for Alessandro Sforza that has been attributed
to his workshop.[39] The triptych's detailed underdrawing,
done with the paintbrush, is also closely related to Rogier
in terms of graphical repertoire and strongly resembles a
number of drawings that have recently been attributed to
Rogier's Brussels follower Vrancke van der Stockt.[40]

*fig. 10*
Memling
Diptych of the *Virgin and Child with
Angels, St George and a Donor*
Munich, Alte Pinakothek

*fig. 11*
Detail of fig. 10

Another commission that Hans Memling received in the 1460s appears substantially more important and artistically far more ambitious; it emanated from the Florentine banker Agnolo (or Angelo) Tani, who ran the Medici's Bruges operations between 1450 and 1464. The painting, a *Last Judgement* triptych now in the Muzeum Narodowe in Gdańsk, is one of the largest works that Memling ever produced (figs. 14, 41);[41] its turbulent history has been discussed at length on a number of occasions. The triptych was ordered from Memling by Agnolo di Jacopo Tani, head of the Medici bank in Bruges, for his chapel in the Badia Fiesolana. The finished work was dispatched by sea in 1473 by Tommaso Portinari, his successor in the Flemish city. It was carried by a Florentine galley operating under the Burgundian flag, which set off from Bruges' outport of Sluis to sail to Pisa via England. Shortly after departing, however, it was captured off Gravelines on 27 April 1473 by the privateer Paul Bennecke from Danzig (Gdańsk). Memling's *Last Judgement* altarpiece was landed in the northern German town of Stade with the rest of the booty, where it was claimed by members of the Danzig crew. In spite of Portinari's protests and written interventions, they subsequently had it installed in the chapel of the Confraternity of St George in Danzig's church of Our Lady.[42] We thus know that the triptych, which would inevitably have taken several years to paint, was completed no later than 1473; it is unclear, however, precisely when Tani first placed the commission.

The Florentine banker had already left Bruges for his native city by the end of April 1464 to get his contract extended. While he was away, Portinari managed to have himself appointed head of the Bruges branch by the Medici in 1465. Relations between Portinari and Tani cannot have been affected by this as dramatically as the literature tends to claim, as professional business contacts between the two bankers continued largely as if nothing had happened. Tani, who retained a financial stake in the Bruges operation, married Caterina Tanagli in Florence in 1466. As Caterina, whose family were wealthy merchants, appears on the closed wings of the altarpiece opposite her husband, and as she had been engaged to Filippo Strozzi until September 1465, it would seem that Memling did not receive the commission for the painting until after the couple's wedding. Furthermore, the aisle chapels in the Badia Fiesolana were completed no earlier than the end of 1466, when Francesco Sassetti was the first to be

*fig. 13*
Memling
Triptych of Jan Crabbe
Vicenza, Museo Civico (centre panel);
New York, The Pierpont Morgan
Library (wings)

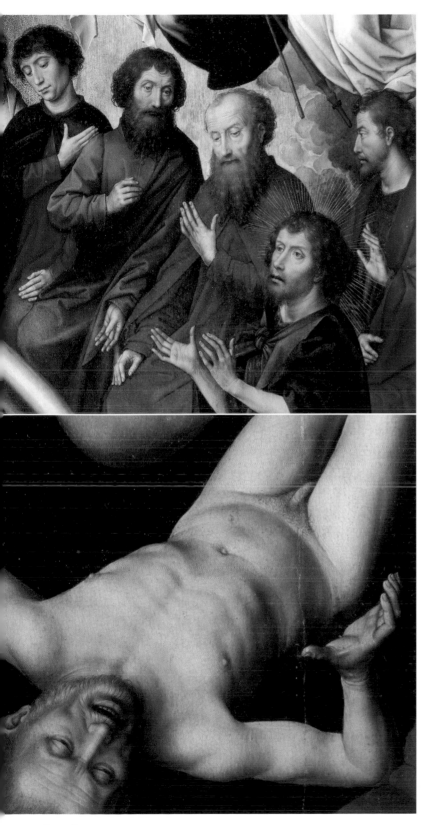

*fig. 14a–f*
Memling
*The Last Judgement* triptych, details
Gdańsk, Muzeum Narodowe

granted endowment rights there, followed shortly afterwards by Tani.[43] Tani may therefore have conceived the idea of installing a Flemish altarpiece in his family chapel – a move that must have seemed nothing short of spectacular given the time and place – some time in 1467, when he realized that he would have to return to Northern Europe on business; the London branch of the Medici bank had run into financial difficulty and he was ordered to go and sort things out.

On 12 December 1467 he drew up a will naming his wife as beneficiary in the event of his death and then set off over land for London, arriving there on 12 January 1468.[44] Although it is not implausible to imagine Tani pausing briefly in Bruges to order the triptych at that point, it is more likely (if we leave aside the possibility that the order was placed by letter) that the altarpiece commission was not placed with Memling until the summer of 1468. Tani's duties in England included the financing of Margaret of York and Charles the Bold's wedding – the London branch of the Medici bank loaned Edward IV 10,000 pounds to help pay for the event. The guarantor was Sir John Donne of Kidwelly, who also went on to commission a triptych from Memling (see below). It is highly probable that Tani came back to Bruges in mid-1468 as part of Margaret of York's retinue.[45]

The opulently staged wedding celebrations, at which Tommaso Portinari paraded at the head of a horseback contingent from Bruges' Florentine merchant community, took place in July 1468. Tani would have had plenty of time to specify his wishes regarding the commission and to negotiate payment and delivery details with Memling. He would also have had to provide the artist with an Italian portrait drawing of his young wife – who had never visited the Netherlands – as the basis for her donor's portrait (the style of which suggests that an artist from the circle of Filippo Lippi might have been responsible for the drawing). He would then have returned to his business commitments in London. Tani spent several more weeks in the Netherlands in the summer of 1469, before finally returning that autumn to Florence and his wife, who bore him a daughter in 1471.[46]

It is intriguing to speculate that during his 1469 visit to Flanders, Tani took the opportunity to ascertain how Memling's work was progressing and to further specify how he wanted the finished painting to look. The artist would then have done his best to accommodate his client's wishes. Memling certainly made far-reaching changes to the composition at a fairly advanced stage of execution; these include the insertion of the Apostle group on either side of the *Deesis* (Christ sitting in judgement with his mother and John the Baptist) and the reconfiguration of the donor's coat of arms. Although we cannot say whether Tani really did visit Memling in person, alterations of this significance can only have occurred on the patron's express instruction.[47]

The composition of Memling's *Last Judgement* is heavily indebted to the polyptych on the same theme that Rogier van der Weyden painted in the mid-1440s for the hospital founded in Beaune by Nicolas Rolin, the powerful Burgundian chancellor;[48] this too may have been a specific request on the part of the Florentine banker. Yet there are signs in this work that Memling was beginning to assimilate the painting of Jan van Eyck, too. The triptych is characterized by its ambitious artistic effects, the elaborate foreshortening of the naked human bodies and the emulation of intricate surfaces and refined reflections; it is as if Memling wanted to show off his painterly skills and to lay claim to a place among the first rank of Flanders' artists.

Whatever the case, this highly prestigious commission seems to have attracted the attention and interest of the Italian businessmen who lived or traded in Bruges. Numerous members of the Florentine and – apparently – the Venetian merchant communities in Bruges seem to have commissioned portraits from Memling while he was still working on Tani's altarpiece; moreover, the souls of the blessed in the *Last Judgement* triptych have the faces of Florentine merchants, possibly in return for those same commissions (see cat. 13 and fig. 14a–b). Memling appears to have introduced landscape backgrounds for the portraits of his Italian customers at an early stage, while continuing to paint his local patrons in front of a neutral background in keeping with their more conservative tastes.[49]

Even Tommaso Portinari – Tani's alleged rival – commissioned Memling around that time to paint himself and his new bride Maria Bandini Baroncelli, probably to mark the couple's wedding in 1470 (pl. 2). Their portraits functioned as the wings of a folding devotional triptych whose centre panel – undoubtedly a Virgin and Child – has been lost. Memling took the devotional diptych developed by Rogier van der Weyden and turned it into a triptych.[50] The highly refined and prestigious work cannot have been intended purely for private worship: it must have been

available to at least a limited extent for public viewing – probably at Portinari's residence, the Hof Bladelin.

It was also around 1470–72 that the Florentine banker – who in the meantime had become a councillor and confidant of Charles the Bold – commissioned Memling to paint a *Passion of Christ* (Turin, Galleria Sabauda), which might first have been displayed in Portinari's private chapel in the church of St James, before passing into Medici ownership in the sixteenth century.[51] The painting consists of a panoramic, fictive view of Jerusalem, within which Memling placed miniature scenes from the Passion, beginning with Christ's entry into the city and ending with the journey to Emmaus. The simultaneous visual narrative appears to be rooted in early fifteenth-century German panel painting, tapestry cycles and Flemish book illumination – particularly the illustration of historical chronicles.[52] Although, strictly speaking, Memling had already applied the simultaneous narrative principle in his *Last Judgement*, it was only in this Passion cycle painted for Tommaso Portinari that he consistently presented historical events in this way. The technique can be found to some extent in works produced by Rogier van der Weyden's workshop – the 'Miraflores' and St John altarpieces (both Berlin, Gemäldegalerie), for instance – and has also been hypothetically linked on occasion with lost early works by Jan van Eyck.[53]

Memling must have worked on Portinari's *Passion of Christ* while he was still putting the finishing touches to his *Last Judgement*, and evidently experienced no difficulty in switching between the latter's monumental mode and the miniature approach of the former. During this masterful and versatile performance, he also found time to try out new and innovative pictorial concepts alongside his more conventional visual repertoire.

Tani's *Last Judgement* and the commissions to which it gave rise among the Italian diaspora in Flanders must have substantially enhanced Memling's reputation as a painter. He appears to have received a whole series of orders in the early 1470s, including the *Virgin and Child with St Anthony Abbot and a Donor* (cat. 4 and fig. 15), which is inscribed with the date 1472. This painting illustrates Memling's special gift for developing new compositions from a limited repertoire of motifs – the configuration of the Virgin and Child and the donor figure both derive from the same models, which the artist also used for the scene on the closed wings of the *Last Judgement* altarpiece. At the

fig. 15
Memling
*The Virgin and Child with St Anthony
Abbot and a Donor* [cat. 4], 1472,
detail of pl. 5
Ottawa, National Gallery of Canada

fig. 16
Jan van Eyck
*The Virgin and Child
with Chancellor Rolin*, detail
Paris, Musée du Louvre

same time, we detect signs that Memling was increasingly coming to terms with Bruges painting. In addition to the formal vocabulary of his Brussels master Rogier van der Weyden, he was now also incorporating in his work motifs from Van Eyck – whose *Virgin and Child with Chancellor Rolin* (fig. 16) may be cited in this instance – and, to a lesser extent, Petrus Christus. He was to take this diverse range of influences and to merge them into a style of his own.[54]

The 'Triptych of the Two Saints John' (fig. 17), completed in 1479 and originally displayed on the high altar of the chapel in St John's Hospital, Bruges, illustrates Memling's achievement in terms of synthesizing his forebears' work: he has taken the influences of Rogier and Van Eyck and independently assimilated them in his own composition, merging them and linking them with his own means of expression. Memling proudly signed the altarpiece on its surviving, original frame: '*Opus Iohannis Memling 1479*'. As one of his two signed works, it forms the joint basis on which art historians have sought to reconstruct his oeuvre.[55]

The central focus of the monumental triptych is an image of the Virgin and Child enthroned beneath an imposing brocade canopy and flanked by Saints Barbara and Catherine, John the Baptist and John the Evangelist. Memling has incorporated episodes from the lives of the hospital's two patron saints in the background of the central panel, where they link in narratively with the principal scenes depicted in the wings. The visual narrative culminates on the left with the beheading of John the Baptist – a composition based on the St John altarpiece from Van der Weyden's atelier. The equivalent scene on the right shows St John the Evangelist on Patmos, his apocalyptic vision presented as a simultaneous visual cycle that is one of the most magnificent and individual pictorial inventions ever.

Memling plainly had in mind the spatial disposition of Jan van Eyck's *Virgin and Child with Canon Van der Paele* – still located at the time in the church of St Donatian (fig. 18)[56] – when laying out the central panel of the triptych. Above all, the compositional type with the enthroned Virgin and Child surrounded by a small group of saints – the *sacra conversazione* format popular in Italy – must have been a crucial source of inspiration. Although Petrus Christus had already adopted this scheme around 1450,[57] it seems chiefly to have been Memling who, having expanded it to include the female saints kneeling on the

*fig. 17*
Memling
Triptych of the Two Saints John,
centre panel
Bruges, Stedelijke Musea,
Memlingmuseum –
Sint-Janshospitaal

ground, established its lasting popularity first in Bruges painting and then in early Netherlandish art as a whole.[58] The decisive influence on Memling's presentation of the scene appears not to have been Christus, but – alongside Van Eyck – compositions by Van der Weyden and his circle, most notably a *Virgin and Child with Saints* now known only through fragments and copies.[59]

Memling must have received the commission to paint a triptych for the high altar of Bruges' most prominent hospital community immediately after completing his *Last Judgement* altarpiece. The mere fact that it was evidently the first time that one of the city's long-established

institutions had ordered a painting from Memling must have been of special significance. St John's was founded in 1188 and was one of three hospitals in Bruges overseen by the city authorities. Following a dispute between the hospital and the city council – a conflict that took on all the dimensions of a power struggle – the institution fell in 1459 under the sole care of the Bishop of Tournai, following which the monks and nuns who made up the hospital community had to perform their duties in Augustinian habits. The situation did not, however, persist: it was agreed in 1463 that city and bishop would henceforth share oversight of St John's, with the bishop permitted to

*fig. 19*
Detail of fig. 20

examine the hospital's finances and the city given a say in the appointment of key personnel.[60] The triptych commission for the high altar was probably connected with a new apsidal choir for the hospital chapel, on which building work began in 1473/4. The new choir was dedicated in 1477 by Ferry de Clugny, who had been ordained as Bishop of Tournai in 1474.[61]

Given the relations between the hospital governors, the Bishop of Tournai and Bruges city council, it is hard to imagine that the commission would have been placed with Memling without prior consultation with the hospital's administrators; nominally, however, it appears to have been the hospital's friars and nuns themselves who acted as patrons for the altarpiece and it is their portraits that appear on the closed wings of the triptych, accompanied by Saints James, Anthony, Agnes and Clare. The hospital possessed relics of these saints, who were also invoked against a variety of illnesses, both of which circumstances explain their presence on the hospital's high altar. They may also have been the patron saints of the depicted hospital staff, whom James Weale identified as prioress Agnes Casembrood with Clara van Hulsen, and master Antheunis Seghers with Jacob Ceuninc; however, neither Jacob Ceuninc nor Clara van Hulsen held an offi-

cial management post at the hospital or belonged to its community in the period from the placing of the commission in 1473/4 to its completion in 1479.[62]

The monumental donors' portraits in the St John altarpiece (fig. 20) are possibly among the latest examples of the placement of the patrons' likenesses on the closed wings – customary Netherlandish practice in the 1430s and 1440s and exemplified in Van Eyck's 'Ghent Altarpiece' and Van der Weyden's *Last Judgement* polyptych in Beaune. They might even have appeared anachronistic at the time. Memling comes up here with an impressive solution to an apparent lack of internal logic: the four mem-

bers of the hospital community kneel facing one another, their hands clasped in prayer, even though there is no sign in the painted wings themselves of the actual object of their devotions. The viewer has to know about the image of the Madonna, conceived in the form of a *sacra conversazione*, that lies hidden in the triptych until being displayed on holy days – only then is the donors' worship encompassed in the iconographic programme. At the same time, the ambiguity of this devotional gesture enables Memling to incorporate the physical space of the chapel itself – to which the painting's jutting tracery lays claim – into the pictorial scheme of his altarpiece. Those who viewed the

altarpiece in its original position will immediately have been struck by the link between the image in the closed wings and the chapel altar, towards which the donor group would have been oriented. This brilliant pictorial artifice drawing the actual altar out of its real space into a supernatural present, does not, paradoxically, enhance the realism of the work. The effect is heightened by the carefully staged lighting, which causes the tracery to cast artfully diffuse shadows on the even rear wall (fig. 19) and is evidently not of this world, falling as it does from the north onto an altar oriented towards the east.

Just as the *Last Judgement* altarpiece for Agnolo Tani won Memling a number of commissions from the local Italian merchant community, the 'Triptych of the Two Saints John' – completed, so the inscription tells us, in 1479 – appears to have elicited a series of follow-up orders. Memling's work for the Hospital of St John seemingly made him acceptable for the first time to local patrons, who now began to commission altarpieces from him for their guild chapels; in addition to the lost wings for the altar of the illuminators' guild (see above), these included an altarpiece with the *Seven Joys of the Virgin* endowed in 1479 by Pieter Bultinc for the tanners' chapel in the choir of Our Lady's in Bruges. Once again, the work was conceived as a simultaneous visual narrative.[63] For other commissions, it was evidently the patron's explicit wish that Memling should essentially reprise the composition of the central panel of the St John altarpiece: examples are the *Virgin and Child with Saints and Angels*,[64] painted for an unidentified patron, and the 'Donne Triptych', which was commissioned by the aforementioned Welsh diplomat Sir John Donne of Kidwelly and his wife Elizabeth Hastings, probably in 1480 (see fig. 43).[65]

Finally, there were orders for small, private altarpieces from other members of the hospital community: also inscribed with the name of Hans Memling and the date

*figs. 21–22*
Memling
Triptych of Jan Floreins, 1479, open and closed
Bruges, Stedelijke Musea, Memlingmuseum –
Sint-Janshospitaal

(1479) on the frame is the *Adoration of the Kings* which, the inscription on the original frame goes on to tell us, was commissioned by Jan Floreins (figs. 21–22).[66] Floreins, who joined the hospital community in 1471/2, belonged to an aristocratic family from Hainaut and probably came to Bruges from Boussu near Mons; he chose scenes from the Childhood of Christ to adorn his private altar. The central panel shows him at the age of 36 as a witness to the Epiphany (see fig. 40), the composition of which Memling borrowed and simplified from the Adoration scene in Van der Weyden's 'Columba Altarpiece' (fig. 23). It is flanked by the Nativity in the left wing and the Presentation in the Temple in the right.

The structure and composition of the triptych echo those of another that Memling probably painted several years earlier (Madrid, Prado), which is also based on Rogier's 'Columba Altarpiece', but which is significantly larger.[67] The closed wings show Saints John the Baptist

and Veronica sitting in front of a landscape that stretches into the distance. John points towards the Mystic Lamb, while Veronica holds up the cloth she used to wipe the sweat from Christ's brow as he carried the Cross and on which his face miraculously appeared. Memling had previously used both of these motifs in a diptych[68] commissioned by the Venetian envoy Bernardo Bembo, who left the Netherlands in 1474 (see cat. 10). In the 'Triptych of Jan Floreins', however, the two figures are framed by a stone arch with marvellous *trompe-l'œil* tracery that seems to imitate the actual architecture of the late Gothic tabernacle fragment which can still be seen in St John's Hospital. The stone archway is decorated with imitation statues representing the Fall of Man and the Expulsion of Adam and Eve from Paradise; their purpose is to illustrate the necessity of Christ's sacrificial death, as implied by the lamb and Veronica's cloth. The images on the closed wings are themselves set in illusionistic marble frames on which the patron's initials – IF – have been painted in the form of a golden cord, while the patron's high social status is revealed by the shields incorporated at the top. The small triptych is one of Memling's most exquisite works in terms of both content and execution, despite the fact that its individual elements had already been developed in other contexts elsewhere in his work.

The *Lamentation* triptych that Adriaan Reins commissioned from Memling to mark his admission to the hospital community in 1479 dates from a year later (see fig. 42).[69] The triptych resembles that of Jan Floreins in terms of its structure, but the overall effect is more modest – something that is especially plain from the less artfully rendered architectural framing in the little altarpiece's closed wings. The frame lacks both the inscription and the coats of arms we see in the 'Floreins Triptych'. Even the conspicuous donor's initials on the closed wings are missing, though they do appear on the frame at the bottom of the central Lamentation scene. The difference in height between the outer panels and the central scene, together with stylistic discrepancies, suggests that the Lamentation panel had already been finished and was completed by the addition of wings showing the donor and his patron saint on the left and St Barbara on the right. The triptych thus seems to bear out the hypothesis that Memling produced certain popular scenes in advance, confident that demand would remain steady; all he would then have had to do would be to personalize the wings for the specific purchaser.

Memling appears in the course of the 1480s to have produced more and more versions of particularly admired compositions in advance, as a substantial proportion of his output from that period onwards is marked by far-reaching standardization, including size. This applied above all to half- and full-length images of the Virgin and Child. He tended to use variations on a basic composition, to which he occasionally added one or more angels. For the background, he alternated between landscapes and interiors (see cat. 23, pl. 25). An interesting example is provided by Memling's composition with the enthroned Virgin and Child beneath a canopy; three different versions survive – two with swags of fruit added for decoration – but the variations between them are marginal. All three include naked *putti*, which are generally interpreted as evidence of the burgeoning influence of Italian Renaissance ornamentation, causing the panels to be given a late date – towards the end of the 1480s.[70] They served as the central panels

of triptychs, the original configuration of which has survived in one case and can be reconstructed in another. The one that has survived is now in Vienna and consists of a triptych with wings showing John the Baptist and John the Evangelist; the closed wings have images of Adam and Eve. The size difference between the centre panel and the wings once again suggests that the work was assembled from elements produced in advance. It has long been known, meanwhile, that the donor figure kneeling on the right before the Virgin and Child was overpainted and that a Cistercian abbot originally appeared there. This might well have been another commission from Jan Crabbe, who died in 1488, leaving the work unpaid for – and probably unfinished – in Memling's workshop. The painter evidently had little trouble in finding another buyer for the left-over picture and merely had to update the donor portrait.[71]

The original arrangement of the second triptych was only recently reconstructed and its patron identified. The central panel, featuring the enthroned Virgin and Child, is now in Florence. Instead of a donor figure, a harp-playing angel appears on the right. The scene formed a triptych with a pair of wings (London) showing John the Baptist and St Lawrence on the inside and a group of cranes on the outside. The work was commissioned from Memling's workshop by the Dominican bishop Benedetto Pagagnotti, probably through intermediaries. The painter turned to a standard composition, which he personalized to a certain extent with wings designed specifically for this patron.[72] The 'Triptych of Benedetto Pagagnotti' clearly shows that while Memling may have painted works for stock – or at the very least resorted to a degree of standardization – this in no way entails a qualitative sacrifice in terms of technical execution; nor is it necessarily evidence of increased input on the part of workshop assistants.

Memling increasingly produced panels of standard dimensions and compositions in the 1480s – speculating on persistent, anonymous demand – which he then incorporated in diptychs and triptychs for individual clients (figs. 10, 24). He nonetheless continued to receive major commissions for larger altarpieces, the iconography of which was conceived according to the donors' specific wishes. Those donors appear around the mid-1480s to have been primarily members of Bruges' patrician class.

First and foremost among these works is the 'Moreel Triptych' (cat. 22, pl. 24), which Memling painted for the

influential Bruges politician, banker and merchant Willem Moreel and his wife Barbara van Vlaenderberch alias Van Hertsvelde. The commission was linked with the Moreels' endowment of a family altar devoted to Saints Maur and Giles at the church of St James in Bruges in 1484/5. They received permission to install a prestigious altarpiece, together with the right to be buried in the church. The year '1484' that appears on the frame thus refers most likely to the year of the endowment rather than the date the altarpiece was completed.

Memling's composition is rather unusual for Netherlandish painting and will undoubtedly have reflected the specific requirements of the foundation. In formal terms, the central scene featuring Saints Christopher, Maur and Giles corresponds with the rows of saints to be found in German and Italian painting; however, there are indications at least that Memling turned for the figure of St Christopher to a lost composition of Van Eyck which was also copied by, among others, Dieric Bouts.[73] The

triptych is one of the earliest examples of the family group portraits that became increasingly fashionable in Flanders in the 1480s and which suggest a shifting attitude on the part of a section of the social élite – specifically the urban patrician class – towards the family and matters of descent.

The 'Moreel Triptych' reminds us in this respect of the so-called 'Altarpiece of Jacob Floreins' (fig. 25), which shows the Virgin and Child enthroned in the interior of a church and gives a prominent place to the portraits of the donors and the couple's children. The painting dates from around the late 1480s and was probably conceived as a single panel. There are clear echoes of Van Eyck's *Virgin and Child with Canon Van der Paele* (fig. 18), while the Madonna's figure and throne derive from a standard model of Memling's, on which the artist produced several variations in the latter part of his career. The traditional identification of the donor as Jan Floreins's brother, the spice merchant Jacob Floreins, who died in 1488, dates back to Weale but can

*fig.* 24
Memling
Diptych of Jean du Cellier
Paris, Musée du Louvre

by no means be considered secure.[74] Although the context in which the painting was commissioned and executed remains a puzzle, we may still assume that it was originally intended as an altarpiece to adorn a private chapel of a high-ranking patrician or merchant family. The clothes and above all the jewellery illustrate the considerable wealth enjoyed by the donor family, several members of which evidently belonged to the priesthood or a monastic order. It is likely to have been the woman in widow's garb who commissioned the painting from Memling and his workshop to commemorate her late husband.[75]

In addition to large altarpieces, the latter half of the 1480s also saw the production of smaller works intended for private worship in the form of devotional diptychs and triptychs. The fact that works of this kind by no means rendered the large and prominent altarpiece obsolete is evident from Willem Moreel and his wife's commissioning of a devotional triptych from Memling at more or

less the same time as their celebrated altarpiece. Meanwhile, the prominent inclusion of coats of arms and mottos on the back of the portrait wing suggests that, despite their small size and use in private devotion, works like this remained prestigious objects which, we can safely assume, had an at least limited public function (see cat. 18).

It is significant in this respect that around the same time that Memling was painting the 'Moreel Triptych' and receiving the commission for the so-called 'Altarpiece of Jacob Floreins', Maarten van Nieuwenhove – another member of an influential Bruges patrician family – also ordered a Marian diptych from him. The painter was evidently drawing his most important clients at this stage primarily from the ranks of Bruges' leading citizens, whereas the Italian merchant commissions that had featured so prominently at the outset of his career, appear to have played only a minor role in his output by the 1480s. The 'Diptych of Maarten van Nieuwenhove' is inscribed with

fig. 25
Memling
Altarpiece of Jacob Floreins
Paris, Musée du Louvre

the date 1487 and was almost certainly displayed in an oratory. It is undoubtedly one of Memling's most original and successful pictorial inventions, even though the Madonna wing actually derives once again from a standard model (see cat. 23).[76]

Compared with the demand with which Memling was confronted in the final decade of his life – primarily on the part of Bruges' high bourgeoisie – he seems to have received virtually no further important commissions from guilds or ecclesiastical institutions. There was an exception, though, in the shape of the 'St Ursula Casket' (finished in 1489), which the artist painted for the community at St John's Hospital (figs. 2, 26). Memling uses six scenes to recount the story of St Ursula and her virgin companions, the miniature images of which stylistically recall the simultaneous narratives he painted for Tommaso Portinari (around 1470) and Pieter Bultinc (1480). The detailed view of Cologne in the background to three of the scenes is very striking and has been cited in the literature as evidence of an early stay in the German city. However, a tradition recorded among the hospital community in the nineteenth century has it that Memling was once sent to Cologne on the hospital's behalf – an account that seems more likely.[77]

Similarly, Memling appears to have worked only occasionally for foreign patrons after the early 1480s. It was not to him but to Hugo van der Goes that Tommaso Portinari turned for a monumental triptych for his family endowment at Santa Maria Nuova in Florence (see fig. 62); other Italians, meanwhile, no longer ordered paintings only from Memling, but also from minor Bruges masters like the Master of the Legend of St Ursula and the Master of the Legend of St Lucy. Demand for portraits, in particular, on which Memling seemed to boast a virtual monopoly at the beginning of his career in Bruges, appears to have waned drastically by the end of the century, with the genre only undergoing a renaissance in the Netherlands in the early part of the sixteenth century (fig. 81).

It was not until the final years of Memling's life that foreign merchants – primarily Spaniards and Germans this time – began to commission Netherlandish panel paintings and especially altarpieces once again; Memling too was able to benefit for a while. Around 1490, he received a commission for a large altarpiece, probably through the intermediary of Castilian wool traders, who enjoyed close business relations with Flanders. The work was to consist

of multiple panels on the theme of the Assumption and Coronation of the Virgin and was destined for the church of the prominent monastery of Santa María la Real in Nájera (La Rioja). All that now survives are three monumental panels with God the Father and an orchestra of angels (Antwerp, Koninklijk Museum voor Schone Kunsten) that originally formed the upper tier of the ensemble and which paraphrased Van Eyck's 'Ghent Altarpiece'. The completed work was enormous and Memling must have produced it with considerable assistance from his workshop and other colleagues; we do not know, however, precisely when the altarpiece was completed or how it was transported to Spain.[78]

The Passion triptych inscribed with the year 1491 in Lübeck was probably Memling's final large commission (see fig. 29); here, too, the date might refer to the year the altar was endowed rather than when the painting was com-

pleted, as the Hanseatic merchants who left Bruges in 1488 did not return until 1491.[79] The altarpiece owes its double-winged configuration to a type customary in the Baltic region and was commissioned by a member of a Lübeck patrician family – the merchant Heinrich Greverade, who was active in Flanders, or his brother Adolf, who enrolled as a theology student at the University of Leuven in 1495. The work was destined for the Greverades' family chapel in Lübeck Cathedral, where Memling's painting was securely documented for the first time in 1504.[80] There are strong indications that the completed painting did not arrive in Lübeck until after Memling's death, as the family also commissioned a Calvary scene in 1494 from local artist Hermen Rode, which does not contain the slightest echo of the Bruges painter's work.[81]

By the time Memling received the Lübeck commission, he was no longer viewed as the only artist in his adopted

city; when, for instance, the Confraternity of the Black Heads – a merchants' association in Reval (now Tallinn) – decided around the same time to commission a prestigious double-winged altarpiece dedicated to their patron saints and featuring their group portrait, they did not turn to Memling, but to a younger contemporary of his, the anonymous Master of the Legend of St Lucy (fig. 30).[82]

It is plain from this survey of Memling's life and work in Bruges from 1465 to his death in August 1494 just how closely his career was intertwined with the historical events of the time. The first fifteen years of his activity in the Flemish city coincided with the final stages of a period of unusual economic and political stability that accompanied the zenith of Burgundian power from the 1450s. Founded on commerce and finance, Bruges' sustained economic prosperity helped to bring wealth to the same Italian merchants and financiers, influential local families and even a few of the city's craftsmen that had been commissioning paintings from Flemish artists since the 1430s. Along with courtiers, churchmen, guilds and confraterniries, this urban élite, taking its cultural lead from the Burgundian nobility, ensured plentiful employment for painters like Memling as they sought to make their mark through, amongst other things, substantial religious endowments.[83]

The political climate of the Burgundian Netherlands and of Bruges in particular was thrown into turmoil by the death of Charles the Bold in January 1477, although the region's economy had already been gradually destabilized by Charles's aggressive pursuit of expansion. It took some time, however, before the crisis also began to affect the more privileged echelons of society. At any rate, the city was able to capitalize politically on the duke's unexpected death by pledging its loyalty to his heir, Mary of Burgundy, in return for the reinstatement of a series of municipal privileges hitherto feared lost for ever.[84] The result was a new-found confidence on the part of both the crafts and the city's most influential families, who appear to have accounted for the majority of Memling's commissions around 1480. It was about this same time that Memling's career seems to have peaked economically.

Whatever the nature of the city's loyalty to Mary of Burgundy, it came to an abrupt end in 1482, when the governess of the Netherlands died suddenly. While her widower, Archduke Maximilian, was confirmed as regent of most of the Burgundian territories, Bruges and the other Flemish cities were only prepared to recognize a regency council, in conjunction with which Maximilian would govern as guardian of his underage son, Philip the Fair. The dispute sparked a drawn-out and increasingly bitter power struggle between the Flemish towns and the man who was to become emperor, and it was to leave a decisive mark on the history of the Southern Netherlands in the ensuing decade.[85] The prolonged conflict, which led in Bruges to repeated armed rebellions against the archduke and to fierce clashes between supporters of the pro-Habsburg party and their opponents, had political and above all serious economic repercussions. Maximilian levied several special taxes, for instance, and in 1484 and again in 1488, he ordered foreign merchants to quit Bruges and to conduct their business from Antwerp instead; he blockaded Bruges' link with the sea and laid siege to the city several times. It was not until 1491 – three years before Memling's death – that Bruges finally submitted to Maximilian of Habsburg's rule.[86]

During those unstable times, therefore, it was primarily wealthy local families who commissioned altarpieces as a public demonstration of their status, rank and prestige, with their chapels in the city's churches as the backdrop. Foreign merchants barely feature as patrons between 1484 and 1491. Memling, as we have seen, seems to have responded to the shift in demand by producing more and more standard compositions, speculating on their appeal to prospective customers. The situation improved again after 1491; part at least of the international merchant community returned to Bruges, and signs of a second cultural flowering gradually began to emerge in the Burgundian Netherlands. Memling, however, died too soon to witness much of this.

fig. 29
Memling
*Triptych of the Passion*
(Greverade Triptych), 1491,
detail: bystanders at the foot
of the cross of the Good Thief
Lübeck, St. Annen-Museum
für Kunst und Kulturgeschichte

*fig.30*
Master of the St Lucy Legend
Altarpiece of the Black Heads
Tallinn, Niguliste Muuseum

It is appropriate that Memling's only documented commission – the wings for the altarpiece of the Bruges book illuminators' guild representing Willem Vrelant and his wife – actually related to portraiture (see above). After all, portraits – be it full-length likenesses of donors or half-length portraits – occupy a particularly prominent place in the artist's surviving oeuvre. Over thirty paintings, or just under a third of all Memling's known works, can be broadly characterized – formally and in terms of content – as portraits in the modern sense. If we also count the nearly twenty surviving full-length donor portraits that appear

in paintings attributed to Memling and his workshop, it becomes plain that over half of his extant oeuvre features portraits of one kind or another. Impressive as that figure may be, it is still misleading in so far as several of Memling's paintings are actually fragments of larger ensembles, some of which at least will originally have included portraits, too.

Memling was plainly the most successful portraitist of his generation in the Burgundian Netherlands – nowhere near as many portraits survive by any of his contemporaries. Not a single autonomous likeness, for instance, has come down to us from Hugo van der Goes, although the handful of surviving donor figures (fig. 31) and ancillary portraits (fig. 32) that he incorporated in his panels testify to what must have been his outstanding achievement in this area, too. Equally few portraits have survived from Memling's immediate circle of minor Bruges masters (fig. 9); and while a variety of donor portraits have been ascribed to Gerard David, who arrived in Bruges in 1484, his surviving oeuvre otherwise includes just one lone portrait (fig. 28).

Memling's success as a portraitist can be attributed to a number of factors. As apprentice and assistant to Rogier van der Weyden, he was able to familiarize himself with his mentor's portrait compositions and painting style – both half-lengths (fig. 6) and full-length donors' portraits. We may also assume that, through Rogier, Memling will have been aware of Robert Campin's portraits (figs. 4–5, 34) and those of other assistants working in Rogier's atelier (fig. 35). Memling continued to draw on Rogier's typology in his own portraiture throughout the almost thirty years of his professional career in Bruges. He took the scheme, for instance, of the half-length portrait diptych and developed it into a variety of spatial formulas that were sufficiently flexible to meet his clients' wishes. But that was not the extent of Memling's borrowings from his teacher in this regard; a work like Rogier's 'Braque Triptych' (fig. 38) should also be seen as an indirect yet crucial precursor of Memling's move towards the half-length portrait with landscape background. Consequently, the view expressed since Panofsky to the effect that Memling's landscape portraits ultimately derive from Italian models like Piero della Francesca's likenesses of Federigo da Montefeltro and Battista Sforza (fig. 65) plainly does not stand up.

In addition to Rogier, whose influence on Memling's portraiture can barely be overstated, the artist had plentiful opportunity in Bruges to familiarize himself with the refined portraits of Jan van Eyck. The illusionism that Memling displays so emphatically in some of his portraits – the way he plays with reality using parapets and *trompe-l'œil* and imitation marble frames – seemingly derives directly from Van Eyck's portraits (figs. 7, 27, 36, 37). Certain aspects of the lighting, meanwhile, and of the way he defines the pictorial space appear chiefly indebted to the portraits of Petrus Christus (see figs. 51–53). As in his religious compositions, Memling successfully blends the achievements of Van der Weyden and Van Eyck in his

*fig. 31*
Hugo van der Goes
*A Donor with St John the Baptist*
Baltimore, Walters Art Museum,
Bequest of Henry Waters

*fig. 32*
Hugo van der Goes
Monforte Altarpiece
Staatliche Museen zu Berlin,
Preussischer Kulturbesitz,
Gemäldegalerie

portraiture to produce a style of his own that was plainly appreciated by his clients.

The *genius loci* must also have contributed significantly to Memling's extraordinary success as a portraitist: Bruges was, after all, the ultimate cosmopolitan metropolis in the Burgundian Netherlands. Members of the Italian *nationes* – above all the Genoese – had been among Jan van Eyck's patrons as early as the 1430s, and thus played a decisive part in establishing the reputation of Flemish art in southern Europe. The many foreigners based in or passing through Bruges also accounted for a significant pro-

portion of Petrus Christus's clients, not least as buyers of portraits.

When Memling arrived in Bruges, he encountered substantial demand for portraits and was evidently quick to meet his potential customers' wishes. Despite this it would probably be mistaken to conclude that the production of Memling's surviving portraits was spread evenly across the years he was active in Bruges. Although the artist received portrait commissions throughout his career, a substantial proportion of his surviving works – the provenance of which often points to Italy – seems to date from

fig. 33
Rogier van der Weyden
*Virgin and Child*;
*Portrait of Philippe de Croÿ*
San Marino (Cal.), Huntington
Art Collections, The Art Gallery;
Antwerp, Koninklijk Museum
voor Schone Kunsten

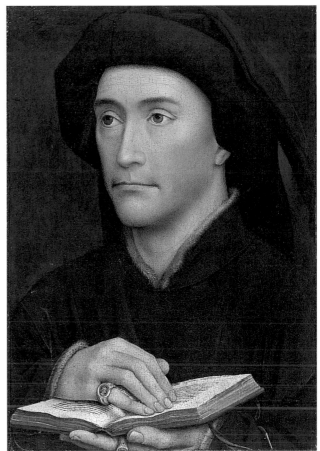

fig. 35
Follower of Rogier van der Weyden
*Portrait of a Man (Guillaume Fillastre?)*
London, Courtauld Institute Gallery

fig. 34
Robert Campin
*Portrait of a Man (Robert de Masmines?)*
Madrid, Museo Thyssen-Bornemisza

the 1470s, with demand for portraits apparently waning in subsequent years. The economic and political crisis that engulfed Bruges by 1482 at the latest will undoubtedly have contributed, as will the liquidation of Medici banking operations in northern Europe and England.

Representatives of other merchant communities – Germans, Spaniards and Portuguese – displayed nowhere near as much interest in portraiture as the Italians had, and would not begin to do so until after the turn of the

century. For their part, members of influential local families were more interested in prestigious portraits in the context of larger, high-profile altarpieces and were thus no more able to plug the gap left by the Italians in terms of demand for individual portraits. We are very fortunate, therefore, that a portrait painter as gifted as Memling should have arrived in fifteenth-century Bruges at a moment where demand for portraits was at its zenith.

*fig. 38*
Rogier van der Weyden
Triptych of Jean Braque
Paris, Musée du Louvre

1  Memling catalogue raisonnés include Voll 1909, Friedländer 1928 (1971); Faggin 1969; Lane 1980; De Vos 1994.
2  Weale 1861, 20–28, 34–6, 45–9, 53–5; Weale 1871, 18–34; Goetinck and Ryckaert 1976, 495–501; De Vos 1994, 407–14; Janssens 1997, 65–89.
3  Bock 1900, 1–52; Borchert 1994; De Vos 1994, 15–73; Lorentz 1995a, 17–20.
4  De Vos 1994, 361–4; Lane 1997, 53–70.
5  Parmentier, 1938, 630–31, De Vos 1994, 21 and 407; Vandewalle 1997, 19–24.
6  Strasser 1961, 97–100; Jahn 1980, 45–46; Groten 1993, 12; De Vos 1994, 407.
7  Dussart 1892, 49; Viaene 1963, 304–6; Viaene 1976, 229; Vandewalle 1997, 20.
8  Strasser 1961, 97–100; Küchler 1978; De Vos 1994, 414.
9  Schouteet 1989, 12; Blockmans 1995, 11–20; Martens 1995, 43–4.
10 Schouteet 1989, 8–9.
11 Van Miegroet 1989, 21–5; Martens 1994b, 18–19; Spronk 1998, 94–6.
12 Martens 1994, 18–22; Martens 1997, 35–41.
13 Schouteet 1989, 6–7 and 236–47.
14 Schouteet 1989, 7, contrary view: De Vos 1994, 22.
15 De Vos 1994, 407, 410–14; Ryckaert 1994, 104–8; Janssens 1997, 67–78.
16 Strohm 1990, 62–3; Martens 1992, 315–19.
17 Vanden Haute 1913, 28 and 35; De Vos 1994, 410–11.
18 Weale 1861, 21–2; Weale 1871, 27–30; De Vos 1994, 411–12; Janssens 1997, 77–8, 80.
19 Janssens 1997, 80.
20 Weale 1861, 31–6; De Vos 1994, 410.
21 De Vos 1994, 43.
22 Janssens 1997, 66–70.
23 Schouteet 1955, 81–4.
24 Strohm 1990, 47–8; Martens 1992, 232–6; Janssens 1997, 78–9.
25 Martens 1992, 236.
26 Martens 1992, 233–4.
27 Martens 1994b, 16; Janssens 1997, 78–9, 87–9; Van der Velden 1997, 88–110.
28 Ryckaert 1994, 106–7.
29 Weale and Brockwell 1912, 19 (doc. 30).

30 Strasser 1961, 97–100; De Vos 1994, 414.
31 Devliegher 1964, 232–6; Martens 1992, 79–85.
32 Martens 1992, 80.
33 Martens 1992, 85 and 484–8.
34 Martens 1992, 327–30; De Vos 1994, 36 and 408–9; Martens 1994, 16; Bousmanne 1997, 52–3.
35 Metropolitan Museum of Art, inv. 17–190.7; see also De Vos 1994, 304; Ainsworth 1994, 79–80, New York 1998, 112–14, no. 10.
36 De Vos 1994, 21, 23 and 90–93, 110.3; Ainsworth 1994, 78–81, Copy: Venice, Galleria dell'Accademia, inv. 141; see also Bruges 1994, 246, no. 97; Devliegher 1997, 31–3.
37 Geirnaert 1987–8, 175–83; Geirnaert 1997, 25–30.
38 Geirnaert 1992, 246–8; Martens 1995, 48–9.
39 See De Vos 1999, nos. 10, 13; Stroo et al. 1997, 131–53.
40 Galassi 1999, 7–24; Ainsworth 2003, 308–10; see, regarding Vrancke, Koreny 2002, 67–122; Koreny 2003, 266–92.
41 De Vos 1994, no. 4.
42 Białostocki 1966, 80–85; Lane 1991.
43 Warburg 1932, I, 187–206, 207–12; Nuttall 1992, 97–112; Rohlmann 1994, 41–52; Nuttall 2004, 54–60.
44 De Roover 1963, 331–3 and 474 n. 80.
45 De Roover 1963, 331–3; McFarlane 1971, 1–12; Campbell 1998, 381–3.
46 De Roover 1963, 475 n. 92; Nuttall 2004, 57–9.
47 Białostocki 1966; Borchert 1995b, 80–83; Faries 1997, 243–59.
48 See De Vos 1999, no. 17.
49 See e.g. cat. 3, 13, 17.
50 Waldman 2001, 28–33.
51 See De Vos 1994, no. 11.
52 Smeyers 1997, 176–94.
53 See De Vos 1999, nos. 12, 22; Belting and Eichberger 1983, 165–82.
54 See Lane 1997, 61–70.
55 De Vos 1994, no. 31.
56 Janssens de Bisthoven 1983, 204–7; Koster 2002, 79–82.
57 Lane 1997, 65–6.
58 Winkler 1965, 155–65. Winkler erroneously attributes this type to Van der Goes.
59 Ward 1971, 27–35; Campbell 1998, 398–400.
60 Geldhof 1976, 169–74.
61 Duclos 1913, 341–2; Esther 1976, 275; Martens 1992, 352–9; Martens 1995b, 169–75.

62 Weale 1871, 45; Lobelle-Caluwé 1987, 44–5; Martens 1994, 15–16; Martens 1995b, 169–70.
63 De Vos 1994, no. 38; Martens 1994, 18.
64 De Vos 1994, no. 35; New York 1998, no. 11.
65 De Vos 1994, no. 39; Campbell 1998, 374–91.
66 De Vos 1994, no. 32; Martens 1994, 15–16.
67 De Vos 1994, no. 13.
68 De Vos 1994, no. 50; Belting and Kruse 1994, 254–5.
69 De Vos 1994, no. 37.
70 De Vos 1994, nos. 53, 77, 89.
71 Demus, Klauner and Schütz 1981, 238–40; De Vos 1994, 215–16.
72 Rohlmann 1994, 67–83; Campbell 1998, 362–9; Nuttall 2004, 123–4.
73 Dieric Bouts, 'The Pearl of Brabant' (Munich, Alte Pinakothek, WAF 76–78); see also Koreny 2002, 53–5.
74 Weale 1871, 47; McFarlane 1971, 31; De Vos 1994, no. 86; Lorentz 1995a, 35–42; Borchert 1995b, 85–8.
75 Comblen-Sonkes and Lorentz 1995, 220–62, here 250–56.
76 See also Spronk et al., *Early Netherlandish Diptychs* (forthcoming).
77 De Vos 1994, no. 83.
78 De Vos 1994, no. 81; Borchert 1995a, *passim*; Borchert, in Bruges 1998, 20–22.
79 Borchert 1993, 91–100; De Vos 1994, no. 90; Borchert 2002, 144–5.
80 Hasse 1975, 3–7; Martens 1994, 29.
81 Borchert 1993, 99–100; Borchert 2002, 144–5.
82 See Martens 2000, 58–82; most recently: Polli and Koppel 2004, 13–17.
83 See Martens 1994b, 18–22; Wilson 1998, 41–84.
84 See Martens 1997, 37, graph 2.
85 Blockmans and Prevenier 1997, 195–226.
86 Blockmans and Prevenier 1997, 226–50; Wiesflecker 1971, 224–47.

Lorne Campbell

# Memling
# and the Netherlandish
# Portrait Tradition

### Donor portraits

Both Memling's 'signed' works include donor portraits. The inscriptions naming Memling as the author of the 'Triptych of the Two Saints John' and the 'Floreins Triptych' (both Bruges, Memlingmuseum; figs. 17, 21–22) may have been renewed or restored but there is no reason to suspect their authority: both triptychs were finished by Memling in 1479.[1] The 'Triptych of the Two Saints John' was executed for the altar of the church in the Hospital of St John. The four donors appear with their patron saints on the outsides of the wings: Jacob Ceuninc and Antheunis Seghers; Agnes Casembrood and Clara van Hulsen. Jacob, who made his profession in 1469–70, was afterwards to be bursar of the community, from 1487–8 until his death in 1489. Antheunis was master of the hospital from 1469–70 until his death in 1475, four years before the altarpiece was completed. Agnes had joined the community in 1445–6 but in 1447, with several other male and female members, she was excommunicated. By 1459–60, however, she was serving her first term as prioress and she was again prioress when the altarpiece was completed. Clara, who was a member of the community for 51 years, died in 1478–9.[2]

The second 'signed' triptych was commissioned by Jan Floreins, who kneels discreetly on the left side of the centre panel (fig. 40). The number 36, written on the wall next to his head, indicates his age: he was therefore born in about 1443. Related in some way to Hendrik van Berghen, Bishop of Cambrai, he probably came from Boussu, west of Mons, and joined the community in 1471–2. The only friar to survive the plague of 1489, he was master between 1489 and 1496–7 and died in 1504–5.[3]

Five paintings of religious subjects with donor portraits are mentioned as Memling's work in sixteenth- and seventeenth-century sources. The first is the *Passion of Christ* (Turin, Galleria Sabauda), cited by Vasari in 1550 and 1568 as Memling's work; it was painted in or shortly after 1470 for Tommaso Portinari and his young wife Maria Bandini Baroncelli.[4] Tommaso was not only a banker in the employ of the Medici but also a courtier and held the position of councillor to Charles the Bold, with whom he was on very friendly terms.[5] The second is the 'St Ursula Casket' (Bruges, Memlingmuseum; see figs. 2, 26), consecrated in 1489 and described by Van Mander in 1604 as by Memling. The two nuns of the Hospital of St John who paid for it are shown kneeling before the Virgin and Child but have

*fig. 42*
Memling
Triptych of Adriaan Reins, 1480
Bruges, Stedelijke Musea,
Memlingmuseum –
Sint-Janshospitaal

not been identified with certainty.[6] The third religious subject is the *Seven Joys of the Virgin* (Munich), painted in 1480 for the tanner Pieter Bultinc and his wife and placed in the Tanners' Chapel in the church of Our Lady. Both Peter Stevens and Antonius Sanderus (1641) stated that it was by Memling.[7] The fourth painting is the 'Triptych of Adriaan Reins' (fig. 42), dated 1480. It was commissioned by another member of the community of the Hospital of St John, who joined in 1479–80, and was mentioned as Memling's work by Sanderus and David Charlart.[8] The fifth painting is the picture from which have been cut the fragments of the *Virgin and Child* (Aurora Art Fund, Inc.), *A Donor and his Son* and *A Donatrix* (both Sibiu; pl. 15); all three fragments were sold in 1676 as works by Hans Memling.[9]

Thirteen more religious paintings with donor portraits are so like the 'signed' and authenticated works of Memling that they are confidently attributed to him. Only the six most significant will be considered here.[10] The great triptych of the *Last Judgement* was commissioned by Agnolo Tani, another Florentine banker, and his wife Caterina Tanagli, who appear on the reverses of the wings (fig. 41). In 1473, the galley on which it was being transported from Bruges to Florence was captured by a Hanseatic privateer and taken to Gdańsk, where the triptych has remained.[11] The dismembered triptych of the *Crucifixion* (Vicenza; New York, Morgan Library; and Bruges, Groeningemuseum; see fig. 13) was painted in about 1470 for Jan Crabbe, Abbot of Ter Duinen near Bruges. He is the donor in the centre panel; on the left wing is his aged mother Anne Willemszoon who, in 1448, when she was sixty and twice widowed, was abducted and forced to marry a gentleman of Zeeland; the young man on the right wing is probably the abbot's nephew Willem de Winter.[12] The 'Donne

Triptych' (London), which appears to have been dated 1478, was commissioned by a Welshman, Sir John Donne, and his wife the English noblewoman Elizabeth Hastings. Accompanied by one of their daughters, they kneel before the Virgin and Child (fig. 43).[13] Willem Moreel, who traded in spices in Bruges, commissioned for his chapel in the church of St James the triptych dated 1484 of Saints Christopher, Maur and Giles (Bruges, Groeningemuseum; cat. 22, pl. 24).[14] On the wings are represented Willem himself, his wife Barbara van Vlaenderberch, their five sons and eleven of their daughters. Jacob Floreins, who is believed to have been a younger brother of Jan Floreins and who became a burgess of Bruges in 1464, also traded in spices and seems to have died in the plague of 1489. It may have been his widow, a Spanish lady, who commissioned the *Virgin and Child with Saints* (Louvre), in which they appear accompanied by seven sons and twelve daughters.[15] Lastly, the great polyptych of the *Crucifixion*, dated 1491, was commissioned for the cathedral of Lübeck by a member of the Greverade family, represented in the lower left corner of the left wing. He is probably Adolf Greverade, who was a merchant but who in 1495 matriculated at the University of Leuven and died in Leuven in 1501.[16]

In all these paintings, the patrons kneel and are easily identified as donors; but in several of Memling's religious subjects he included representations of recognizable people who observe or even take part in the narrative. They too may well be portraits, of the donor's relatives, friends or associates. On the extreme right of the centre panel of the 'Triptych of the Two Saints John' (fig. 17) stands a man who is dressed in the habit worn by the brothers of the Hospital of St John and who is presumably one of the community. Behind Jan Floreins in the 'Floreins Triptych' stands a young man, possibly one of his nephews (fig. 40). In the *Martyrdom of St Ursula* on the 'St Ursula Casket', the elderly couple standing behind the saint (fig. 26b) are dressed in contemporary though unfashionable clothes and have been identified as Memling himself and his wife Anne, who had died in 1487, two years before the casket was consecrated.[17]

In the *Last Judgement*, the damaged head of the naked soul who kneels in St Michael's scales bears the features of Tommaso Portinari and a great many of the men among the blessed and damned could well be other banker colleagues of the donor Agnolo Tani. In the 'Donne Triptych', the man behind the column in the left wing looks like a portrait; and in the centre panel of the Lübeck *Crucifixion* the three men standing below the cross of the good thief must be likenesses that the donor and his contemporaries would have recognized. In a triptych of the *Adoration of the Kings* (Prado), there are no portraits of praying donors but, in the right wing, the prophetess Anna and the young man behind the high priest bear the features of Anne Willemszoon and her young companion (Willem de Winter?), almost exactly as they appear in the 'Triptych of Jan Crabbe'. Anna's head is simply a reversal of the portrait of Anne in the left wing of the Crabbe triptych. It seems probable that, in the centre panel of the Prado triptych, the man third from the left, and perhaps the half-concealed youth third from our right, are also portraits. All these figures are distinguished from those who truly participate in the narrative because they are not in fancy dress but wear contemporary clothes.[18]

A series of half-length portraits is clearly by the same painter, for they are related in style and of comparably high quality. Twelve of these show subjects at prayer and must be wings from diptychs or triptychs; nineteen are independent portraits. In the first group are two diptychs, one of which, the diptych of the Bruges patrician Maarten van Nieuwenhove, dated 1487 (cat. 23, pl. 25), has survived intact,[19] while the other, the diptych of the Virgin and Child adored by an unidentified donor (Chicago), was reunited during the last century.[20] One triptych can be reconstructed: the left wing, *St Benedict*, is in the Uffizi; the centre panel, a *Virgin and Child*, is in Berlin; the right wing, the portrait of Benedetto Portinari, dated 1487, is also in the Uffizi (see pl. 30).[21] Benedetto was a nephew of Tommaso Portinari and he too lived for a while in Bruges; he must have sent his triptych back to Italy soon after it was painted, for the landscape behind his portrait was copied in the background of a *Virgin and Child* (London) painted in Italy, probably in the 1490s and attributed to Perugino's pupil Andrea di Aloigi.[22] All three panels of Benedetto's triptych have the same dimensions, which implies that the left wing was folded over the centre panel and that the right wing, the reverse of which shows Benedetto's device and motto, was then folded on top of the left wing.

The existence of two more such triptychs can be surmised from the survival of both wing panels from each: the portraits of Tommaso and Maria Portinari (New York, Metropolitan Museum; pl. 2), painted early in the 1470s;[23] and the portraits of Willem and Barbara Moreel (Brussels;

cat. 18, pl. 19),[24] probably painted shortly before their large triptych dated 1484 (cat. 22, pl. 24). The Portinari panels were still united with their lost *Virgin and Child* in 1501 and 1544, when the triptych was described in the will of the donors' son Francesco as 'a small tabernacle with three hinged panels in which are painted the images of the most glorious Virgin and the testator's father and mother'.[25]

The remaining five half-length donor portraits are of praying men. Two of them face right: unidentified young men painted in about 1475 (London; fig. 39 and pl. 26)[26] and in about 1485 (Madrid, Museo Thyssen; cat. 25, pl. 28).[27] The latter's clothes seem to indicate that he was a Spaniard.[28] The other three face left. The first, dated 1472, represents the musician and composer Gilles Joye (Williamstown; cat. 3, pl. 4), a canon of the church of St Donatian in Bruges, where he was buried. During the 1460s he had also served as a chaplain at the Burgundian court.[29] His executors were permitted to hang 'a wooden board of his reputation on his portrait near his tomb in the sacristy'.[30] The second is the small portrait of a man (The Hague; cat. 21, pl. 23), painted in about 1480 and identified by a coat of arms on the reverse, later overpainted with another shield, as a member of the de l'Espinette family from Franche-Comté.[31] The coat of arms beneath the overpaint could equally be that of the de Visen, who also came from Franche-Comté.[32] Charles de Visen, who married in 1457 and died in 1486, had been one of Charles the Bold's *sommeliers de corps* and the keeper of his *menus joyaux*: he lived in the duke's chamber and looked after its furnishings, including the jewels and the books that he used from day to day. Charles de Visen was also a noted combatant at court tournaments and held important military offices.[33] The man in the Hague portrait could be Charles de Visen; he seems to have a broken nose and may have sustained this injury in Burgundian service. The last of these half-length donor portraits is the even smaller portrait of a young man, painted in about 1490 (Upton House, Warwickshire; cat. 26, pl. 31).[34]

### Independent portraits

A further nineteen paintings are independent portraits. One is a double portrait of an elderly couple, which has been divided into its two component parts (Berlin–Louvre; cat. 5, pl. 6) and which was probably painted in the 1470s.[35] Two further portraits of an old man (New York, Metropolitan Museum; pl. 10a) and an old woman (Hou-

ston; cat. 9, pl. 10b) are thought to have been cut from another such double portrait, painted probably in the 1480s.[36] Two of the nineteen works are portraits of women, both facing left: the so-called 'Sibyl', dated 1480 (Bruges, Memlingmuseum; cat. 17, pl. 18);[37] and a very damaged fragment, perhaps of about the same date (New York, Metropolitan Museum).[38] The remaining fifteen portraits are of men, nine of whom face left and six of whom face right – which may imply, but does not necessarily prove, that those six were once paired with portraits of women facing left.

Let us consider the men, none of whom can be positively identified, in an approximately chronological order. None of these portraits is dated; they have to be placed on grounds of costume and style. The earliest group, probably of around 1470, comprises the portraits at Frankfurt (cat. 1, pl. 1)[39] and in the Frick Collection (cat. 2, pl. 3)[40] and the head, cut into an oval, presumably from a half-length portrait (formerly in the Barlow collection; cat. 6, pl. 7).[41] The Windsor *Man* (cat. 12, pl. 13)[42] and the Washington *Man with an Arrow* (cat. 13, pl. 14)[43] are perhaps of about 1475. The *Man with a Spotted Fur Collar* (Uffizi; cat. 8, pl. 9) may be placed in the second half of the 1470s,[44] with the Brussels *Portrait of a Man* (cat. 7, pl. 8)[45] and the *Man with a Pink* (New York, Morgan Library; cat. 20, pl. 22).[46] The last is almost exactly the same size as the 'Sibyl' of 1480 but, since the two compositions do not balance particularly well, they are unlikely to have formed a pair. The *Man* from the Corsini collection, now in the Uffizi (cat. 11, pl. 12), was copied by an Italian, probably late in the fifteenth century.[47] The sitter was presumably Italian and his picture, like the similar portraits of a *Young Man* (Venice; cat. 16, pl. 17)[48] and the *Man with a Coin of the Emperor Nero* (Antwerp; cat. 10, pl. 11),[49] may be placed around 1480. The *Young Man* from the Lehman Collection (New York, Metropolitan Museum; cat. 15, pl. 16) was known to painters working in Florence towards the end of the fifteenth century, who imitated the composition and copied the columns and the landscape. This would imply that the sitter was another Italian who sent the portrait home to Italy shortly after it was painted, perhaps around 1480.[50] To the later 1480s may be assigned the portrait of Benedetto (?) Portinari, missing from the Uffizi since 1944; the sitter has been identified from descriptions of the reverse, which was very similar to the reverse of the portrait of Benedetto dated 1487 on the right wing of his triptych, and from his

resemblance to that painting.[51] Yet another portrait in the Uffizi, showing a man wearing a robe with a brown fur collar, appears to be from about the same period (cat. 24, pl. 29),[52] while the very damaged *Man Holding a String of Beads* (Copenhagen; pl. 32) would seem to be the latest of all, perhaps painted in about 1490.[53] As the beads may be a paternoster and as the donor in Memling's *Virgin and Child with Saints and Angels* (New York, Metropolitan Museum) is shown not praying but telling his beads,[54] it is claimed that the Copenhagen portrait could be the wing of a diptych or triptych. If it is, its closest parallel would be the portrait of Charles de Visen (?); here, the Copenhagen picture will be considered as an independent portrait.

## Copies
Other portraits, close in style to Memling's work but not of comparable quality, are classified as copies after lost originals by him. One such lost portrait was of Antoine, the 'Grand Bâtard' of Burgundy, an illegitimate brother of Charles the Bold, a figure of considerable importance in international politics and a discerning patron of the arts. The original was painted in about 1470; two good copies (Chantilly; fig. 47, and Dresden) have on their reverses the sitter's device and motto.[55] The second lost portrait was of Jacques of Savoy, Count of Romont, the ninth son of Louis II, Duke of Savoy, who spent much of his life at the courts and in the armies of his Burgundian cousins. It is known from one painted copy (Basel; fig. 46), on the reverse of which are painted Jacques's name and coat of arms. The lost original would have been painted before, though not long before, 1478: in that year, Jacques, born in 1450, became a Knight of the Golden Fleece and thereafter would have worn the collar of the Order.[56] The last two portraits, known from rather poor and less trustworthy copies, were of Edward IV, King of England, and his wife Elizabeth Woodville, whom Memling would have

encountered during their exile in Bruges in 1470–71.[57] The early sixteenth-century version of Edward's portrait in the Royal Collection (fig. 44) shows him wearing a robe of velvet cloth of gold of the pattern that Memling used on cloths of honour behind the Virgins in the 'Donne Triptych' (fig. 43) and at least three other paintings.[58] Indeed it was one of Memling's favourite textile patterns and it is quite likely that, confronted by a king living in exile and relative poverty, he decided to invent for him a suitably magnificent robe. Another version of this likeness, known from an engraving of about 1472, showed Edward crowned and holding a sceptre and an orb.[59] The incompetent versions of the portrait of his queen (fig. 45) show her wearing a golden bonnet under a 'butterfly' head-dress of the type which in 1470 was just coming into fashion in England but which never seems to have found much favour in Flanders.[60]

### Rejected attributions

Several other portraits, which do not appear to be copies, have been given to Memling but are not sufficiently good or sufficiently like the authenticated portraits for the attributions to be sustained. They are the damaged portraits of young men at Montreal (cat. 19, pl. 20)[61] and Zurich (pl. 21),[62] whose heads are more distorted than anything by Memling; and the *Young Woman with a Pink* (New York, Metropolitan Museum), perhaps of about 1475, which may be an allegorical figure rather than a straightforward portrait but which in any case is too badly drawn and too coarsely painted to be by Memling.[63] Even if the fashions for high foreheads and thin arms are taken into account, it cannot be by the same artist who painted Maria Portinari. All three paintings should be reassigned to imitators or followers of Memling. Finally, the portrait of Jacob (?) Obrecht (Fort Worth; cat. 28, pl. 34), dated 1496, seems to have been painted in Antwerp.[64]

### Composition

It now becomes possible to make some generalizations about Memling's portraits and to analyse the ways in which he individualized, but at the same time idealized, his subjects.[65]

He evidently preferred, for his independent portraits, a 'seven-eighths' to a three-quarters view. A head in pure three-quarters view presents the far eye with its tear-duct tangent to the contour of the nose and its opposite corner

*fig. 46*
After Memling
*Portrait of Jacques of Savoy*
Basel, Kunstmuseum

tangent to the contour of the face: the London *Young Man at Prayer* is a good example (pl. 26). In his half-length as in his full-length donor portraits, Memling was obliged to turn his subjects towards the objects of their devotions, in three-quarters or even 'five-eighths' views: Sir John and Lady Donne provide instances of this last pose, between three-quarters and pure profile (fig. 43). In the independent portraits, however, he usually followed his own preference for the 'seven-eighths' view. The Corsini portrait of a man (pl. 12) and the 'Sibyl' (pl. 18) are examples.

Memling usually centred his sitter's head. In some cases, the centre of the portrait's width lies in the pupil of the near eye; in most cases, the centre lies within the area of the near eye. The Lehman portrait is exceptional in that the centre lies between the eyes. Only the Antwerp, Corsini and Lehman men and Jacques of Savoy look towards the spectator (fig. 46; pls. 11, 12, 16). Because of the placing of the pupils and the catchlights, only the Antwerp sitter seems to meet the spectator's gaze.

In his half-length donor portraits, Memling necessarily included the hands, which are joined in prayer. Only Barbara Moreel and the Chicago donor cross their thumbs, though this pose is fairly common in Memling's full-length donor portraits. In his half-length independent portraits, he seems always to have included at least one hand. Fifteen such portraits survive and four copies: ten show two hands (separated in four instances, e.g. fig. 44 and pl. 1; pressed together in six instances, e.g. figs. 45, 46 and pl. 18); nine show only one hand (e.g. fig. 47; pls. 12, 14). The hands are confined to a corner (eleven examples, e.g. pls. 1, 14) or placed off centre (eight examples, e.g. figs. 46, 47; pls. 12, 18). Six of the men have attributes: a folded paper and a pink (pl. 22); an arrow (pl. 14); a coin of Nero and a leaf (pl. 11); a folded paper (pl. 12); beads (pl. 32); a ring (fig. 44).[66]

The hands normally appear to be resting on the frame, which serves as a sort of parapet. In four cases a parapet is painted above the frame. In two compositions, the Uffizi *Man with Spotted Fur Collar* (pl. 9) and the *Grand Bâtard*, known from copies (fig. 47), the parapet supports the hand. In the third, the *Jacques of Savoy*, if the copy is trustworthy (fig. 46), Memling experimented with a short parapet in the lower right corner which fills only a third of the composition's width but serves to support both hands. In the fourth, the Corsini portrait (pl. 12), the hand overlaps the parapet and seems to touch the frame. In the 'Sibyl' (pl. 18), the only independent portrait that has preserved its original frame, the tips of the fingers protrude onto the frame. If more original frames had survived, it might have been possible to discuss in greater detail this aspect of Memling's interest in illusion.

When patrons commissioned their portraits and agreed on prices, they would of course have determined not only the sizes of their portraits but also the poses and the types of background. Maarten van Nieuwenhove would have paid a lot more for his diptych than the unidentified young man in the portrait at Upton House simply because Maarten's portrait is nearly eight times bigger in area (pls. 25, 31). The unidentified youth, moreover, has a plain background; and plain backgrounds must have been cheaper than landscapes. Memling could offer plain backgrounds, interiors, interiors with views over landscapes or uninterrupted

landscape vistas. Plain backgrounds occur in one of the reconstructed double portraits, the New York–Houston *Elderly Couple*, eight of the half-length independent portraits (e.g. pls. 14, 18), three of the independent portraits known from copies (figs. 44, 45, 47) and four of the half-length donor portraits (e.g. pl. 4). An interior without a window is found only in one donor portrait, the London *Young Man* (pl. 26). Interiors with views onto landscapes appear in the Berlin–Louvre *Elderly Couple* (pl. 6), in only one of the independent portraits, the Lehman *Young Man*, but in six of the donor portraits (e.g. pl. 19a). An uninterrupted landscape stretches behind one of the half-length donors, Charles de Visen (?), but also behind nine of the sitters in the independent portraits (e.g. pls. 1, 12), including the *Jacques of Savoy*, known only from a copy (fig. 46). Just as Memling had decided to include parapets in five of his independent portraits – two with plain backgrounds and three with landscape backgrounds – he introduced fictive frames behind his subjects in the donor portraits of the Portinari couple, which have plain backgrounds, and in the portraits of unidentified men in Frankfurt and in The Frick Collection, which have landscape backgrounds. All four are early paintings of about or shortly after 1470, when Memling seems to have been particularly interested in the creation and denial of illusions of space: compare the donor portraits of the Gdańsk *Last Judgement* (fig. 41).

## Idealization and individualization

There is a family resemblance among Memling's portraits, for he tends always to enlarge eyes and mouths, to elongate noses and to smooth away angularities of contour. Sudden contrasts of light and shadow are generally avoided. In his half-length portraits, he distorts very much more boldly than in his full-length donor portraits. Where the donors are in close proximity to idealized figures of saints, he avoids making too disruptive a contrast between the sacred and profane figures. In the half-length portraits, however, the faces are too large in proportion to the heads, so that the crania appear diminished (pls. 12, 18). The enlargement is made both vertically and horizontally and the features, the most interesting parts of the face, are emphasized. Measure the distance between the eyes and the chin and compare the distance between the eyes and the top of the head. These should be approximately equal, as they are in nature and in Memling's full-length portraits of donors (figs. 40, 43). Then measure the widths of the eyes and the distance between the eyes, which, if allowance is made for the turning of the head, should be approximately the same. Memling usually diminishes the far eye, enlarges the near eye and increases the space between the eyes, which is even wider than the near eye. This gives a false impression of recession. The nose is longer and broader and the mouth is wider, in conformity with the enlarged eyes; the mouth recedes too abruptly at the far corner, again enhancing the false sense of recession. The eyebrows, eyelids, eyelashes and eyeballs and the lips are painted with great refinement of detail, which further stresses their importance. Asymmetries between the eyes, the eyebrows or the corners of the mouth seem sometimes to be stressed in the interests of getting a vivid likeness. The placing of the subject's headgear or an emphasis on the patterns made by his hair distract attention from the anomalies of scale, which are rarely disturbing in Memling's authentic portraits.

The portraits of Willem and Barbara Moreel in the 'Moreel Triptych' are exceptional in that their heads, unlike those of their children, are slightly distorted so that their faces are enlarged and their crania diminished (pl. 24, detail). Normally, because they are close to five saints who are represented on the same scale, Memling would have given their heads normal proportions. Here, however, for Willem and Barbara, though not for their children, he was probably working from the portraits on the wings of their half-length triptych where they were isolated and where Memling had applied his usual distortions for likenesses in half-length (pl. 19).

In the two earliest independent portraits, the unidentified men in Frankfurt and in The Frick Collection (pls. 1, 3), the distortions are even more marked because Memling has forced the noses further into profile than the other features, in order to give them more immediately recognizable contours. The mouths, positioned in relation to the points of the noses, have moved out of alignment with the eyes: the centres of the mouths are no longer vertically below the centre point between the eyes, with the result that both men appear to have projecting jaws. The lost original of the portrait of the 'Grand Bâtard' seems to have been distorted in much the same way (fig. 47). The Frankfurt portrait, where the eyes are unusually small and close together and where they look in slightly diverging directions, is perhaps over-ambitious in combining nearly full-face views of the eyes and mouth with a nearly profile

*fig. 47*
After Memling
*Antoine, the 'Grand Bâtard de Bourgogne'*
Chantilly, Musée Condé

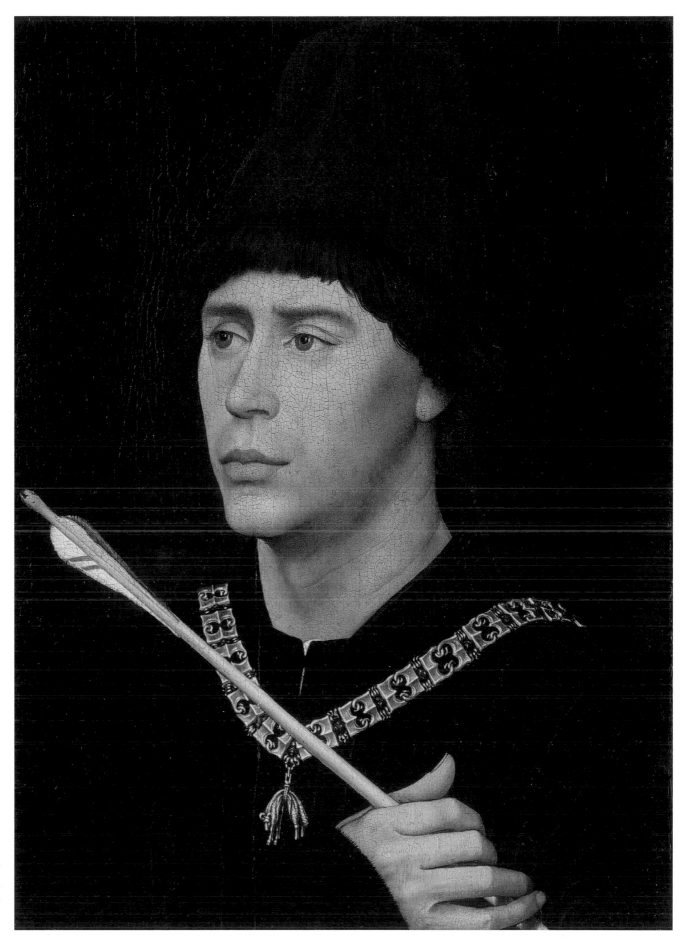

*fig. 48*
Rogier van der Weyden
*Antoine, the 'Grand Bâtard
de Bourgogne'*
Brussels, Musées Royaux des
Beaux-Arts de Belgique

view of the nose. The space between the far eye and the contour of the head is distressingly unresolved, too obviously removed from nature. In his later portraits, Memling twists the noses less dramatically and the distortions are more acceptably managed.

The eyes do not always look in precisely the same direction and the slightly diverging gaze can give a certain mobility of expression: the face will seem to change its aspect as the spectator focuses on one eye or the other. The pupils are often very small and the irises are generally large: which may indicate that Memling placed his sitters in a very strong light; but which may also imply that he liked to increase the area of the irises so that he could record in greater detail the beauties of the patterns and changes of colour. The irises often float clear of the lower lids: this applies to twelve of the independent portraits as well as the Louvre *Elderly Woman* (pl. 6b) and the *Jacques of Savoy* (fig. 46) and to six of the half-length donor portraits (pl. 4). In all the others, except the copies of the *Edward IV* (fig. 44), the irises are tangent to the lower lids but, because the thicknesses of the eyelids, viewed from above, are exaggerated, highlighted and falsely pale, the irises can still give the impression of floating (pl. 18). The floating iris, sometimes considered a mark of beauty, induces an expression of elevated exaltation, of constantly looking upward.

Memling does not seem to have wanted to probe the personalities of his subjects, who may have preferred not to be probed. The two about whom most is known are Antoine, the 'Grand Bâtard', and Gilles Joye. According to Chastellain's chronicle, Antoine was a knight of high courage and one of the most handsome people of his time, wonderfully ceremonious and punctilious.[67] This description agrees less well with Memling's portrait, admittedly known only from copies (fig. 47), than with the earlier painting by Rogier van der Weyden (Brussels; fig. 48), closer in date to Chastellain's text. Though Rogier was not strongly inclined to be analytical, his portrait conveys, by a wonderful use of distortion and pattern, something of Antoine's ardent disposition.

No one could guess from Memling's portrait of Gilles Joye (pl. 4) that he was a witty, mischievous and lecherous cleric, who was constantly reproved by his superiors. During mass on Christmas Day 1450, when he was twenty-five, he and two friends had concocted ribald verses about all their colleagues at St Donatian's and these had been

*fig. 49*
Master of Frankfurt
*Self-Portrait with his Wife*, 1496
Antwerp, Koninklijk Museum voor
Schone Kunsten

'*jocose recitata*' at dinner. In 1454, he was told to mend his ways, moderate his language and get rid of his mistress, '*vocatam in vulgo Rosabelle*'.[68] An 'excellent poet' as well as a musician, Joye certainly composed the music for the song *Ce qu'on fait a catimini*; he may also have written the text, which uses ingenious plays on French and Latin words for obscene and blasphemous effect. *A catimini* means 'on the sly' but *catamini*, deriving from the Greek, could also mean catamenia, menstruation. The word is set against the second person plural ending for Latin verbs in the passive voice, *-mini*. '*Ce qu'on fait a catimini / Touchant multiplicamini*': *multiplicamini*, moreover, echoes the words of God in the first book of Genesis – '*Crescite et multiplicamini*' in the Vulgate; 'Be fruitful, and multiply' in the Authorized Version. 'What is done stealthily concerning multiplication …' '*Mais qu'il soit bien tenu secret / Sera tenu pour excusé / In conspectu altissimi*' – '… as long as it is a well-kept secret, will be excused in the sight of the Most High'. In the second stanza, Latin deponent verbs are cleverly deployed: '*Et pourtant operamini / Mes filles, et letamini …*' – 'And now, my girls, labour [or, alternatively, worship] and be joyous …'. In the third stanza, the medieval Latin verb *ingrosso* – I make thick – is used to mean 'make pregnant'. '*Et se vous ingrossamini / Soit in nomine Domini / Vous aurez à proufit ouvré / et vous sera tout pardonné / Mais que vous confitemini*' – 'And if you are made pregnant, Be it in the name of the Lord. You will have laboured profitably and all will be forgiven as long as you make confession.'[69] Of course, Memling's portrait was the wing of a diptych or triptych and was placed near Joye's tomb, for which it may always have been intended. Eventually, his executors were to attach to it a sonorous Latin inscription in praise of the canon.[70] Though Memling makes Joye look suitably solemn and even ascetic, there is little sign of his humanity, let alone his genius as a composer of music and poetry.

### Tradition and innovation

Instructive comparisons can be made between portraits of Maria Portinari by Memling and by Hugo van der Goes,[71] or between Memling's portraits of women and Gerard David's bland and fairly objective donor portrait of Marie Caignet on the right wing of his 'Triptych of Jan de Sedano' (Louvre; fig. 50), probably painted during Memling's lifetime.[72] The Master of Frankfurt's *Self-Portrait with his Wife* (Antwerp; fig. 49) was painted in Antwerp in 1496, two years after Memling's death; it shows how, in the period around 1500, portraitists were relaxing some of the conventions of pose and composition.

Memling has been fortunate in that fairly large numbers of his portraits have survived. It is impossible to estimate how many may have been lost but it would appear that time has spared fewer portraits by his mentor Rogier van der Weyden and by his great contemporary Hugo van der Goes. Hardly any fourteenth-century Netherlandish painted portraits are still in existence, though copies, often of wretched quality, and documentary evidence attest to the fact that flourishing traditions in portraiture existed in the Low Countries before the time of the Van Eycks. Because so little survives, any attempt to discuss trends and developments in Netherlandish portraiture must be at best provisional, at worst futile. The subject is further bedevilled by the notion of 'Northern Realism' – the misconceived idea that artists in the lands beyond Italy pursued the imitation of reality with the same stolidity as their Florentine contemporaries. In fact, the leading artists of France and the Low Countries had achieved by about 1400 astonishing levels of technical brilliance and had passed far beyond imitation to highly sophisticated degrees of invention. Jan van Eyck and his contemporaries must have assumed that a competent artist would be able to imitate reality convincingly and that, having mastered representation, he would deploy his abilities in pursuit of further aims: to delight, disturb, move or enlighten his public.

Memling came from Seligenstadt. It is generally believed that he received his first training in that region and that he then went to Brussels to work with Rogier van der Weyden. In Rogier's studio, he would have learned about Netherlandish techniques and traditions, about principles of design and ways of using distortion and ambiguity for expressive effect. After Rogier's death in June 1464, Memling moved on to Bruges, where he became a burgess on 30 January 1465. He seems to have retained connections with the Van der Weyden workshop, which continued to function under the direction of Rogier's descendants, and with some of Rogier's other associates, for example the Master of the Prado Adoration. When Memling arrived in Bruges, the name and work of Jan van Eyck would have been held in reverence and Petrus Christus, who in his earlier years had been in contact with Jan's assistants and imitators, survived until 1475–6 (figs. 51–53). Between that time and 1484, when Gerard David arrived from Holland,

*fig. 51*
Petrus Christus
*Portrait of a Carthusian*, 1446
New York, The Metropolitan
Museum of Art, The Jules Bache
Collection

*fig. 52*
Petrus Christus
*Portrait of a Lady*
Staatliche Museen zu
Berlin, Preussischer
Kulturbesitz,
Gemäldegalerie

*fig. 53*
Petrus Christus
*Portrait of a Young Man*
London, National Gallery

Memling can have had no serious rivals in Bruges, though he lost one exceedingly important patron, Tommaso Portinari, to Hugo van der Goes.

Memling brought to Bruges from other traditions new ideas on portraiture. His half-length double portraits are similar to paintings produced in Germany, though full-length double portraits had been known in the Low Countries in the fourteenth century and Jan van Eyck had painted in 1434 his full-length portrait of Giovanni (?) Arnolfini and his wife (London).[73] This was probably still in Bruges in Memling's time; it was certainly known to his contempo-

rary, the illuminator Loyset Liédet.[74] The half-length double portrait, however, may have been new to Bruges.

Memling's practice of putting portraits among the onlookers in paintings of religious subjects had a long history and can certainly be related back to Rogier van der Weyden, who included a self-portrait in his lost *Scenes of Justice*, painted for the Town Hall of Brussels, and, in his triptych of the *Seven Sacraments* (Antwerp), portraits of the donor, Jean Chevrot, Bishop of Tournai, and several of his associates.[75] Memling's portraits of people actually playing the parts of persons mentioned in the Gospel nar-

*fig. 54*
Dieric Bouts
*Portrait of a Man
(Jan van Winckele?)*, 1462
London, National Gallery

rative, for example Anne Willemszoon, who impersonates the prophetess Anna in the *Presentation in the Temple* on the right wing of the Prado triptych of the *Adoration of the Kings*, have precedents in German painting. In Mainz, near Memling's home in Seligenstadt, there were in two different churches two early fifteenth-century paintings including portraits of the Emperor Sigismund as one of the Three Kings and as King David.[76]

Precedents for Memling's portraits of people in interiors can be found in Van Eyck's *Giovanni (?) Arnolfini and his Wife*, dated 1434, Petrus Christus's *Edward Grimston*, dated 1446 (lent to London) and Dirk Bouts's *Portrait of a Man (Jan van Winckele?)*, dated 1462 (London; fig. 54).[77] The very artificial idea of placing a half-length figure in front of a distant panoramic landscape may have been evolved by Rogier, who used it in his 'Braque Triptych' of about 1452 (Louvre; see fig. 38).[78] Even if few portraits with landscape backgrounds are known that are certainly earlier than Memling's Frankfurt and Frick portraits, the shortage of comparative material, and especially of dated or datable material, means that the search for 'firsts' is doomed to frustration and can result only in further inaccuracies and uncertainties.

Memling's distortions, however, and his play with levels of reality must have been inspired by Jan van Eyck and Rogier van der Weyden. Jan, Rogier and Memling were all interested in the spatial relationships between the portrait and its frame.[79] Rogier's men and women frequently appear to rest their hands on the frames of their portraits; their hands are often compressed into small triangles or parallelograms which echo the pyramidal compositions of the portraits and which, by limiting the areas of high tone created by the flesh of the hands, prevent them from distracting attention from the heads (fig. 48). Memling sometimes follows Rogier's lead (cf. the Washington portrait; see fig. 61) but, being less concerned with linear pattern and more interested in spatial illusion, he develops on Jan van Eyck's experiments with parapets and with hands that appear to project across the frame. Memling uses various means to keep the hands under control: sometimes he simply omits one hand; or he loses sections of hands within sleeves or behind frames; or he gets rid of fingers below the knuckles by making the hands emerge from behind a frame or parapet on which are rested only the tips of the fingers. This stresses the plane of the frame.

In his religious paintings, Memling often stresses the plane of the frame and then simultaneously counters this emphasis by building out, in the lower parts of his compositions, platforms that seem to be in front of the frame. On the exterior of the Gdańsk *Last Judgement*, the niches occupied by the statues of the Virgin and Child and St Michael appear to be in the plane of the frames until we register that the plinths project from that plane and that the donors on their platforms are at some distance from the statues and their plinths, on our side of the apparent division between us and the statues (fig. 41). Similarly, in the 'Sibyl' (pl. 18), the tips of her fingers emerge out of the picture, cross the parapet and end in front of the frame, on which the tips of the fingers are painted.

The recent cleaning of the Washington *Man with an Arrow* has led to a remarkable discovery: a fly sits, apparently on the frame, between the man's thumb and his shirt (pl. 14).[80] The foreshortened thumb seems to project across the frame. The original frame is lost but, if it was like the frame of the 'Sibyl',[81] it would have had no thickness at that point. The fly has nowhere to put its feet and cannot be in the fictive space of the picture or in the real space of the frame. Memling's play with illusion is here at its most subtle. If, as seems likely, the arrow continued across the frame, the spatial relationships were exceedingly complicated. The proportions of the head have been purposefully distorted in the interests of vivid likeness. The arrow and the hat-badge of the Virgin and Child on a crescent moon provide indications of the man's identity, which nevertheless continues to elude us. Freed now of its disfiguring nineteenth-century additions and restored to its original splendours of composition and colour, the *Man with an Arrow* and his fly provide a most instructive example of the ways in which Memling develops upon the examples of Jan van Eyck and Rogier van der Weyden, in which he creates and then denies illusions and manipulates appearances of reality. The fascination with which contemporaries and later generations have regarded, and will continue to regard, his portraits is due in large part to his powers over reality and illusion.

1 De Vos 1994, nos. 32 and 31.

2 Martens 1994, 14–15; for the excommunication of Agnes, see M. Vleeschouwers-van Melkebeek, *Compotus sigilliferi curie Tornacensis. Rekeningen van de officialiteit van Doornik 1429–1481*, 3 vols., Commission royale d'histoire, Brussels 1995, I, 257 (3519).

3 G. H. Flamen, 'Le frère Jean Floreins, maître spirituel de l'Hôpital Saint-Jean, à Bruges', *Annales de la Société d'Émulation pour l'étude de l'histoire & des antiquités de la Flandre* XXXI (4e sér. IV) (1880), 18–52. Jacob Floreins, apparently Jan's younger brother, became a burgess of Bruges in 1464, when he was described as a native of Boussu: see R. A. Parmentier, *Indices op de Brugsche Poorterboeken* (Geschiedkundige publicatiën der stad Brugge, II), 2 vols., Bruges 1938, II, 568–9.

4 De Vos 1994, 62 and 105–9, no. 11.

5 R. J. Walsh, *Charles the Bold, last Valois Duke of Burgundy 1467–1477, and Italy*, Ph.D. dissertation, Hull 1977, 273–85.

6 De Vos 1994, 62 and 296–303, no. 83.

7 De Vos 1994, 63 and 173–9, no. 38.

8 De Vos 1994, 63–4 and 170–2, no. 37.

9 De Vos 1994, 64 and 307–9, no. 85; Goetghebeur 1997.

10 The remaining seven are: the *Virgin and Child with St Anthony and a Donor*, dated 1472 (Ottawa: cat. 4); the *Virgin and Child with Saints and Angels and a Donor* (New York, Metropolitan Museum: De Vos 1994, no. 35; New York 1998, 116–17); the *Lamentation* (Rome, Galleria Doria Pamphilj, acquired in 1854 from the Roman painter Luigi Cochetti, 1802–84: De Vos 1994, no. 25; E. A. Safarik, *Galleria Doria Pamphilj, Masterpieces, Paintings*, Florence and Rome 1993, 34–5); the *Virgin and Child with St George and a Donor* (London: De Vos 1994, no. 51; Campbell 1998, 354–8); the triptych of the *Virgin and Child with Saints and a Donor* (Vienna: De Vos 1994, no. 53); the diptych of the *Virgin and Child with Saints and Jean du Cellier* (Louvre: De Vos 1994, no. 62; Comblen-Sonkes and Lorentz 1995, 263–82); and the diptych of the *Virgin and Child with Angels, St George and a Donor* (Munich: De Vos 1994, no. 87). The badly damaged portrait of a member of the de Rojas family (De Vos 1994, no. 2), sold at Sotheby's, London, 10 July 2002 (no. 8), is also left out of account until further investigations clarify the question of condition and the problem of the subject's identity.

11 De Vos 1994, no. 4; Farics 1997.

12 De Vos 1994, no. 5; Geirnaert 1997. The last ring of the wing panels was formed in 1442 (reports by Peter Klein, 27 August and 27 September 2004).

13 De Vos 1994, no. 39; Campbell 1998, 374–91.

14 De Vos 1994, no. 63.

15 De Vos 1994, no. 86; Comblen-Sonkes and Lorentz 1995, 238–62; see also note 3 above for the record of his becoming a burgess of Bruges in 1464, when, at the instance of Pieter Bladelin, the usual charges were waived: '*Gratis 12s., par le commandement de monseigneur de Leestmakere*'.

16 De Vos 1994, no. 90; see also P. G. Bietenholz, 'Adolf Greverade of Lübeck', in *Contemporaries of Erasmus, A Biographical Register of the Renaissance and Reformation*, ed. P. G. Bietenholz and T. B. Deutscher, 3 vols., Toronto, Buffalo and London 1985–7, II, 128–9.

17 Lobelle-Caluwé 1997.

18 De Vos 1994, no. 13; Garrido 1997.

19 De Vos 1994, no. 78.

20 De Vos 1994, no. 55.

21 De Vos 1994, no. 79.

22 Rohlmann 1994, 87.

23 De Vos 1994, no. 9; New York 1998, 162–4. The last annual rings of the oak panels on which they are painted were formed in 1423 (Tommaso) and 1448 (Maria): see Klein 1997, 288–9.

24 De Vos 1994, no. 22; Stroo et al. 1999, 200–214. The last rings in these panels were formed in 1461 (Willem) and 1457 (Barbara): see Stroo et al. 1999, 213 n. 2.

25 L. A. Waldman, 'New documents for Memling's Portinari Portraits in the Metropolitan Museum of Art', *Apollo* (February 2001), 28–33.

26 De Vos 1994, no. 45; Campbell 1998, 370–73.

27 De Vos 1994, no. 72.

28 Compare the painting thought to represent Diego Hurtado de Mendoza (1415–79), first Duke of Infantado, by the Master of Sopetrán (Prado: M. del Carmen Garrido & J. M. Cabrera, 'El dibujo subyacente y otros aspectos técnicos de las tablas de Sopetrán', *Boletín del Museo del Prado* III [1982], 15–31).

29 De Vos 1994, no. 18.

30 Strohm 1994, 42–3.

31 De Vos 1994, no. 40. The last ring in the panel was formed in 1465: see Klein 1997, 289. He was perhaps Antoine de l'Espinette, an esquire who by 1496 was married to Aloïse de Vautravers (R. de Lurion, *Nobiliaire de Franche-Comté*, Besançon 1890, 296). Several members of the Vautravers family had been in the service of the Dukes of Burgundy, who granted them many privileges; in 1476, Claude de Vautravers had received Charles the Bold at his castle of Domblans near Lons-le-Saunier (F.-F. Chevalier, *Mémoires historiques sur la ville et seigneurie de Poligny*, Lons-le-Saunier 1767–9, II, 508–14; A. Rousset and F. Moreau, *Dictionnaire géographique, historique et statistique des communes de la Franche-Comté…, Département du Jura*, 6 vols., Besançon 1853–5 and Lons-le-Saunier 1856–8, III, 5–6, and VI, 306–9; Lurion, cited above, 785–6; etc.).

32 Jean de Visen, who had been between 1437 and 1440 Receiver of All the Finances of Philip the Good and who died in 1460, used a seal with the arms '*un chevron et un chef chargé de trois grelots ou coquilles*' (J. d'Arbaumont, *Armorial de la Chambre des Comptes de Dijon, d'après le manuscrit inédit du Père Gautier*, Dijon 1881, 124–5). If the objects on the chief are *grelots* or bells, then the correspondence with the overpainted coat of arms is complete.

33 Charles de Visen married in 1457 Jacqueline, daughter of Jean Le Tourneur, another intimate of Charles the Bold (W. Paravicini, *Invitations au mariage. Pratique sociale, abus de pouvoir, intérêt de l'état à la cour des ducs de Bourgogne 1399–1489*, Stuttgart 2001, 102–3). Mentioned by both Olivier de la Marche and Philippe de Commynes, Charles de Visen was for several years captain of the castle of Châtillon-sur-Seine.

34 De Vos 1994, no. 80.

35 De Vos 1994, no. 14; Comblen-Sonkes and Lorentz 1995, 286–95. The last ring in the Berlin panel was formed in 1430: see Klein 1997, 288.

36 De Vos 1994, no. 60; New York 1998, 168–9. The last ring in the Houston panel was formed in 1461: see Klein 1997, 288.

37 De Vos 1994, no. 36.

38 De Vos 1994, no. 21.

39 De Vos 1994, no. 7. The last ring in the panel was formed in 1442: see Klein 1997, 289.

40 De Vos 1994, no. 12. The last ring of the panel was formed in 1433 (report by Peter Klein, 27 August 2004).

41 De Vos 1994, no. 10.

42 De Vos 1994, no. 30.

43 De Vos 1994, no. 29.

44 De Vos 1994, no. 28.

45 De Vos 1994, no. 43; Stroo et al. 1999, 180–87. The last ring in the panel was formed in 1447: see Stroo et al. 1999, 187 n. 2.

46 De Vos 1994, no. 26. Maryan Ainsworth kindly informs me that the portrait was cleaned in 2003 and that the dimensions of the panel and the painted surface are, respectively, 39.5 x 28.4 and 37.8 x 27 cm. The last ring of the panel was formed in 1445 (report by Peter Klein, 27 August 2004).

47 De Vos 1994, no. 44.

48 De Vos 1994, no. 49.

49 De Vos 1994, no. 42; cleaned in 2002.

50 De Vos 1994, no. 48; New York 1998, 166–7. The last ring in the panel was formed in 1461: see Klein 1997, 289.

51 De Vos 1994, nos. 57 and 79 (triptych).

52 De Vos 1994, no. 56.

53 De Vos 1994, no. 69.

54 De Vos 1994, no. 35.

55 De Vos 1994, no. A6; for the Chantilly picture, see also Comblen-Sonkes 1988, 58–76, pls. LXXVI–LXXXIII.

56 De Vos 1994, no. A1. On the sitter, see L. Colot, 'Jacques de Savoie, Comte de Romont, homme lige de la maison de Bourgogne', *Publication du Centre européen d'études burgundo-médianes*, 20, *Rencontres de Milan 21 au 23 septembre 1978*, Basel 1980, 89–102. His widow had in her collection of portraits '*Ung de Jacques de Savoye premier mary de feue Madame de Luxembourg*': see 'Inventaire des tableaux de Marie de Luxembourg au château de La Fère (29 janvier 1551)', *Nouvelles archives de l'art français*, 3e sér., XI (1895), 80–83.

57 Hepburn 1986, 60–67.

58 Campbell 1998, 358, 384.

59 Hepburn 1986, 60–61, 67, pl. 49.

60 Hepburn 1986, 54–60, frontispiece, pls. 41, 44.

61 De Vos 1994, no. 46.

62 De Vos 1994, no. 47.

63 De Vos 1994, no. 73; New York 1998, 174–6. The last ring in the panel was formed in 1465: see Klein 1997, 289.

64 De Vos 1994, no. 93.

65 See Campbell 1990, 1–39, for more detailed considerations of the definitions of portrait, likeness, individualization, idealization and characterization.

66 These are the portraits in the Morgan Library, Washington and Antwerp, the 'Corsini' portrait in the Uffizi, the portrait in Copenhagen and the copy of the *Edward IV*.

67 [Le Quesnoy, October 1458:] '*Le bastard de Bourgoingne, qui moult estoit chevalier d'ung eslevé couraige et ung des beaux personnaiges de son temps, pompeux merveilleusement et de hault vouloir…*' See George Chastellain, *Chronique. Les fragments du Livre IV révélés par l'Additional Manuscript 54156 de la British Library*, ed. J.-C. Delclos (Textes littéraires français, 394), Geneva 1991, 130.

68 Strohm 1990, 27–9.

69 See Strohm 1994, 43 fig. 11, for the relevant pages from the 'Mellon Chansonnier'; H. Mayer Brown, *A Florentine Chansonnier from the Time of Lorenzo the Magnificent. Florence, Biblioteca Nazionale Centrale MS Banco Rari 229* (Monuments of Renaissance Music, VII), Chicago and London 1983, Text Volume, 306–7.

70 Strohm 1994, 42.

71 Campbell 1990, 16–23.

72 Jan de Sedano, who came from Santa Maria del Campo, settled in Bruges where he married, in about 1486, Marie, daughter of the Bruges merchant Willem Caignet. Between 1488 and 1492, Sedano seems to have resided in Antwerp but he moved back to Bruges. In the triptych, Jan is accompanied by a small boy, who holds a cross to indicate that he is dead. The triptych must have been painted in the early 1490s. See Hélène Adhémar, *Les Primitifs flamands*, I. *Corpus … 5, Le Musée National du Louvre, Paris*, vol. I, Brussels 1962, 101–13. For Marie Caignet and the date of her marriage, see Raymond Fagel, *De Hispano-Vlaamse wereld, De contacten tussen Spanjaarden en Nederlanders 1496–1555* (Archives et Bibliothèques de Belgique, Numéro spécial 52), Brussels and Nijmegen 1996, 219–20.

73 Campbell 1990, 53–4; Campbell 1998, 174–221.

74 Campbell 1998, 178–80.

75 Campbell 1990, 3.

76 Dr von Hagen, ed., *Das Leben König Sigismunds von Eberhard Windecke* (Die Geschichtschreiber der deutschen Vorzeit in deutscher Bearbeitung, Fünfzehntes Jahrhundert, 1), Leipzig 1886, 285.

77 Campbell 1990, 113–15; Campbell 1998, 46–51.

78 Campbell 1990, 120–21; De Vos 1994, 367.

79 Campbell 1990, 69–74.

80 I am extremely grateful to Catherine Metzger and to John Hand, who have most generously allowed me here to refer to this as yet unpublished discovery.

81 See the description and section in H. Verougstraete-Marcq and R. Van Schoute, *Cadres et supports dans la peinture flamande aux 15e et 16e siècles*, Heure-le-Romain 1989, 146–7.

*Paula Nuttall*

# Memling
# and the European
# Renaissance Portrait

In 1465 Memling established himself as an independent artist in Bruges. Like other outsiders before him – notably Jan van Eyck and Petrus Christus – who had also built successful careers there, his choice of Bruges must have been influenced by the city's pre-eminence as an international commercial centre and the prospect of artistic patronage afforded by the many foreign merchants who were either resident there, or simply passing through.[1] It was a judicious choice: Memling found a ready market for his work amongst the expatriates, particularly the Italians; indeed, figures calculated by Maximiliaan Martens suggest that around 20% of his output was produced for foreign patrons.[2]

Some of Memling's most important large-scale works were made for foreigners. The altarpiece of the *Last Judgement* (Gdańsk, Muzeum Narodowe), possibly his first major commission, datable to about 1469, was painted for the Florentine banker Agnolo Tani, formerly the manager of the Medici bank in Bruges; intended for Tani's chapel in the Badia of Fiesole, it was part of a cargo captured by a Hanseatic privateer *en route* to Italy and taken to Danzig.[3] The altarpiece of the *Crucifixion* (Lübeck, St. Annen Museum), dated 1491 and possibly Memling's last major commission, for the Greverade family chapel in Lübeck cathedral, was commissioned by Heinrich Greverade, a Hanseatic merchant in Bruges, or his brother Adolf.[4] On a more modest scale, the English courtier Sir John Donne, who made numerous visits to Bruges, commissioned a private devotional triptych of the *Virgin and Child with Saints* (London, National Gallery, see fig. 43).[5] The Florentine Tommaso Portinari, manager of the Bruges branch of the Medici bank, commissioned Memling's *Passion of Christ* (Turin, Galleria Sabauda), perhaps for a local church;[6] and a member of the Bolognese Loiani family commissioned Memling's small polyptych of *Earthly Vanity and Divine Salvation* (Strasbourg, Musée des Beaux-Arts).[7] The vast Marian altarpiece for the abbey of Nájera near Logroño, of which only the panels of *Christ in Glory with Musician Angels* survive (Antwerp, Koninklijk Museum), is traditionally thought to have been commissioned by a family from Nájera, involved in the wool trade with the Low Countries. Recently, however, it has been suggested that this altarpiece was commissioned for a more exalted patron, relying on Spanish wool traders as intermediaries.[8]

As well as acquiring work from Memling on their own account, members of the foreign community also acted

*fig. 55*
Memling
*Portrait of Maria Portinari*,
detail of pl. 2
New York, The Metropolitan
Museum of Art, Bequest of Benjamin
Altman

fig. 56
Memling
Triptych of Benedetto Portinari, 1487
Staatliche Museen zu Berlin,
Preussischer Kulturbesitz,
Gemäldegalerie (centre panel);
Florence, Galleria degli Uffizi (wings)

on behalf of clients at home. The eminent Florentine prelate Benedetto Pagagnotti, for example, commissioned a superb private devotional work from Memling, the triptych of the *Virgin and Child with Saints John the Baptist and Lawrence* (Florence, Uffizi, and London, National Gallery), without apparently ever having visited the Netherlands himself. He probably used as an intermediary his nephew Paolo Pagagnotti, a merchant known to have visited Bruges.[9]

Of all the works Memling produced for foreigners, portraits were by far the most popular, particularly among the Italians. Small-scale, portable and – obviously – personal, a portrait possessed the double attraction of recording the owner's appearance while also constituting a souvenir of his time in Bruges. Some of Memling's foreign patrons chose to have their portraits incorporated into half-length devotional triptychs or diptychs, a distinctively Netherlandish type often associated with Rogier van der Weyden, who may have been its inventor,[10] but also much favoured by Memling. Tommaso Portinari commissioned a triptych, probably around 1470, with portraits of himself and his young wife Maria Baroncelli (pl. 2 and figs. 55, 89) as pendants to a now-lost image of the Virgin and Child.[11] His nephew Benedetto Portinari, employed in the family business in Bruges, in 1487 also commissioned

figs. 57–58
Memling
*The Virgin and Child
with a Donor,*
details of pl. 27
The Art Institute of Chicago,
Mr & Mrs Martin A. Ryerson
Collection and Gift of Arthur Sachs

*fig. 59*
Memling
*Portrait of a Man with a Coin of the
Emperor Nero (Bernardo Bembo?)*
[cat. 10], detail of pl. 11
Antwerp, Koninklijk Museum voor
Schone Kunsten

a half-length devotional triptych incorporating his portrait with images of the Virgin and Child and St Benedict (fig. 56).[12] Memling's half-length diptych of the *Virgin and Child with a Donor* in Chicago may represent a Spanish patron (figs. 57–58; pl. 27),[13] and it has been suggested that the *Young Man at Prayer* in the Thyssen Collection (pl. 28), also once part of a devotional ensemble, was either Spanish or Italian.[14]

For the most part, however, foreign clients (like the majority of Netherlandish patrons) preferred the simpler – and less costly – alternative of an independent portrait. Memling depicted two more members of the Portinari family (well represented in late fifteenth-century Bruges), possibly brothers, in this format, in portraits now in the Uffizi and of unknown whereabouts (see pl. 29).[15] A further half-dozen or so portraits by Memling depict sitters who may have been foreigners, predominantly Italians. This is suggested in some cases by provenance (the *Man with a Spotted Fur Collar* in the Uffizi [pl. 9]; the *Portrait of a Young Man before a Landscape* in the Venice Accademia [pl. 17] and the *Portrait of a Man* in The Frick Collection [pl. 3] – the last of which has a north Italian provenance), by the existence of early copies testifying to a work's presence in Italy (*Portrait of a Man with a Letter* in the Uffizi [pl. 12] and the *Portrait of a Man* in the Lehman Collection [pl. 16]) or, in the case of the *Man with a Coin of the Emperor Nero* (pl. 11 and fig. 59) by attributes.[16] Together with his strikingly Mediterranean looks, the Roman coin which he holds (at this date, *c.* 1480, still largely the preserve of Italian humanists and collectors) and the prominent palm tree behind him have long been regarded as indicators that the sitter was Italian, and numerous attempts have been made to associate him with such family names as Palmieri, Palma or Neroni.[17] Recently, Hilde Lobelle-Caluwé made another, intriguing, suggestion, noting the connection between the motifs of the palm and the laurel sprig in the foreground (which perhaps originally extended onto the frame, making it more prominent), and the personal *impresa* of the Venetian patrician Bernardo Bembo.[18] Ambassador of Venice to the Burgundian court in 1473, Bembo was certainly a client of Memling's, being the

*fig. 60*
Giovanni Bellini
*Portrait of a Man (Pietro Bembo?)*, 1504
The Royal Collection © H. M. Queen Elizabeth II

*fig. 61*
Rogier van der Weyden
*Portrait of a Lady*
Washington, National Gallery of Art, Andrew W. Mellon Collection

owner of the diptych of *St John the Baptist and St Veronica* (Munich, Alte Pinakothek, and Washington, National Gallery of Art), and in 1473 would have been aged forty, which is plausibly the age of the sitter.[19] Given the Italian predilection for Memling's portraits, it is more than likely that Bembo commissioned his likeness as well as a devotional work.[20] Moreover, as will be seen below, there are further, stylistic reasons for associating this portrait with Bembo.

It is notable that this group includes many of Memling's finest portraits: evidently the foreigners demanded, and received, of Memling's best. Moreover it is clear that they kept abreast of local fashions in portraiture, and commissioned the same types of work as the local élite. With their plain dark backgrounds, the portraits of Tommaso and Maria Portinari, believed to have been painted shortly after their marriage in 1470, reflect the type popularized by Rogier van der Weyden, which was particularly fashionable in mid-fifteenth-century Burgundian court circles. By the late 1480s, when Benedetto Portinari commissioned his triptych (fig. 56), there had developed a preference for more descriptive settings and for the inclusion of attributes reflecting the sitter's status. Although set in a loggia rather than a richly appointed interior, the 'Triptych of Benedetto Portinari', with its luxurious still-life detail of prayerbook and textiles, can be likened to Memling's exactly contemporary 'Diptych of Maarten van Nieuwenhove' (pl. 25), which displays the same fascination with the appurtenances of material culture. Just as earlier Tommaso had emulated Burgundian courtiers like Philippe de Croÿ, so now his young nephew commissioned a work which may consciously have been intended to rival the superb portrait diptych painted by Memling for the scion of a noble Bruges family.

### The appeal of Memling's portraits

It is not difficult to see why Memling was in such demand among locals and foreigners alike. As a portraitist, he was unrivalled in late fifteenth-century Bruges.[21] The best-preserved of his portraits, such as the *Tommaso Portinari* (pl. 2), are miracles of naturalistic observation and painterly virtuosity: with the most subtly nuanced flesh tones, Memling conveys both sculptural form and surface texture. He records with analytical precision the sheen of smooth skin and the small scar on Tommaso's jaw, traces the fine lines around the eyes, brushes in the eyebrows almost hair for

*fig.* 62
Hugo van der Goes
The Portinari Altarpiece
Florence, Galleria degli Uffizi

hair, notes the catchlights and even the tiniest red capillaries in the eyes themselves. At the same time, Memling's ability to record appearance and to capture a likeness was tempered with subtle flattery, as is revealed by comparison of his portraits of Tommaso and Maria Portinari with Hugo van der Goes's less glamorous rendition of them in the 'Portinari Triptych' (Florence, Uffizi; see figs. 62, 94), where no effort is made to underplay sharp bones and large noses.[22] Memling enhanced the appearance of his sitters, and typically endowed them with an air of relaxed yet dignified nobility without overdue hauteur (compared with earlier Netherlandish portraits they are more elegant than those of Van Eyck or Petrus Christus, and more accessible than those of Van der Weyden). His portraits are also often masterly exercises in design, in which understated simplicity masks careful calculation. In the Lehman portrait, for instance, the sitter's hands are arranged in a way that subtly echoes the curve of his head, his curls are paralleled in the slight upward curve of his thumb, while the dark plum of his costume is picked up in the red marble of the columns, and their vertical forms are echoed in the fluting on his doublet. Moreover, the refined facture of Memling's portraits, in which as much care and delicacy are lavished on details of costume, still life or landscape as on the face itself, must have further enhanced their desirability as artefacts.

Memling's chief contribution to portraiture, however, was in his use of the landscape background, sometimes viewed through a window, as in the Lehman and Thyssen portraits (a motif already current in Netherlandish portraits, notably Petrus Christus's *Portrait of a Young Man* of *c.*1450 [fig. 53] and Bouts's *Portrait of Jan van Winckele* of 1462 [fig. 54], both in the National Gallery, London),[23] but more typically seen extending behind the sitter, either under an open sky or through the arch of a loggia. Whether or not Memling should be credited with inventing this distinctive portrait type, the roots of which may lie in devotional works such as Rogier's 'Braque Triptych' (see fig. 38) and Jan van Eyck's 'plateau' compositions, he certainly made it his own.[24] As a design formula it is felicitous, a balanced counterpoint between top and bottom, foreground and background: the head offset by the neutral expanse of sky, and the neutral area of the shoulders enlivened by the landscape detail behind. The hands rest on a ledge or on the edge of the picture frame, and the shoulders are often cropped at the sides, producing a close-up effect comparable to that achieved by zooming on a camera, as if the sitter is appearing at a window formed by the frame itself. This illusionistic *double entendre* is sometimes taken further, with the addition of a fictive painted frame behind the sitter, as in the Frick portrait (pl. 3), which has the effect of projecting the figure into the viewer's own space.

It is worth considering whether Memling's use of the landscape background – effectively his hallmark portrait type – was shaped by Italian demand. Judging from the number of portraits by him of this type associated with Italians, it was clearly one they favoured. The depiction of landscape was itself an admired attribute of Netherlandish painting in Italy, praised for instance in Bartolomeo Fazio's commentary on Jan van Eyck's famous

*fig. 63*
After Memling
*Portrait of a Man with a Letter*
Petworth House, Sussex

*fig. 64*
Pietro Perugino
*Self-Portrait*
Florence, Galleria degli Uffizi

painting of *Women Bathing* at Urbino.[25] Landscape, like portraiture, was an aspect of the representation of reality with which Italian painters at this date were actively engaged; like portraiture, too, it was an art form for which there was Classical authority, namely Pliny's descriptions of antique landscape paintings. In the light of this, it may not be too wide of the mark to suggest that awareness of Italian acclaim for this aspect of Netherlandish painting prompted Memling (familiar with the tastes of his Italian patrons) to evolve a new portrait type incorporating landscapes, which catered expressly for the tastes of his most important group of foreign clients.[26]

Punctuated with picturesque buildings, minute figures, and such details as horsemen or swans floating on water, these landscapes – like the handsome features of the sitters themselves – are easy on the eye, bringing to mind Michelangelo's famous comment that the Netherlanders paint 'such things as may cheer you and of which you cannot speak ill … [such as] the green grass of the fields, the shadow of trees, and rivers and bridges, which they call landscapes'.[27] Michelangelo's remark, reported in the *Roman Dialogues* of 1547 by the Portuguese artist Francisco de Holanda, was meant disparagingly, born of an artistic climate in which it was not the business of painting to be easy on the eye (in which portraiture itself, for that mat-

ter, was an inferior art form).[28] Memling's public, however, Italian, Iberian or Netherlandish, prized the very qualities which Michelangelo later condemned: the conquest of visual reality was a very recent one, and audiences for art were still entranced with the encylopaedic and the empirical, qualities with which sophisticated audiences in mid-sixteenth-century Italy had long since become jaded. In the late fifteenth century, the combined visual effect of pleasing landscape detail and miraculously rendered flesh, hair and costume in Memling's portraits must have appeared little short of perfection.

## The influence of Memling's portraits in Italy

It is not surprising that, as the leading portraitist in Bruges, Memling found particular favour with the Italian community, but appreciation of his skills extended to Italians who never visited the Low Countries. The distinguished Venetian collector Cardinal Domenico Grimani in 1521 owned a self-portrait and the portraits of 'a man and wife together in the Flemish manner [*alla Ponentina*]', all by Memling, described in 1521 by Marcantonio Michiel.[29] Although Michiel's attributions are not always reliable, the mere fact that he believed the portraits to be by Memling is testimony to the Flemish master's reputation in Italy a quarter-century after his death.

*fig. 65*
Piero della Francesca
*Portraits of Battista Sforza and Federigo da Montefeltro*
Florence, Galleria degli Uffizi

*fig. 66*
Antonello da Messina
*Portrait of a Man (the 'Condottiere')*
Paris, Musée du Louvre

fig. 67
Workshop of Verrocchio
*Virgin and Child*
Paris, Musée du Louvre

fig. 68
Domenico Ghirlandaio
*Portrait of an Old Man and his Grandson*
Paris, Musée du Louvre

Such esteemed portraits naturally exerted an influence on local painters. The *Portrait of a Man with a Letter* in the Uffizi (pl. 12) was faithfully copied by an Italian painter in a version now at Petworth House (fig. 63), perhaps because its owner required a replica, or perhaps as the sort of exercise in virtuosic emulation which Italian painters seem to have enjoyed. (Pietro Summonte, writing to Marcantonio Michiel, relates how the fifteenth-century Neapolitan painter Colantonio made a copy of a Netherlandish portrait of the Duke of Burgundy 'in such a manner that one could not distinguish his copy from the model'; in early sixteenth-century Milan, Giovan Francesco Caroto likewise sought competitively to reproduce a much-admired portrait newly arrived from Flanders.)[30] Memling's *Portrait of a Young Man* in the Lehman Collection (pl. 16) was closely imitated in the design of the *Self-Portrait* of Perugino in the Uffizi (fig. 64); its background detail of polished marble columns and landscape was also reproduced in a *Virgin and Child* from Verrocchio's circle in the Louvre.[31] The two trees on either side of the figure in the background of Memling's *Man with a Spotted Fur Collar* (pl. 9) were copied in the so-called *Portrait of Matteo Sassetti* by the young Fra Bartolommeo.[32] These acts of artistic homage are testimony not only to the fascination Memling's portraits exerted, but to the fact that although they were private works, kept in the homes of the patronal élite, they were – at least on occasion – accessible to Italian painters.

During the 1470s, portraits by Memling began to be brought back from Bruges by their owners, or sent to their families in Italy. Their arrival coincided with a period of unprecedented interest in portraiture, fuelled in part by humanist scholarship and the cult of Antiquity, and by rising consumer demand, but also by a growing awareness of sophisticated painted examples from the Netherlands. In Italy portrait painters still clung to the restrictive and hieratic profile view, long since outmoded in the North, where by 1430, if not earlier, artists had developed the more revealing – and more realistic – three-quarters view. Northern portraitists also included the sitter's hands, and introduced devices such as parapets to create the illusion of the sitter occupying a space that is an extension of the viewer's own, while the tonal and textural potential of the oil medium completed the lifelike effect. The realism of Northern portraits had been admired by Italian commentators since the mid-fifteenth century, but it was only in the 1470s, as Netherlandish models became increasingly available in Italy, that the three-quarters view began to replace the profile.[33]

It did so with astonishing rapidity. Some artists, notably Antonello da Messina and the Venetians, favoured the strong lighting and plain dark backgrounds found in the portraits of Van Eyck and other earlier painters, but also employed by Memling. Since this type of portrait was widespread in the Netherlands, it is extremely difficult to pinpoint Memling's specific influence on Italian examples, although Antonello's so-called *Condottiere* in the Louvre (fig. 66) and his *Portrait of a Man* in the Thyssen Collection possess affinities with Memling's portraits of this type, as does Andrea Solario's *Portrait of a Man*, also in the Thyssen Collection.[34] This may be partly accidental: the sober black doublet and glimpse of white linen at the neck is like the dress worn by many of Memling's sitters, and produces a similarly restricted palette; the fine-boned features are comparable to those of Memling's Italian clients. Yet the sculptural form of the heads, the delicacy with which the features are modelled and the catchlights indicated in the eyes, the meticulously observed highlights and fine tendrils of the hair, and the cropping of the shoulders to create a close-up effect suggest that the resemblances are more than coincidental.

Memling, however, painted as many portraits with naturalistic settings as with plain backgrounds, and the influence of these – trend-setting and distinctive in the Netherlands as well as in Italy – is much more easily identified. One of his favoured devices, that of placing the sitter in an interior with a window giving onto a landscape vista, as in the Lehman and Thyssen portraits, seems to have been especially popular in Florence, where artists explored a number of variants of the interior-exterior setting for portraits. Mainardi employed the motif of polished marble columns giving onto a landscape in his *Portrait of a Young Woman* in Berlin, suggesting that he knew the Lehman portrait, either directly or perhaps through his father-in-law Ghirlandaio (who, it will be remembered, is often credited with the authorship of the *Virgin* in the Louvre which cites this motif); Mainardi's delight in rendering virtuoso detail also suggests the study of Memling.[35] Ghirlandaio himself employed the corner of a room with a window vista in his *Portrait of an Old Man and his Grandson* (fig. 68).[36] In his portrait of *Francesco Sassetti and his Son Teodoro* (New York, Metropolitan Museum)[37] the sitters are placed in front of a fictive frame, in the manner of Memling's *Portraits of Tommaso and Maria Portinari*, and fictive frames and stone mouldings also appear in the Thyssen Collection's *Portrait of Giovanna Tornabuoni*.[38]

More distant reminiscences of Memling may be detected in Botticelli's work. The so-called *Portrait of Smeralda Bandinelli* in the Victoria & Albert Museum is set in an interior, with the sitter appearing as if at a window, her hand resting on the embrasure; in the background on the left, another window with a colonette may be a distant echo of the Lehman portrait;[39] fictive stone mouldings, as in the New York Portinari portraits, are employed in the *Portrait of a Woman* in the Galleria Palatina, Florence (possibly a copy after Botticelli's original), to project the sitter into our space.[40]

It was, however, Memling's hallmark portrait type with the pure landscape background which enjoyed the greatest success. Indeed, it is difficult to think of a portrait painter active in Italy in the last quarter of the century who did not respond to it. Even Botticelli, who according to Leonardo da Vinci was notoriously uninterested in the depiction of landscape, adopted it in his *Portrait of a Young Man with a Medal of Cosimo de' Medici* (fig. 69).[41]

Besides its generic reliance on Memling – the head with stray curls silhouetted against the sky, the distant vista – Botticelli's portrait, in which the sitter displays a portrait medal, bears an intriguing resemblance to Memling's *Portrait of a Man with a Coin of the Emperor Nero* (pl. 11 and fig. 59). This may be mere coincidence, yet if the identification of the sitter in Memling's portrait as Bernardo Bembo is correct, the kinship of the two portraits becomes less coincidental. Following immediately from his embassy to Burgundy, in 1475 Bembo was appointed Venetian ambas-

*fig. 69*
Sandro Botticelli
*Portrait of a Young Man with a Medal*
*of Cosimo de' Medici*
Florence, Galleria degli Uffizi

*fig. 70a–b*
Leonardo da Vinci
*Portrait of Ginevra de' Benci,*
obverse and reverse
Washington, National Gallery of Art,
Ailsa Mellon Bruce Fund

sador to Florence (which coincides with the presumed date, on stylistic grounds, of Botticelli's portrait). Bembo may well have taken with him to Florence his recently acquired portrait by Memling, a prized possession, no doubt much discussed in cultivated circles, which he would surely have shown off, and which Botticelli may have seen.[42]

It is not only Botticelli whose work can be brought into relation with Memling's portrait. In Florence, Bembo famously engaged in a platonic love-affair with a married lady, Ginevra de' Benci, who was immortalized by Leonardo da Vinci in the portrait now in Washington, apparently painted for Bembo himself (fig. 70), since his motto appears on its painted reverse, together with his palm and laurel *impresa*.[43] Leonardo's *Ginevra de' Benci* is manifestly indebted to Memling, and given the Bembo connection, it is tempting to see the Antwerp portrait as its specific model. Leonardo was far too subtle and inventive an artist, even this early in his career, to copy outright, but there are elements of the landscape vignette in the *Ginevra* which could reflect Memling's portrait: the single tree on the near side of the lake, its slender trunk silhouetted against the water like Memling's palm, the low promontory with its two rounded trees, the zig-zagging outline of the shore, and the hazy, overlapping forms of the distant hills and trees.[44]

Indebted to Memling though it is, Leonardo's *Ginevra de' Benci* also departs from its model in some striking ways. The head, in Memling's portraits characteristically silhouetted against a pale backdrop of sky, is here set against the dark foliage of a juniper bush (a pun on Ginevra's name), perhaps deliberately flouting the Memling 'norm'. Although in its present form the proportions of sitter to frame are not dissimilar to those in a typical Memling portrait, this resemblance is deceptive, as the portrait has been cut, and it probably originally included more of the body and gave more emphasis to the hands than in Memling's portraits.[45] Such an inventive reworking of Memling's popular portrait type, at a date when the type itself was still a novelty in Italy, and when his contemporaries had barely begun to assimilate its basic formula, is typical of Leonardo's brilliantly idiosyncratic approach.

For the most part, Italian painters were content to imitate Memling rather than to attempt to surpass him. The *Portrait of a Man with a Ring* (fig. 71) by Cossa, active in Ferrara and Bologna, who died in 1478, is perhaps contem-

*fig. 71*
Francesco del Cossa
*Portrait of a Man with a Ring*
Madrid, Museo Thyssen-Bornemisza

porary with the *Ginevra*.[46] Like Botticelli's *Young Man with a Medal* (also of similar date), it is a more straightforward reworking of Memling's type, although a fantastical rocky landscape typical of the Ferrarese school has been substituted for Memling's lush scenery, and the dramatically foreshortened hand protruding over the parapet is more reminiscent of Van Eyck (notably the '*Léal Souvenir*' portrait in London) than Memling. Later in the century, Ghirlandaio's *Portrait of a Lady* in Williamstown and Piero di Cosimo's paired portraits of Giuliano da Sangallo and Francesco Giamberti testify to the enduring popularity of the type in Florence,[47] and Neroccio de' Landi's *Portrait of a Lady* (fig. 72) and Pinturicchio's *Portrait of a Boy* (fig. 73) to a comparable vogue in central Italy.[48] Venetian examples include Giovanni Bellini's *Portrait of a Man* in

the Royal Collection (sometimes identified as Bernardo Bembo's son Pietro), Carpaccio's *Portrait of a Man* in the Museo Correr, Andrea Solario's *Man with a Pink* (London, National Gallery) and Jacometto Veneziano's jewel-like pair of portraits of Alvise Contarini and his wife in the Metropolitan Museum (figs. 74–75).[49] Jacometto's portraits additionally recall Marcantonio Michiel's description of the portraits of 'a man and wife together' by Memling, 'in the Flemish manner' – possibly an allusion to the comparative unfamiliarity of conjugal portraits in Italy at this date – and it is worth speculating whether they were inspired by this lost work. Another pair of portraits of 'a man and wife together', which was surely intended to invite comparison with Netherlandish works and which has been discussed in relation to Memling's portraits, is

Piero della Francesca's diptych of Federigo da Montefeltro, Count and later Duke of Urbino, and his wife Battista Sforza, widely believed to have been painted in 1472, the year of the duchess's death.[50]

Among Memling's most faithful followers was Perugino, who, in his own presumed self-portrait, paid homage to Memling's Lehman portrait, and whose portrait of the Florentine merchant *Francesco delle Opere* (fig. 76) of 1494 is an impressive approximation of a Memling model.[51] The debt is evident in the proportions of the sitter to the pictorial field, the silhouetting of the wiry curls (very like those of Benedetto Portinari) against the sky, the hands resting as if on the picture frame, and the landscape with its Northern-style buildings, stretch of water and puff-ball trees, with delicately stippled highlights on their foliage. Immense care has been taken to reproduce not only the typical components of a Memling portrait, but the coloration, delicate brushwork, and refined visual effect.

Perhaps encouraged by his master Perugino, the young Raphael was an equally diligent student of Memling, as is clear from his early self-portrait in the Royal Collection (fig. 77).[52] Raphael's fluency in imitating the style, execution and design of Memling's portraits – still, around 1500, the paradigm in Italy – was undoubtedly the product of a direct engagement with his works, not only portraits but devotional images, such as the 'Bembo Diptych', which he probably saw in Urbino, in the possession of Pietro Bembo, around 1505.[53] The *Portrait of a Young Man* in Munich, thought to be a copy of another, early self-portrait, incorporates the trees from the *Baptist* panel, as well as another motif borrowed from Memling, the loggia setting with polished marble columns framing the figure.[54] This motif, also used in Raphael's *Lady with a Unicorn* in the Galleria Borghese, may derive from the portrait of Benedetto Portinari (fig. 56), which he could have seen in Florence.

Benedetto Portinari's portrait was certainly known to Leonardo, who was a friend of his, and who himself used the motif of the loggia setting and columns framing the figure in the *Mona Lisa* of *c.* 1503 (although due to the panel having been subsequently cut down, only the bases of the columns are now visible).[55] In fact the *Mona Lisa* (fig. 79), without doubt the most famous European Renaissance portrait, beneath its *sfumato* veil is recognizably derived from Memling in its compositional formula and the elements (if not the forms) of its landscape – winding roads, bridges and expanses of water. Yet, as in the *Ginevra*, Leonardo makes free with Memling's formula: rather than 'zooming in' on the head and shoulders he expands the space around the figure, and extends the figure itself to waist length, twisting it into a pose of graceful informality and revealing the arm of the chair on which she sits. Greater attention is also paid to the hands, elegantly folded on the arm-rest, than was possible in the more cramped space of Memling's portraits.

Raphael followed Leonardo's example in the *Portraits of Agnolo and Maddalena Doni* (fig. 78) of *c.* 1507, which are set in front of landscape backgrounds clearly still inspired by Memling, but whose more generous proportions and elegantly draped hands reveal his debt to Leonardo's new paradigm.[56] Resonances of Memling may still be discerned in the portrait by Raphael's Roman rival Sebastiano del Piombo of *Ferry Carondelet and his Secretaries* (fig. 80) of about 1512,[57] with its motifs of columns, vista and carpet-covered table, but – as with Leonardo and Raphael – the increasing breadth and expressive mode of this portrait signal a changing aesthetic. The more ample and grandiloquent portrait of the sixteenth century had been born, and the portraits of Memling could not compete with their novelty.

*fig. 82*
Simon Marmion
*St Jerome and a Donor*
Philadelphia Museum of Art,
John G. Johnson Collection

*fig. 83*
Master of Moulins (Jean Hey)
*Portrait of a Princess*
New York, The Metropolitan
Museum of Art, Robert Lehman
Collection

## Responses to Memling's portraits outside Italy

It is extremely difficult to assess the impact of Memling's portraits elsewhere in Europe. Relatively little is known about portraiture in countries other than Germany and allowance must also be made for the accidents of survival. In France (with the notable exception of Fouquet), and still more in Spain, independent portraits from the fifteenth century are comparatively rare. Memling's influence in these countries may be seen in the work of artists who had trained in, or who had close contact with, the Netherlands, such as the French painter Simon Marmion, based in Valenciennes, who was familiar with Netherlandish art and who frequently worked for Netherlandish patrons. Marmion's *St Jerome and a Donor* (fig. 82) employs details reminiscent of the 'Van Nieuwenhove Diptych' – an open prayerbook, a stained-glass window bearing the sitter's arms, and a landscape vista.[58] The half-length donor portrait with saint is not known to have been used by Memling, however, and may have another source, possibly French. It is also found in works by the Master of Moulins, notably the *Portraits of Pierre II of Bourbon and Anne of France* (Paris, Louvre) and the *Portrait of a Donor with a Saint* (Glasgow, City Art Gallery).[59]

The Master of Moulins, plausibly identified as the Netherlandish painter Jean Hey, is thought to have trained with Hugo van der Goes and to have been active at the Bourbon court of Moulins in the 1490s.[60] Many of his portraits include landscapes, viewed through windows or arches, or in the Glasgow portrait, in the open air. Up to a point they can be seen as reworkings of Memling's ideas,

*fig. 84*
Michael Sittow
*Portrait of Diego de Guevara*
Washington, National Gallery of Art,
Andrew W. Mellon Collection

but they probably also draw on other sources. The *Portrait of a Princess* (possibly the young Margaret of Austria) in the Lehman Collection (fig. 83) is set in the corner of a room with detailed landscape vistas on either side, generically recalling Memling.[61] Yet the composition is closer to Petrus Christus's *Portrait of a Young Man* in London (fig. 53), while the stony window embrasure with its bold geometric sense of volume and line is more reminiscent of Van der Goes, who is known to have painted at least one portrait incorporating a window vista, and who may well have formulated his own version of this compositional type independently of Memling.

Michael Sittow, born in the Hanseatic city of Reval (modern Talinn, Estonia), is known to have trained in

Bruges in the 1480s, possibly with Memling; in 1492 he embarked on a career at the court of Isabella the Catholic in Spain, after her death in 1504 working in the Netherlands for Philip the Fair and Margaret of Austria, and also returning for periods to Reval.[62] He was clearly familiar with Memling's portrait types, favouring a dark background, the cropping of the shoulders at the sides, and the placement of the hands on the edge of the frame, as in the *Portrait of a Man* in the Mauritshuis, probably painted in Reval around 1510, or the *Portrait of Christian II of Denmark* (Copenhagen, Statens Museum for Kunst) of 1515.[63] Sittow's most consummate variation on Memling's portraits is the *Portrait of Diego de Guevara* in Washington (fig. 84), half of a devotional diptych, in which spatial continuity with the pendant panel of the *Virgin and Child* (Berlin, Gemäldegalerie) is implied by the carpeted ledge on which the sitter's hand rests, a typically Memlingesque device.[64]

Outside Italy, the impact of Memling's portraits was most strongly felt in Germany, notably in areas such as the Rhineland and the Baltic, where commercial traffic with the Low Countries facilitated contact with Netherlandish art. The landscape background was, for instance, adopted in Cologne by the Master of the Life of the Virgin in his *Portrait of a Man* in Karlsruhe,[65] in Lübeck by Hermen Rode in his *Portrait of a Man* in the Brera,[66] and on the Middle Rhine, by Anton Neubauer in his *Portrait of a Young Man* in Darmstadt.[67] It did not, however, enjoy the kind of vogue in Germany (where indeed the preference was overwhelmingly for plain backgrounds) that it did in Italy, and instances of its use are relatively rare.

More popular was the interior setting with a window vista, although since this type is not exclusively associated with Memling, fewer claims can be made for his influence: for instance, Dürer's *Self-Portrait* of 1498 in the Prado recalls Memling's types, such as the Lehman or Thyssen portraits, but not so potently as to imply a direct source.[68] It is often very difficult to know whether a work alludes to Memling specifically or merely generically, or indeed whether he is one of several sources. The early *Portrait of Frederick the Wise* attributed to Hans Traut (fig. 87), active in Nuremberg, is typical of Memling's portraits in the pose and the arrangement of the hands; it is set in the corner of a room with a mullioned window beyond which is a vista of water, buildings and a bridge, recalling elements of the portrait of Maarten van Nieuwenhove (pl. 25), but the low,

fig. 85
Michael Wolgemut
*Portrait of Levinus Memminger*
Madrid, Museo Thyssen-Bornemisza

fig. 86
Master of the Aachen Altarpiece
*Portrait of Johann von Melem*
Munich, Alte Pinakothek

beamed ceiling is more reminiscent of Petrus Christus, notably the *Portrait of Edward Grimston* in London.[69] In the portrait of the merchant Johann von Melem attributed to the Master of the Aachen Altar (fig. 86), active in Cologne, the motif of the convex mirror reflecting the view from the window recalls both the Van Nieuwenhove and Chicago diptychs (pls. 25, 27), although here again there are also reminiscences of Petrus Christus, notably the *St Eligius* in New York. The portrait of the Ravensburg merchant Johann Gamspirch by an unknown Upper Swabian artist (Heidelberg, Kurpfälzisches Museum) is set in a high room, with distant landscape vistas on either side, viewed on the sitter's right through a pair of polished marble colonettes similar to those in Memling's Lehman portrait, although the central curtain backdrop is not an arrangement which Memling is known to have favoured.[70]

Memling is vividly recalled in the *Virgin and Child with a Donor* by Hermen Rode (fig. 88), whose receptivity to him has already been noted.[71] Memling's inspiration is evident in the colonettes and landscape behind the sitter, and also in the form itself, derived from the devotional portrait diptych. Unlike its folding Netherlandish prototypes, however, Rode's is painted on a single wide panel, a format commonly employed for double portraits in Germany. Double portraits of married or betrothed couples seem to have been more common in Germany than in the Netherlands, and this wide-format type was particularly popular. Memling himself, in a reversal of his more familiar role as a disseminator of Netherlandish forms, appears to have introduced this Germanic type to the Low Countries in his *Portrait of an Elderly Couple* (now divided between the Berlin Gemäldegalerie and the Louvre; pl. 6).[72]

Rode's panel departs from Memling, however, in the use of a patterned textile as a foil for the Virgin. The fondness of late fifteenth-century German portrait painters for placing their sitters against curtains or textile hangings with landscape vistas to one side seems to be a local variation on the interior settings of Netherlandish portraits.[73] Examples of this type are numerous, and include Michael Wolgemut's *Portrait of Levinus Memminger* (fig. 85) and Wolfgang Beurer's *Portrait of a Man*, both in the Thyssen Collection,[74] Anton Beurer's *Portraits of a Man and Woman* in Frankfurt, Dürer's *Portrait of Oswold Krel* in Munich and Tucher portraits in Weimar and Kassel.[75] Their landscape vistas are often more mountainous than the gentler lowlands of Memling, anticipating the full-blown landscape

fig. 87
Attributed to Hans Traut
*Portrait of Frederick the Wise,*
*Elector of Saxony*
Frankfurt, Städelsches Kunstinstitut
und Städtische Galerie

*fig. 88*
Hermen Rode
*The Virgin and Child with a Donor*
Lübeck, St. Annen-Museum
für Kunst- und Kulturgeschichte

backgrounds of Cranach's *Portraits of Johannes and Anna Cuspinian* of *c.* 1502 (Winterthur).

Memling's portraits did not enjoy such extensive influence in Germany as in Italy, nor did they tend to be as faithfully emulated. It is possible that their impact was diluted by existing local traditions and by other Netherlandish sources, such as the portraits of Petrus Christus or Bouts, or equally, that Memling was simply not as popular with German clients. The available evidence suggests that the Italians, more than any other foreign 'nation' represented at Bruges, were by far Memling's most devoted

international patrons, especially with regard to portraits, and there is a correlation between this and the impact of his portraits in Italy itself. Nevertheless, as this brief discussion of German responses shows, his influence here, if more diffuse, was not negligible. Cranach's great Cuspinian portraits, with which the new century opens, can be regarded as the German counterparts of Raphael's almost contemporary Doni portraits – ample, monumental figures who sit at ease in their landscape settings; like them, they also bear witness to Memling's role in the evolution of the portrait in Renaissance Europe.

1. On the international community in Bruges, see V. Vermeersch (ed.), *Bruges and Europe*, Antwerp 1992; Vandewalle 2002.

2. 25% of Memling's paintings have known patrons, and the nationality of 54.2% of their owners is either known or can be presumed. Of this 54.2%, 33.9% were foreign owners – that is, 20% of the known patrons of Memling's paintings were foreigners. Martens 1997, 35–7.

3. De Vos 1994, no. 4; Rohlmann 1994, 41–9; Nuttall 2004, 53–60.

4. De Vos 1994, no. 90; T.-H. Borchert, 'Entre commerce et négoce: Bruges et l'art européen', in Vandewalle 2002, 144. The commission may have been placed jointly with Heinrich's brother Adolf, a priest in Lübeck who had formerly studied at the University of Leuven.

5. De Vos 1994, no. 39; Campbell 1998, 374–91.

6. De Vos 1994, no. 11; Rohlmann 1994, 63–5; Nuttall 2004, 64–5.

7. De Vos 1994, no. 64; M. Rohlmann, 'Memling und Italien: Flämische Malerei für die bologneser familie Loiani', in Verougstraete and Van Schoute 1997, 92–104.

8. De Vos 1994, no. 81; Borchert 1995; Borchert 1997.

9. Rohlmann 1994, 67–83; Rohlmann 1995, 438–45.

10. See Campbell 1990, 120.

11. De Vos 1994, no. 9; Waldman 2001, 28–33.

12. De Vos 1994, no. 79; Rohlmann 1994, 86–7.

13. De Vos 1994, no. 55. Originally suggested by Faggin 1969, no. 28, on the basis of its Spanish provenance.

14. De Vos 1994, no. 72. Eisler 1989, 108, 112, considers him to have been Spanish on the basis of an old label on the reverse (now lost), which appears to have been written in Spanish; De Vos 1994, 262–3, favours an Italian identity on the grounds of costume and hairstyle.

15. De Vos 1994, nos. 56, 57; Rohlmann 1994, 87–9; Nuttall 2004, 70. Perhaps intended as a pair, the sitters are sometimes identified as Benedetto Portinari and his older brother Folco. See cat. 24.

16. De Vos 1994, nos. 28, 49, 12, 40, 44, 48.

17. De Vos 1994, no. 42; Rohlmann 1994, 85–6.

18. Bruges 1998, 17.

19. De Vos 1994, no. 50; Campbell 1981, 471.

20. Similarly, Alessandro Sforza, Lord of Pesaro, commissioned his portrait as well as a small triptych of *The Crucifixion* from Van der Weyden's workshop during a visit to the Netherlands in 1457–8. See G. Mulazzani, 'Observations on the Sforza triptych in the Brussels Museum', *Burlington Magazine* CXIII (1971), 252–5.

21. See the discussion of Memling as a portraitist in De Vos 1994, 365–70.

22. See Campbell 1990, 22.

23. See Campbell 1998, 46–51, 104–9.

24. Campbell 1990, 120; De Vos 1994, 367. On the Eyckian plateau composition, see M. Meiss, 'Highlands in the Lowlands: Jan van Eyck, the Master of Flémalle and the Franco-Italian tradition', *Gazette des Beaux-Arts* LVII (1961), 273–314.

25. Nuttall 2004, 37, 195–209. For Fazio, see M. Baxandall, 'Bartholomeus Facius on painting: a 15th-century manuscript of the "De Viris Illustribus"', *Journal of the Warburg and Courtauld Institutes* XXVII (1964), 90–109.

26. The suggestion (Panofsky 1953, I, 349; De Vos 1994, 367; Lorentz 1995, 70) that the type originated in Italy is unlikely considering that the purported archetypes – Filippo Lippi's double portrait in New York and Piero della Francesca's 'Montefeltro Diptych' (Florence, Uffizi) – are themselves clearly Netherlandish in inspiration. Moreover, the comparative sophistication of landscape painting in the Netherlands relative to Italy at this date makes it most unlikely that such ideas would have developed in Italy independently, although Piero may have been prompted to introduce a landscape background in the 'Montefeltro Diptych' by the example of Van Eyck's *Women Bathing*, rather than through exposure to Memling's portraits.

27. R. Klein and H. Zerner, *Italian Art, 1500–1600. Sources and documents in the history of art*. Englewood Cliffs 1966, 35.

28. Campbell 1990, 227–8; Nuttall 2004, 1–2.

29. Frimmel 1888, 100. In the same collection was a portrait of Isabella of Portugal, Duchess of Burgundy, dated 1450 and stated to be by Memling, but more likely to have been a version of a lost original by Van der Weyden. The portraits of 'a man and wife together' have been related to Memling's *Portrait of an Elderly Couple* now divided between Berlin and the Louvre (cat. 5); Faggin 1969, 109. Michiel mentions two portraits, presumably on two separate panels, which makes this unlikely, since the *Elderly Couple* originally comprised a single panel. See L. Campbell, 'A double portrait by Memling', *Connoisseur* 194 (1977), 186–9. Lorentz 1995, 71 suggests that the sitters were Italian.

30. F. Nicolini, *L'arte napoletana del rinascimento*, Naples 1925, 162; Vasari 1878–85, V, 282; Campbell 1990, 121; Nuttall 2004, 143, 210.

31. Campbell 1983; the *Portrait of Perugino* has also been attributed to Lorenzo di Credi and to the young Raphael.

32. E. Fahy, 'The Earliest Works of Fra Bartolommeo', *Art Bulletin*, LI, 1969, 148.

33. See Campbell 1990, 69–86, 232; Thiébaut 1993, 92–109; Nuttall 2004, 209–29.

34. Ekserdjian and Stevens 1988, 22, 114; Campbell 1990, 232; Thiébaut 1993, 92–95.

35. Brown 2001, 194–5.

36. Campbell 1990, 186; Cadogan 2000, 276; Nuttall 2004, 218–20.

37. Cadogan 2000, 278–9.

38. Cadogan 2000, 277–8; Nuttall 2004, 220.

39. Lightbown 1978, II, 28–9; Brown 2001, 172.

40. Lightbown 1978, II, 210–11; *Botticelli. From Lorenzo the Magnificent to Savonarola* (exhibition catalogue, Paris, Musée du Luxembourg), Paris 2003, 128.

41. Lightbown 1978, II, 33–5.

42. Suggested by Barbara Lane in a paper given at the symposium 'Jan van Eyck, early Netherlandish painting and the south of Europe' at the Groeningemuseum, Bruges, 2002, to be published in the acts of the symposium and also to be discussed in her forthcoming book on Memling.

43. J. M. Fletcher, 'Bernardo Bembo and Leonardo's portrait of Ginevra de' Benci', *Burlington Magazine* CXXXI (1989), 811–16; Brown 1998, 104, 117–21.

44. On the *Ginevra* and Netherlandish painting, see further P. Hills, 'Leonardo and Flemish painting', *Burlington Magazine* CXXI (1980), 615; Brown 1998, 110–11, Nuttall 2004, 224–7.

45. Brown 1998, 106, Brown 2001, 142–6.

46. R. Molajoli, *L'Opera completa di Cosmè Tura e i grandi pittori ferraresi del suo tempo; Francesco del Cossa e Ercole de' Roberti*, Milan 1974, no. 93; Ekserdjian and Stevens 1988, 46.

47. Brown 2001, 186–8; Bruges 2002, 259, no. 97.

48. Campbell 1990, 90; M. W. Alpatow, *Die Dresdner Galerie: Alte Meister*, Dresden 1966, 29–31.

49. Shearman 1983, 43; M. Cancogni and G. Perocco, *L'Opera completa del Carpaccio*, Milan 1967, no. 3; J. Dunkerton et al., *Giotto to Dürer: early renaissance painting in the National Gallery*, London and New Haven 1991, 99; Brown 2001, 134–7.

50. R. Lightbown, *Piero della Francesca*, New York, London and Paris 1992, 231–4. The Eyckian character of the landscape background, however, raises the possibility that Piero adapted the idea from the panorama in Van Eyck's *Women Bathing*.

51. Campbell 1990, 233.

52. Shearman 1983, 209–11; J. Woods Marsden, *Renaissance Self-portraiture*, New Haven and London 1999, 111–12.

53. D. A. Brown, *Raphael in America* (exhibition catalogue, National Gallery of Art), Washington 1983, 153–7.

54. H. von Sonnenburg, *Raphael in der Alten Pinakothek* (exhibition catalogue, Alte Pinakothek), Munich 1983, 107–8.

55. Brown 2001, 146 n. 8; Nuttall 2004, 228.

56. R. Jones and N. Penny, *Raphael*, New Haven and London 1983, 29–30.

57. M. Hirst, *Sebastiano del Piombo*, Oxford 1981, 51.

58. M. Ainsworth, 'New observations on the working technique in Simon Marmion's panel paintings', in *Margaret of York, Simon Marmion and the Visions of Tondal*, ed. T. Kren, Malibu 1992, 243–53.

59. A. Châtelet, *Jean Prévot, le Maître de Moulins*, s.l. 2001, 92, discusses these in relation to the Marmion portrait in Philadelphia and notes that the type was also used by Fouquet.

60. C. Sterling, 'Jean Hey, le Maître de Moulins', *Revue de l'Art* 1–2 (1966), 27–33. For a recent summary of opinions, see C. Reynolds, 'Master of Moulins', in *The Dictionary of Art*, London 1996, XX, 731–4.

61. New York 1998, 181.

62. Trizna 1976, 1–55; M. Weniger, 'Bynnen Brugge in Flanderen: the apprenticeships of Michel Sittow and Juan de Flandes', in Verougstraete and Van Schoute 1997, 115–31.

63. Trizna 1976, 25, 45–9, 92, 96; Bruges 1994, no. 93; Bruges 2002, no. 57. Also of this type is a portrait said to be of Isabella the Catholic (location unknown) which has been attributed to him: see Trizna 1976, 95.

64. Trizna 1976, 96–7; Hand and Wolff 1986, 231.

65. Buchner 1953, 30–31; H. M. Schmidt, *Der Meister des Marienlebens und sein Kreis*, Düsseldorf 1978, 189. It has been argued that this work may predate Memling's earliest portraits, and that it was not influenced by him but was evolved independently by the Master, perhaps from a Rogier van der Weyden model similar to the 'Braque Triptych'. It is worth speculating whether such ideas were already circulating in the Cologne area during Memling's formative years.

66. See Buchner 1953, 19; Gmelin 1996, 506–7.

67. Buchner 1953, 146–7. The artist (otherwise unknown, but presumably active on the Middle Rhine or in Franconia) is named in an inscription on the reverse; it has also been attributed to the young Dürer.

68. F. Anzelewsky, *Dürer, his art and life*, Fribourg 1980, 88–9.

69. Buchner 1953, 129–31.

70. Buchner 1953, 58.

71. Buchner 1953, 20; Gmelin 1996, 506–7.

72. De Vos 1994, no. 14; Lorentz 1995, 71–4.

73. Intriguingly, similar motifs appear (although predominantly in images of the Virgin) in Venetian painting at a similar date; given the trade between Venice and Germany, it may be that the motif is a shared one, although whether Venetian or German in origin is difficult to say.

74. Lubbeke 1991, 150–55, 392–5.

75. See Lubbeke 1991, 151 for the suggestion that Dürer may have learned this type through contact with Anton Beurer during his travels in the Middle Rhine, where it was common.

*Maryan W. Ainsworth*

# Minimal Means, Remarkable Results
## *Memling's Portrait Painting Technique**

For nearly thirty years at the close of the fifteenth century, Hans Memling cornered the market on the production of portraits in Bruges. His fame spread abroad, and, as Paula Nuttall describes in her essay in this catalogue, it was especially Italian clients and painters who held Memling in such high esteem. Lorne Campbell focuses on the specific characteristics of Memling's portraits, their aesthetic qualities, and the artist's innovations in this genre. He especially notes Memling's indisputable ability simultaneously to individualize and to idealize his sitters. This would certainly have been a selling feature for prospective clients who would have wanted to be recorded for posterity in the most positive way. How do we approach and appreciate Memling's achievement in portraiture today?

A closer look here at certain paintings shown at the three venues of this exhibition and related ones at the Metropolitan Museum of Art (that due to the stipulations of their bequest could not be lent) allows for a reconsideration of Memling's approach to portraiture. In particular, new findings based on the recent technical examination of a number of these works provide a better understanding of Memling's chronological development and accomplishment in this genre.

As Lorne Campbell has written in his catalogue essay, Memling employed a standardized approach toward his portraits, just as Petrus Christus had done before him in Bruges.[1] Certain portraits appear to have originated from stock patterns of head pose, shape and size. The individualization of the sitters occurred in the later stages of the painting process when Memling paid close attention to details of their physiognomy. Therefore, when these final touches have been worn away due to the vicissitudes of time, to repeated or insensitive cleanings, or simply to frequent handling and changes in environment where the paintings were not given appropriate care, their appearance is compromised. While some of Memling's portraits have come through the ages in extremely fine state of preservation – the Metropolitan Museum's *Portraits of Tommaso Portinari and Maria Baroncelli* (fig. 89 and pl. 2), the Thyssen-Bornemisza *Man at Prayer* (cat. 25, pl. 28), or the 'Diptych of Maarten van Nieuwenhove' (cat. 23, pl. 25) are excellent examples of this – other portraits have not fared as well. At the very least, it should be pointed out that only a precious few have survived with their original frames intact. The 'Van Nieuwenhove Diptych', the *Portrait of Gilles Joye* (cat. 3, pl. 4) and the *Portrait of a Young Woman ('Sibyl')*

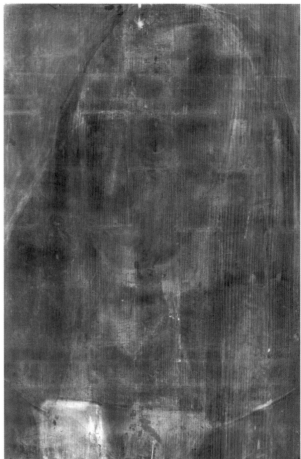

fig. 90
Memling
*Portrait of an Old Man*
New York, The Metropolitan
Museum of Art,
Bequest of Benjamin Altman

fig. 91
X-radiograph of
*Portrait of an Old Woman* [cat. 9]
Houston, Museum of Fine Arts,
The Edith A. and Percy S. Straus
Collection

(cat. 17, pl. 18) are among these rarities, even though the inscription on the banderole of the frame of the *Young Woman* was added later.

Some portraits have been separated from their mates – the Morgan *Man with a Pink* (cat. 20, pl. 22) exists alone without the pendant that likely represented his betrothed. The *Elderly Couple* (cat. 5, pl. 6) once formed a continuous double portrait, but the two panels joined by dowels were split apart at some point and ended up in different museum collections in Berlin and Paris. Both the Metropolitan Museum *Old Man* and the Houston *Old Woman* have been cut down on all of their edges, presumably when they were taken out of original frames and fitted for new ones of different dimensions (fig. 90 and pl. 10b).[2] The *Portraits of Tommaso Portinari and Maria Baroncelli* once flanked a now lost central panel that represented the Virgin and Child.[3]

Although it seems to us today a scandalous act to deliberately alter the appearance of a painting by Hans Memling, such modifications apparently were condoned in the past in order to update a likeness, or to make it more relevant for a subsequent owner. For example, it is apparent in the x-radiograph of the *Old Woman* (fig. 91) that Memling originally painted her hands resting at the lower left

edge of the composition in order to match the corresponding pose of her husband, the *Old Man* whose hands rest at the lower right edge.[4] This, and their compatible measurements, led to the conclusion that they originally formed a pair. At some later point when the two were separated, and the woman's portrait was perhaps damaged, her hands were painted out.[5] An arrow was added in between the thumb and the forefinger of the left hand of the Lehman *Portrait of a Young Man* (cat. 15, pl. 16), extending from the lower left to upper right of the picture, and a halo surrounded the man's head, leading Gustav Waagen in 1857 to identify the subject of this painting as a St Sebastian.[6] These later additions were removed in a restoration of 1913 before Robert Lehman bought the picture, but in raking light a faint image of them may still be seen.[7] In the National Gallery Washington *Portrait of a Man with an Arrow* (cat. 13, fig. 92) the golden arrow was added to Memling's original conception of the portrait. But as the pigments proved to be consistent with the period of the painting,[8] it was concluded that the arrow was probably inserted very early on, even in the sitter's lifetime, perhaps indicating an award won by the man in a shooting competition of an archery guild.[9] It could well be that when the *Portrait of a Young Woman* (cat. 17, pl. 18) had lost her iden-

fig. 92
Memling
*Portrait of a Man with an Arrow*
[cat. 13], detail of pl. 14
Washington, National Gallery of Art,
Andrew W. Mellon Collection

tity for subsequent owners of the painting, she was converted into the Sibyl of Persia by the late sixteenth- or early seventeenth-century texts of the cartouche at the upper left in the painting and on the frame.[10]

Even those paintings that today remain in remarkably fine condition are subject to changes that have occurred naturally over time. The Portinari portraits, probably produced around the time of the couple's marriage in 1470,[11] are astounding in their verisimilitude, a fact due to Memling's mastery of execution and to the preservation of the finishing glazes on the surface of the paintings that enhance the lifelike modelling of the forms. The details of physiognomy are so closely observed that even the stubble of Tommaso's emerging beard and the nick in his chin are faithfully rendered. None the less, the portraits do not appear now as they once did. The decorative pattern on Tommaso's jacket has darkened so that it is submerged in the surrounding dark field and indecipherable in normal lighting conditions. Likewise, the jacket itself as well as the black hat or hennin of Maria Baroncelli have sunk and darkened to such a degree that these forms are no longer silhouetted against the background but appear to merge with it.

The portrait of Maria Baroncelli also reveals certain *pentimenti* that indicate Memling's thought process as he proceeded with working up the painting. The tiny ring of dark dots that appear around her neck show an elevated position of her extraordinary necklace at an earlier stage of the painting. This string of black pearls would not have been apparent upon the completion of the painting but has become increasingly visible over time due to the growing transparency of the overlying flesh tones. Likewise, as one can make out partially with the naked eye, and as the x-radiograph of the portrait confirms (fig. 93), Memling first intended Maria's cone-shaped hennin to extend more vertically over the top edge of the *trompe-l'œil* frame. In addition, transparent lappets of the hennin originally revealed the woman's left ear. The artist amended this plan, adding black velvet lappets that softly brush Maria's shoulders, and he repositioned the hat to fill the upper right corner of the picture, allowing the diaphanous veil to cascade pleasingly down the length of the picture at the right side. The x-radiograph also shows that Memling's first inclination was to embellish the hennin with pearl-decorated letters 'T' and 'M' within triangular borders, denoting Tommaso and Maria. The changes in the hennin as well as the adjustment from a black v-necked insert in the bodice of the dress to a more alluring transparent décolletage were likely made at Maria's request. The pearl-embellished hennin, the extraordinarily elaborate necklace and the gold ring with its two precious gems must have been prized possessions, for Memling's contemporary, Hugo van der Goes, included the same luxury items in his portrait of Maria, along with the more modest dress, in his later 'Portinari Altarpiece' (fig. 94).

Close technical examination of Memling's portraits helps one not only to appreciate the artist's working process and extraordinary mastery of handling and execution, but also to chart his chronological development. Consultation of the infra-red reflectogram assemblies, the x-radiographs, dendrochronology of the oak panels on which the paintings are made and microscope examination of Memling's painting technique further aids in establishing answers to questions of dating and attribution. Attempts to follow the progression of Memling's portraiture have been hampered by the fact that only a small group can be reliably dated by information on the frames or through other forms of documentation. The dating of the majority of the portraits has been based on specific characteristics of style and costume. But as some scholars have already pointed out,[12] Memling's works in general do not always follow an obvious linear development in terms of these criteria, and the portraits offer particular challenges in this regard.[13] Memling perhaps responded to specific requests from his clients for such details of the composition as the addition of landscape backgrounds and certain features of costume. Further complicating matters is the fact that most portraits present few other pictorial elements on which a dating may reliably be based.[14] Because of this, a consideration of other information coming from the technical examination of the paintings that reveals aspects of Memling's handling and execution can be particularly helpful.

It is surprising that for an early Netherlandish painter of such fame relatively little technical investigation of his oeuvre has been carried out. A small number of Memling's portraits has been studied through dendrochronology (although some have very recently been added to the list, see Appendix, Peter Klein's report).[15] In any event, as Peter Klein readily points out, the dendrochronology only provides an aid to the determination of a date. That is, it only tells the earliest possible felling date of the tree cut to

*fig. 93*
X-radiograph of
*Portrait of Maria Portinari*
New York, The Metropolitan
Museum of Art, Bequest of
Benjamin Altman

provide the oak panels on which the paintings were made. It does not establish the definitive date that the artist first applied brush to panel.[16]

Investigations through infra-red reflectography, which reveals the underdrawing or the artist's first sketch on the panel, are by no means complete for all of Memling's paintings.[17] However, a comparative study has shown a perceptible stylistic development in the underdrawings of his works of religious and allegorical themes.[18] In these paintings, Memling not only altered his medium from brush and black pigment to the later employment of a dry drawing tool such as black chalk or charcoal, but he also moved from a more meticulous handling clearly representational of form to a looser, far more abstract calligraphy. This kind of development is not so clear with the portraits, which at most show minimal underdrawing merely indicating the placement of the head, its facial features and the hands, but little else. While it is possible that Memling used an underdrawing material not made visible by infrared reflectography, it is more likely that the reason for the paucity of apparent underdrawing in Memling's portraits is the artist's routine working methods. Memling began his portraits with any one of a group of common templates for the head pose to which he added the distinguishing features of the sitter in the later painting stages. In order to individualize each portrait, he must have had a drawing in hand that showed the distinct traits of the sitter's physiognomy. Or, it is possible that the client came to Memling's studio after the artist had worked in the initial stages of the painting on the panel and sat for him while he painted in the facial features and provided the subtle modelling that would bring the portrayal of the sitter to life.

The Frankfurt *Portrait of a Man in a Red Hat* (cat. 1, pl. 1) or the Williamstown *Portrait of Gilles Joye* (cat. 3, pl. 4) are good examples of the scanty information that can be gleaned from the infra-red reflectogram assemblies of Memling's early portraits. In both, extremely fine brushstrokes are restricted to the contours of the figure, here and there showing slight shifts at the position of the shoulders, as in the *Gilles Joye* portrait. Likewise, in Memling's later *Portrait of a Young Woman* of 1480 there is barely perceptible underdrawing in the face; it only serves to place the features with the most discrete touches, and more boldly to firm up the contour of the head at the left side (fig. 95).[19] In an advance beyond the technique of the Frankfurt and Williamstown portraits, however, Memling here used the underdrawing to establish the contours of the bodice and sleeves of the dress of the woman in broad, free brushstrokes. He placed the strokes of vertical parallel hatching so closely together at the inside of the sleeve of the proper right arm that the individual lines merge into a zone of shadow or undermodelling of the form. Memling achieved the same undermodelling in the bodice at the woman's left breast and the inside of her left arm. Through the reflectogram assembly, the form comes vividly to life in places where the overlying paint has darkened to such a degree that we are no longer able to sense the three-dimensional form clearly. The infra-red reflectogram assembly also shows how Memling shifted the edges of the trailing veil of the woman's hat at the left, and at the last stages of work painted the veil over the face and shoulders, thus enhancing the illusionistic effect of the diaphanous material.

When underdrawings *are* visible in Memling portraits, they often show a jumbled mass of seemingly random scribbled lines. Sometimes, as in the case of the hands and the head in the *Portrait of Maarten van Nieuwenhove* (pl. 25 and fig. 96), these marks can be seen by the naked eye because of the increasing transparency of the overlying flesh-coloured paint over time.[20] The infra-red reflectogram assembly reveals how Memling revised the position of the head, the collar and the sleeves in the development from the underdrawing to the initial painted stages. Because of the elaborate nature of the Nieuwenhove portrait and its more complicated perspective structure, which joins the portrait with the pendant of the Virgin and Child, one can also discern the ruled orthogonal lines laying out the proposed perspective scheme.[21] This necessitated the turn of the figure more toward the left and the shift in the position of the windows at the upper left in order to accommodate the perspective scheme. The bold brush undermodelling in the sleeves of the costume, the painting of the proper left oversleeve at the elbow over the completed window frame and its adjustment in width along the lower edge of the composition, as well as the alteration in the painted stage of the book on the ledge to a thicker volume with furled pages are all indications of Memling's working procedures for this ambitious diptych.[22] In Memling's later works, therefore, it is not only a preliminary underdrawing, but also indications of undermodelling for the final painted layers that are in evidence in the infra-red reflectogram assemblies.

*fig. 95*
Infra-red reflectogram assembly
of *Portrait of a Young Woman* ('Sibyl')
[cat. 17], 1480
Bruges, Stedelijke Musea,
Memlingmuseum –
Sint-Janshospitaal
(IRR: Metropolitan Museum of Art)

*fig. 96*
Intra-red reflectogram assembly
of the portrait of Maarten van
Nieuwenhove [cat. 23]
Bruges, Stedelijke Musea,
Memlingmuseum –
Sint-Janshospitaal
(IRR: Metropolitan Museum of Art)

X-radiography, which shows the artist's use of lead white paint to establish the structure and preliminary stages of the flesh tones of the face, can be more helpful than infrared reflectography in establishing the relative date of Memling's portraits. Not enough x-radiography has yet been carried out in order to view this question comprehensively, but recently new findings have added clarity to this issue.[23] The results of x-radiography may best be understood when compared with details of Memling's execution and handling on the surfaces of the portraits. Perhaps the poles of Memling's technique, handling and execution in portraiture are most easily recognized through a comparison of the *Portrait of Tommaso Portinari* and the Morgan *Portrait of a Man with a Pink* (figs. 97–102). The Morgan portrait is not so well known as it usually hangs on a dark wall behind a door in what once was Mr Morgan's study at the J. Pierpont Morgan Library. Dirk De Vos discussed the painting in his 1994 monograph more briefly than other works, as little information on it was available at the time.[24] Other than the fact that the panel still retained its original edges, appeared to be heavily worn, and was covered by a considerably yellowed varnish, few technical features were conveyed. As the sitter faces right and holds a red carnation, De Vos supposed that the portrait formed half of a diptych, with the man's betrothed originally at the right. Scholars have debated the place of the painting in the chronology of Memling's oeuvre. Conway considered it among the earliest portraits, probably executed between 1467 and 1472. Friedländer concurred with the early date, proposing *c.* 1475. De Vos himself proposed around 1475–80.[25]

What at once may have suggested an early date to some is the rendering of the man's hands in the lower right corner. Their elegant pose and the extremely elongated fingers call to mind portraits of Rogier van der Weyden, such as the *Portrait of Francesco d'Este* in the Metropolitan Museum of Art. The long-supposed, and in my mind convincing, proposal that Memling spent the early part of his career in Rogier van der Weyden's workshop in Brussels before registering as a citizen in Bruges in 1465, is supported by such imitative borrowings. However, this does not guarantee an early date for the Morgan portrait. Indeed, Memling's *Portrait of a Young Woman* ('Sibyl') (pl. 18) is equally indebted to Rogier's *Portrait of a Lady* in the National Gallery, Washington, but the former is dated 1480 on its original engaged frame, indicating its date in Memling's mature, not early period.[26] Until the thick, yellowed varnish, which had long obscured the Morgan *Man with a Pink*, was removed in a restoration in 2003 by Hubert von Sonnenburg, it was very difficult to make further judgements about the specific characteristics and qualities of the painting.

The *Portrait of Tommaso Portinari* painted in about 1470 when the sitter married Maria Baroncelli may serve here as an example of Memling's early portraits. The confrontation of the Portinari and Morgan portraits at once demonstrates Memling's use of a common pattern for his sitters. Although the Portinari portrait portrays a smaller head in a larger panel and the Morgan example a larger head in a smaller panel (both of which show original intact edges), the two exhibit the same pose and three-quarters turn of the head. In addition, the two show a remarkable similarity in the structure of the face, including the pronounced pouch of flesh to the right of the mouth, next to a markedly concave depression of the cheek. The nose in each is slightly to the right of centre of the foreshortened mouth. The Portinari portrait, however, exhibits more complicated drawing. For example, in the Portinari portrait there is a convergence of lines where the proper left eye meets the nose. In the Morgan head, this is avoided in favour of a broader approach. Upon a closer look, in every way the Portinari portrait is more sharply defined, and its features more graphically depicted; the modelling is smooth and taut, and the brushwork imperceptible. As De Vos has noted in his comments about Memling's early portraits, there is a certain cold, polished appearance of wax figures here.[27] By contrast, like Memling's other later works, the Morgan portrait exhibits a more painterly approach: there is supple brushwork, a looser virtuoso execution and a surface that is not overly smooth. Though painted more broadly, the portrait still shows an extreme precision in the definition of the features of the face, only here with a new economy of means. The features are lightly touched in with the minimal number of strokes necessary to achieve the form. The face is very thinly painted and unlike the Portinari portrait, which gives the impression of being more solidly constructed in thin layer after layer in a decidedly sculptural way.

Looking even more closely through the microscope, we can see how Memling's technique varied in the two works. The Portinari head is built up with multiple thin layers of lead white, pink and greyish tones in strokes that are fully

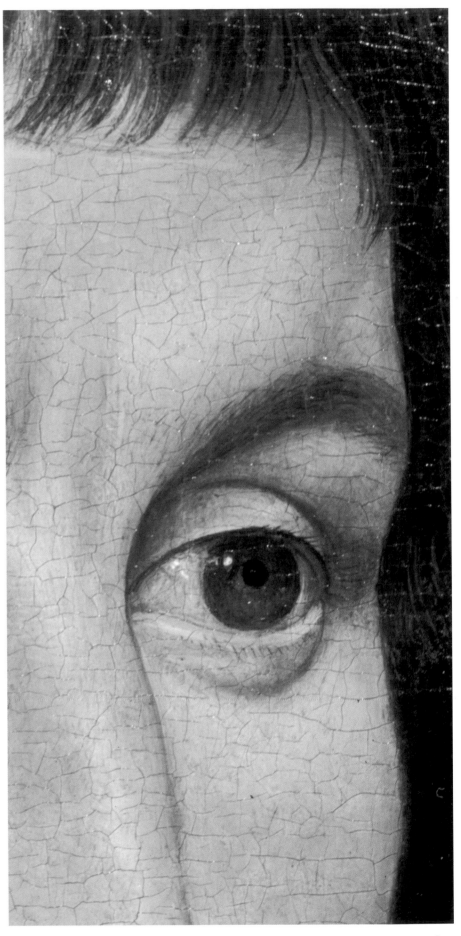

*fig. 97*
Memling
*Portrait of Tommaso Portinari*, detail of pl. 2
New York, The Metropolitan
Museum of Art, Bequest of
Benjamin Altman

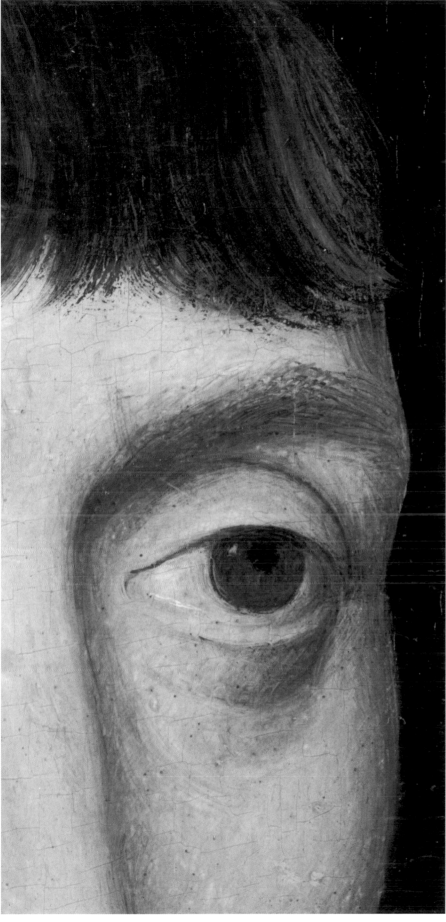

*fig. 98*
Memling
*Portrait of a Man with a Pink* [cat. 20],
detail of pl. 22
New York, The Pierpont
Morgan Library

blended. The only clearly perceptible brushwork appears in the neck and pastose touches on the right ear. The greyish tone in the shadow of the face and the emerging beard are scumbled over so that the brushwork is not so apparent. This lends to the head a certain highly finished, porcelain quality where considerable effort is given to the final touches that are well blended in. By comparison, the Morgan man's head appears flatter and less sculptural. Although Memling relies on some of the same structural conventions as those used in the Portinari portrait, his execution is markedly abbreviated. Over a relatively thin ground, he broadly applied a pinkish-white layer. Very pale greyish strokes in parallel and cross-hatching define the shadow of the cheek. Loose, disengaged brushstrokes, some worked wet-in-wet, form the emerging beard and moustache. The more laboured technique in the Portinari portrait as compared to the Morgan example may be seen especially in the area of the eyes and eyebrows. Although there are similar brown lines in each that define the contours of the eyes, they are far more carefully delineated in the Portinari example. Here, too, great attention is given to the white of the eye, which is variegated with touches of blue, grey and hot pink near the tear duct. The glint of the eye placed at the upper left of the pupil is prominently featured. Eyebrows are thinly brushed in with individual strokes. By contrast, simplicity reigns in the Morgan portrait where only slight greyish tonal gradations are added to the whites of the eyes; a tiny white dot to the left of the pupil provides the glint of the eye; and the eyebrows are quickly and deftly painted wet-in-wet. The brushwork here appears spontaneous, but with great precision of execution and remarkable control of the most efficient and meaningful placement of strokes to achieve the desired form. In general, the same technique is used in each painting to define the lips – a pale pink brushed in with vertical strokes on the lower lip and horizontal strokes on the upper lip, and a simple dark line running through the centre – but again the paint in the Portinari example is more carefully blended than it is in the Morgan portrait. Hands in each portrait in general are more loosely rendered than the heads. In the Portinari portrait individual strokes are even visible, but these hands show a much cooler tone with less contrast than is evident in the Morgan man's hands (figs. 99, 100). The latter's hands are a pinkish grey – the pink painted over a darker layer beneath with lead white and hotter pink applications toward the fingertips.

Unblended strokes are deftly juxtaposed in order to establish convincing form. It is a sign of Memling's attention to detail that the letter in the hand is meant to be 'read' as letters and words appearing through the paper from the reverse side. Not decipherable, these illusionistic strokes are fashioned with a stiff brush or the butt end of the brush into the still-wet white paint.

The differences in approach here – the Portinari portrait's more sculptural and sharper definition of form as compared to the broader, flatter handling of the Morgan portrait – are readily apparent in the x-radiographs of the two paintings (figs. 101, 102). The *Portrait of Tommaso Portinari* is characterized by the use of thin strokes of lead white restricted to the description of the features of the face, the definition of the furrows of the brow, the creases of flesh to the left of the proper right eye, and the touches of highlights on the inside of the ear, bridge and tip of the nose, and the upper and lower edges of the lips. *Maria Baroncelli*, the pendant to *Tommaso Portinari*, amplifies this in its application of lead white which is sparingly applied to the highlights of the face (fig. 93). By contrast, the Morgan portrait shows a more broadly brushed on and evenly applied layer of lead white as one sees as well in the x-radiograph of the Van Nieuwenhove portrait dated 1487 (fig. 103). Such an overall thick and roughly brushed-on application of lead white is also evident in the x-radiographs of other late-dated paintings, such as the Virgin and Child pendant to the Van Nieuwenhove portrait, or the *Virgin and Child* in the Capilla Real, Granada.[28]

The varied approaches indicate a development in Memling's painting technique. The earlier Portinari portrait is produced by a series of thin glazes superimposed on the structure formed by restricted use of lead white applications, leading to a solid three-dimensional-looking and porcelain quality of the surface. The Morgan portrait streamlines this more labour-intensive technique by beginning with an overall coating of the flesh tone to which the definition of the features of the face are added on the surface, often in disengaged strokes of lighter and darker paint that are juxtaposed or placed adjacent to each other instead of blended in layer over layer.[29] The virtuoso handling and execution of the Morgan portrait as I have described it here is characteristic of Memling's late portraits. Its closest dated comparison is the portrait of Willem Moreel, who kneels on the left wing of the 'Moreel Triptych' (pl. 24 and detail, fig. 104). Dirk De Vos rightly

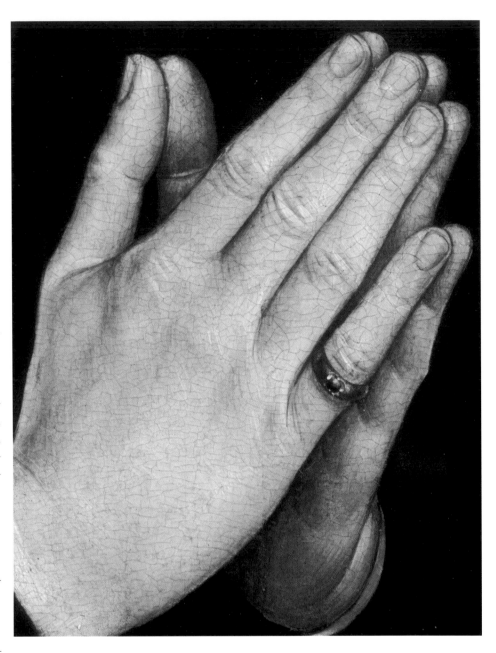

*fig. 99*
*Portrait of Tommaso Portinari,*
detail of pl. 2

*fig. 100*
*Portrait of a Man with a Pink* [cat. 20],
detail of pl. 22

*fig. 101*
X-radiograph of
*Portrait of Tommaso Portinari*

*fig. 102*
X-radiograph of *Portrait of a Man*
*with a Pink* [cat. 20]

describes the brushwork of the 'Moreel Triptych' as show-ing 'the first signs of the freer handling of the paint: the strokes are now concentrated on the surface, especially in the modelling of the heads'.[30] The triptych can be dated after 1484, when the couple was granted permission to set up an altar dedicated to St Maurus and St Giles at St James's Church in Bruges. The Morgan portrait, there-fore, must date from the latter half of the 1480s, that is, considerably later than has been previously proposed and in line with the *Portrait of Maarten Nieuwenhove* of 1487 and the Thyssen *Portrait of a Man at Prayer* (pl. 28) with which it is directly comparable in its features of handling and exe-cution. The exquisite mastery of the brushwork – loose, spontaneous, but completely assured in the placement of the strokes – allows Memling to bring the unknown Mor-gan sitter to life with an extraordinary economy of means.

It is as if the features of the face were merely breathed onto the prepared panel.

It is now possible to use the findings of the above com-parison to evaluate the proposed dating of other por-traits by Memling. Entirely consistent with the charac-teristic application of lead white that we have seen in the early Portinari portraits is the Frankfurt *Portrait of a Man in a Red Hat* (pl. 1), which Jochen Sander has dated to the early 1470s.[31] Although the *Portrait of an Elderly Couple* (pl. 6), has been considered among Memling's earliest works as well as a product of around 1480, the evidence of the x-radiographs supports an early date.[32] Further securing an early date for these works is the *Portrait of Gilles Joye* (fig. 105), dated 1472 on its original frame, which shows a consistent treatment of the lead white paint, restricted to the highlights and carefully

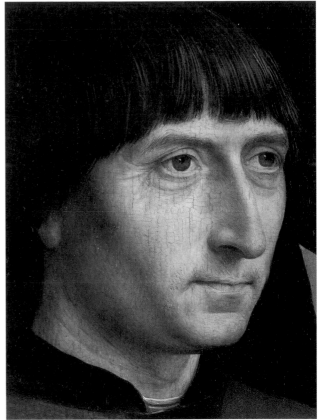

applied to delineate facial features such as the eyes and wrinkles of the forehead.

This group of similar treatment in the early paintings now allows us to look at some portraits that are especially problematic in terms of their dating. The Metropolitan Museum *Portrait of an Old Man* and his mate, the Houston *Portrait of an Old Woman* (figs. 90–91), have been dated as early as 1465–70 by Friedländer and Bauman, around 1480 by Verhoeven and as late as 1480–90 by Dirk De Vos.[33] Yet the x-radiograph of the *Old Man* (fig. 106), now studied with new comparative material at hand, reveals the same

sparing use of lead white and linear approach to the features of the face that indicate an early date in the 1470s.[34] Another controversial painting in terms of its date is the Lehman *Portrait of a Young Man* (fig. 107), presumably one of the Italian patrons of Memling, which has been dated as early as the 1470s and as late as the 1480s. With an earliest felling date of the tree from which the panel came of 1474, and a minimal storage and seasoning time of two years, this portrait could have been painted as early as about 1476, which would tie it more closely to the early group of portraits to which it certainly appears to belong in terms

*fig. 105*
X-radiograph of
*Portrait of Gilles Joye* [cat. 3]
Williamstown (Mass.), Sterling and
Francine Clark Art Institute

of its treatment of the use of lead white in the build-up of the paint layers. This would allow for a more comfortable period of time in which the portrait could have been of direct influence on the works of Perugino and Verrocchio, as Paula Nuttall has suggested.

What then of those paintings which are not aligned with the poles of Memling's development, but reveal stages of his transition from one to the other? One such painting is the Frick *Portrait of a Man before a Landscape* (pl. 3), a painting that is little discussed in the literature. It has been considered among the early portraits because of its *trompe-l'œil* framing device, which like the Portinari portraits and the *Man in a Red Hat* (pls. 1, 2) projects the figure forward into the viewer's space. If this compositional device is not as successful here as it is in the other portraits, it is due to the

fact that the panel has been cut down on all of its edges. It was wider especially at the left and the right, which would have allowed for a more convincing *trompe-l'œil* frame enhanced by the shadows at the upper right and left corners, which have been truncated by the trimming of the panel edges. This beautifully rendered and sensitive portrait is unfortunately abraded, making it somewhat difficult to compare the handling of the flesh tones with the early and extremely well-preserved *Portrait of Tommaso Portinari*. However, if we look at the x-radiograph of the Frick painting (fig. 108), greater clarity emerges about its place in Memling's oeuvre. The use of lead white in the modelling of the flesh tones is neither the restrictive application of the Portinari portrait, nor the overall loosely brushed-in application of the Morgan portrait (compare figs. 101,

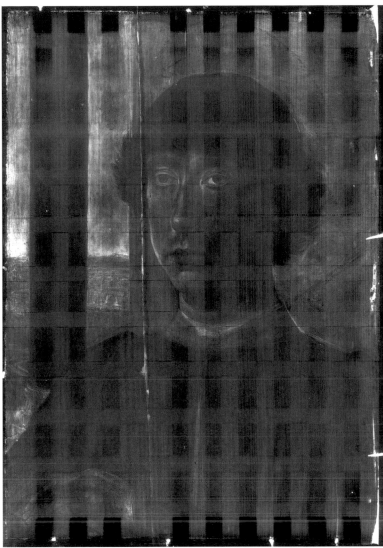

*fig. 106*
X-radiograph of *Portrait of an Old Man*
New York, The Metropolitan
Museum of Art,
Bequest of Benjamin Altman

*fig. 107*
X-radiograph of
*Portrait of a Young Man* [cat. 15]
New York, The Metropolitan
Museum of Art, Robert Lehman
Collection

102 and 108). The application of lead white paint is broader than in the former, and not as precise in its delineation of the features of the face. The lower lids of the eyes, the crow's-feet creases of flesh at the outside edges of the eyes, the bony structure of the ear, all are not described in the distinctly linear fashion that they are in the x-radiography of the Portinari portrait. Furthermore, the brow, the bridge and tip of the nose, and the chin are all more broadly painted. Such an execution is heading in the direction of the handling and execution found in the Morgan portrait, but hardly yet to that degree of loose application.[35] A date in the mid-to-late 1470s, therefore, would seem to be most reasonable.

Even more problematic in terms of recognizing and understanding Memling's latest works is the *Portrait of Jacob (?) Obrecht* (pl. 34, fig. 109), on view at the New York venue of this exhibition. Long unknown in a private collection, it was first brought into the oeuvre of Memling by Dirk De Vos, who published the portrait in 1987. In 1993 it was sold at auction at Sotheby's in New York when it was acquired by the Kimbell Art Museum. While acknowledging that 'a portrait this robust does not appear anywhere else in his oeuvre', and there are 'no readily convincing points of comparison', De Vos none the less made arguments in favour of an attribution to Memling.[36] In his view, 'the exceptional quality of the work, its strong spatial character, the morphological detail of the facial features and the execution of the transparent surplice' all showed signs of Memling's authorship.[37] He further pointed to the tactile quality of the fabrics, the powerful anatomy of the hands and modelling of the head and the reddish-brown marbling of the frame as striking a common chord with Memling's characteristic handling and execution. The work is dated on the frame '1496', that is two years after Memling's death, but this might possibly be explained, De Vos suggested, as the dedication date of the picture, or the date of the completion by another artist of a diptych or triptych that included this panel.

The high quality of the portrait is undeniable, and its handling and execution are impressively bold and convincing in terms of building up the forms of the portrait. In a comparison with the other paintings in this exhibition, the Obrecht portrait holds up very well indeed. But is this work truly representative of Memling's late style? In this study we have looked at the results of the technical investigation of a number of Memling's paintings seeking to find a chronological development in his handling and execution. We have observed that the underdrawing in the early portraits appears to be carried out in black chalk or charcoal in summary notations, if in fact any underdrawing can be detected at all. In the later works of the 1480s (the Bruges *Portrait of a Young Woman* and the 'Van Nieuwenhove Diptych', for example) the underdrawing is boldly executed in brush, and now serves not only as an underdrawn sketch of the form of the sitter, but also as an undermodelling especially in the costumes. Those features that can be detected in the reflectogram assemblies of the portraits are complemented by the information from x-radiography. Lead white is used in the early portraits to build up the form in a three-dimensional, sculptural fashion; it is restricted to applications that indicate the highlights of the face, leaving other areas by contrast untouched. Lead white strokes also delineate the features of the face and sharpen the contours of forms. Over this structure formed by the application of lead white paint, Memling added thin layers of paint in order to build up the form, achieving the final results with fully blended brushstrokes.

The later paintings begin to show the development of an abbreviated technique, culminating in works such as the *Portrait of Maarten van Nieuwenhove* of 1487. Here Memling laid in an overall flat application of lead white, introducing (as the x-radiographs show) the flesh tone layer at once. Over this he sparingly applied strokes of different colours, juxtaposed to create the features of the face with an extraordinary economy of means. Underdrawing in these works often serves also as undermodelling, and Mem-

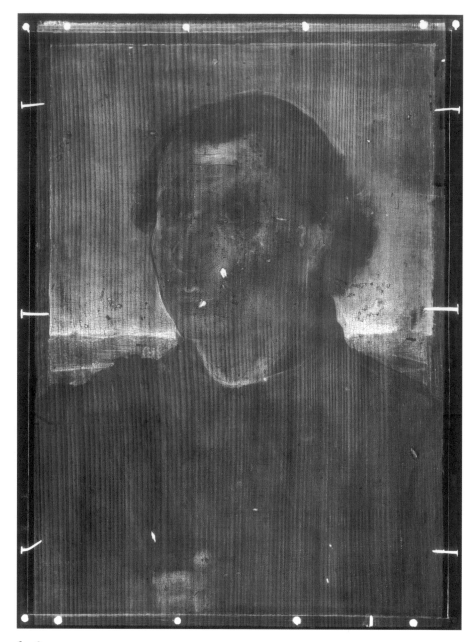

*fig. 108*
X-radiograph of
*Portrait of a Man* [cat. 2]
New York, The Frick Collection

*fig.* 109
Infra-red reflectogram assembly
of *Portrait of Jacob (?) Obrecht* [cat. 28]
Fort Worth, The Kimbell Art
Museum

ling's shifts and changes during the working process may be readily observed in the infra-red reflectograms.

How then does the *Portrait of Jacob (?) Obrecht* compare with these new observations about Memling's paintings? At once apparent in the infra-red reflectogram assembly (fig. 109) is that the face and the hands are opaque and thickly painted; unlike the Van Nieuwenhove portrait, no underdrawing is visible to the naked eye as a result of the thin and increasingly transparent overlying flesh tones. Aside from the possible shift of the position of the proper right eye of Obrecht, the only detectable underdrawing in regard to the head is the preliminary idea for the contour of the face at the right. Nowhere, as in the Van Nieuwenhove portrait or the Bruges *Portrait of a Young Woman*, does the underdrawing serve as undermodelling in an intermediary level of the paint structure. Thin contour lines and some parallel hatching appear in the sleeves of Obrecht's garment, but they are neither of the completely loose, scribbly searching lines as in the Van Nieuwenhove portrait nor the thicker undermodelling we are accustomed to seeing in the costumes of sitters of the 1480s. The x-radiograph of Obrecht (fig. 110) shows this denser modelling of the hands and the rather sparingly applied lead white to select features of the face in the highlights that is more indicative of Memling's early than his late paintings (superimposed is the image from the back of the painting). These observations all lead to the conclusion that, while an impressive portrait, made all the more important because of the possible identification of the sitter,[38] this painting is unlikely to have been produced by Hans Memling. Somewhat imitative in style, it must be the work of a follower.

This brief investigation into some of the features of the painting technique, execution and handling of Memling's portraits, I hope, will serve as an attempt at a method by which we can better discern the artist's development in this genre. Such revelations as we have seen here through technical investigations allow us perhaps to come closer to understanding Memling's intentions and certainly to appreciating his extraordinary efficiency in producing portraits for his many clients. That he achieved such fame in his own time both locally and abroad was due to his approach: an economy of or even minimal means employed to achieve remarkable results.

*fig. 110*
X-radiograph of
*Portrait of Jacob (?) Obrecht* [cat. 28]
Fort Worth, The Kimbell Art
Museum

* Special thanks are due to the following colleagues who gave permission for the study of the Memling portraits under their care and permission to publish the results here: Hilde Lobelle, Colin B. Bailey, Richard Rand, Egbert Haverkamp-Begemann, Rhoda Eitel-Porter, Ubaldo Sedano and Jochen Sander. I am grateful to the late Hubert von Sonnenburg for numerous discussions over questions of Memling's technique. Charlotte Hale kindly produced new x-radiographs of some of the Metropolitan Museum Memling portraits as well as those from the Pierpont Morgan Library and The Frick Collection. I also thank Alison Gilchrest for additional processing of some of the infra-red reflectogram assemblies and the x-radiograph of the Houston *Old Woman* that are published here for the first time. Christina Ceulemans at the Institut Royal du Patrimoine Artistique in Brussels, and Juan Trujillo, Teresa Christiansen and Susan Bresnan in the Photo Studio of the Metropolitan Museum of Art provided new prints of the technical documents for use here.

1  M. Ainsworth (with contributions by M. P. J. Martens), *Petrus Christus Renaissance Master of Bruges* (exhibition catalogue, New York, Metropolitan Museum of Art), New York 1994, 49–50.

2  A close study of the wood grain of the oak panels of the *Old Man* and the *Old Woman* does not indicate that the two were cut from the same panel as sometimes has been supposed. I am grateful to George Bisacca for his expertise in this examination.

3  L. A. Waldman, 'New Documents for Memling's Portinari Portraits in the Metropolitan Museum of Art', *Apollo* 153 (February 2001), 28–33.

4  Infra-red reflectography and x-radiography of the *Portrait of an Old Man* show that the sitter's left hand was originally painted over his right.

5  The x-radiograph also reveals a dense white application over the hand that may have been a white fur cuff of a sleeve of the type that can be seen in the portrait of Maria Portinari in Hugo van der Goes's 'Portinari Altarpiece' (Florence, Uffizi). Slightly to the right in the x-radiograph is another whitish application that may represent a wide belt at the woman's waist. See this essay fig. 94 for comparison with Hugo's portrait of Maria Portinari.

6  Waagen 1857, 440.

7  Martha Wolff in Sterling *et al.* 1998, 74–8.

8  Martha Wolff in Hand and Wolff 1986, 190 and n. 11.

9  For various theories on the addition of the arrow, see *ibid.*, 191.

10  De Vos 1994, no. 36.

11  De Vos 1994, no. 9; New York 1998, 162–5, no. 27.

12  Périer d'Ieteren 1994, 67; Stroo *et al.* 1999, 186.

13  De Vos 1994, 370, 391–2.

14  This was expressed by Stroo *et al.* 1999, 186.

15  See Klein 1997.

16  For the most recent explanation of dendrochronology, see Klein 2003.

17  Aside from the various recent collection catalogues in which some Memling paintings have been studied, see Périer-d'Ieteren 1994, Ainsworth 1994 and Faries 1997.

18  *Ibid.*

19  I undertook the study of the underdrawing in the Bruges *Portrait of a Young Woman* in 1993 thanks to the kind permission of Hilde Lobelle, then curator of the Memlingmuseum. The infra-red reflectogram assembly is published here for the first time.

20  This investigation was also carried out in 1993 thanks to the kind permission of Hilde Lobelle; the results are published here for the first time.

21  For articles devoted to the perspective scheme of the 'Van Nieuwenhove Diptych', see the bibliography under cat. 23.

22  Additional findings about the relationship of the right and left halves of this diptych will be discussed in depth by Ron Spronk and Catherine Metzger in the upcoming exhibition catalogue on Netherlandish diptychs at the National Gallery in Washington and the Antwerp Koninklijk Museum voor Schone Kunsten in 2006.

23  As Cyriel Stroo pointed out in his 1999 catalogue of the collection at the Musées Royaux des Beaux-Arts in Brussels, 'It is probable that, following further technological and dendrochronological analysis, the chronology of Hans Memling's portraits will have to be reviewed as a whole.' Stroo *et al.* 1999, 186.

24  De Vos 1994, no. 26.

25  For the dating proposed by these scholars, see *ibid.*

26  De Vos 1994, 365–6, figs. 59–60.

27  De Vos 1994, 388.

28  See especially the head of the Virgin. For an illustration see De Vos 1994, 384, fig. 148.

29  Dendrochronology of the two portraits does not contradict the relative dating that is suggested by the varied technique of the paintings. According to Peter Klein, the estimated felling date for the tree from which the Portinari portrait panel comes ranges from 1432 to 1438. The date for the same of his mate, *Maria Baroncelli*, is 1457–63, suggesting that the pendant portraits were produced (after the seasoning and drying of the wood) some time in the early 1470s. The earliest felling date of the tree from which the panel of the Morgan portrait is made is 1454, with a more plausible felling date between 1458 ... 1460 ... 1464 + x. With a minimum of two years' seasoning and storage time, a creation date from 1456 upwards would be plausible. Under the assumption of a median of 15 sapwood rings and 2 years for seasoning, a creation date of 1462 upwards would be possible (letter of Peter Klein, 27 August 2004). I am grateful to Peter Klein for his willingness to carry out dendrochronology of Memling portraits in New York (Morgan Library and Frick Collection) in August 2004.

30  De Vos 1994, 244, and plate on p. 242.

31  Sander 1993, 296–305, and 300, fig. 192.

32  For images of the x-radiographs of the man and the woman together, see Comblen-Sonkes and Lorentz 1995, pls. 272, 273. For the quite diverse opinions about the dating as well as the most recent discussion, see *ibid.*, 284, 186–7 and 290.

33  See De Vos 1994, no. 60.

34  In this case, the Metropolitan Museum's *Old Man* cannot be dated by dendrochronology because it is set into another panel and shows no original edges. Dendrochronology of the Houston *Portrait of an Old Woman* is open to interpretation. It can be dated as late as 1480 according to one reading, but the earliest possible felling date of the tree is 1470. With a minimum of two years' drying and storage time for this small piece of wood, Peter Klein agrees that anytime from 1472 on would be possible and cannot be refuted by the data (e-mail communication with the author, July 2004).

35  The findings here parallel those of the x-radiograph of the Brussels (MRBA) *Portrait of a Man* (Stroo *et al.* 1999, 182, fig. 92), suggesting that this portrait too likely dates to the mid- or late 1470s, not as early as 1472 as Stroo and Syfer-d'Olne have suggested.

36  De Vos 1994, no. 93.

37  *Ibid.*

38  See however Till-Holger Borchert's questions concerning the identification of the sitter in his entry for cat. 28.

Plates

pl. 1

**Portrait of a Man in a Red Hat**

*c. 1465–70*

Panel, 41.8 x 30.6 cm

Frankfurt, Städelsches Kunstinstitut und Städtische Galerie, inv. 945

[cat. 1]

pl. 2a–b

## Portraits of Tommaso and Maria Portinari

*c.* 1470

Panel, each 44.1 x 34 cm

New York, The Metropolitan Museum of Art, Bequest of Benjamin Altman,

inv. 14.40.626–627

pl. 3
**Portrait of a Man**
*c.* 1470–75
Panel, 33.5 x 23 cm
New York, The Frick Collection, inv. 67.1.169
[cat. 2]

**pl. 4**
**Portrait of Gilles Joye**
Dated 1472
Panel, 37.3 x 29.2 cm
Williamstown (Mass.), Sterling and Francine Clark Art Institute, cat. no. 408
[cat. 3]

pl. 5
## The Virgin and Child with St Anthony Abbot and a Donor
Dated 1472
Panel, 92.7 x 53.6 cm
Ottawa, National Gallery of Canada, inv. 6191
[cat. 4]

pl. 6a–b

## Portrait of an Elderly Couple

*c.* 1470–75

Panel, 36.1 x 29.4 cm and 35.4 x 29.3 cm

(*Man*) Berlin, Staatliche Museen zu Berlin, Preussischer Kulturbesitz, Gemäldegalerie, inv. 529c

(*Woman*) Paris, Musée du Louvre, inv. RF 1723

[cat. 5]

pl. 7
**Fragment of a Male Portrait**
*c.* 1470–75
Panel, oval, diameter 19/21.6 cm
Private collection
[cat. 6]

pl. 8
## Portrait of a Man before a Landscape
*c.* 1470–75
Panel, 35.4 x 25.8 cm
Brussels, Musées Royaux des Beaux-Arts de Belgique, inv. 1358
[cat. 7]

pl. 9
**Portrait of a Man with a Spotted Fur Collar**
*c.* 1475
Panel, 38 x 27 cm
Florence, Galleria degli Uffizi, inv. 1102
[cat. 8]

pl. 10a–b
## Portrait of an Old Man; Portrait of an Old Woman
*c.* 1475–80
Panel, 25.4 x 18.4 cm and 26.5 x 17.8 cm
(*Man*) New York, The Metropolitan Museum of Art, Bequest of Benjamin Altman, inv. 14.40.648
(*Woman*) Houston, Museum of Fine Arts, The Edith A. and Percy S. Straus Collection, inv. 44.530
[*Woman:* cat. 9]

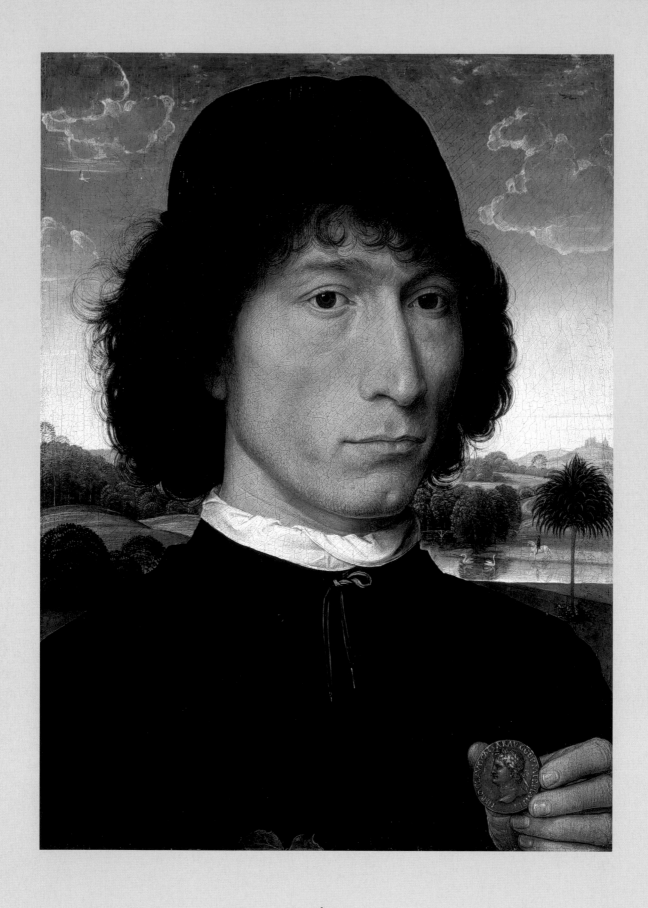

pl. 11

**Portrait of a Man with a Coin of the Emperor Nero (Bernardo Bembo?)**

1473–4?

Panel, 31 x 23.2 cm

Antwerp, Koninklijk Museum voor Schone Kunsten, inv. 5

[cat. 10]

pl. 12
## Portrait of a Man with a Letter
*c.* 1475
Panel, 35 x 26 cm
Florence, Galleria degli Uffizi, inv. 9970
[cat. 11]

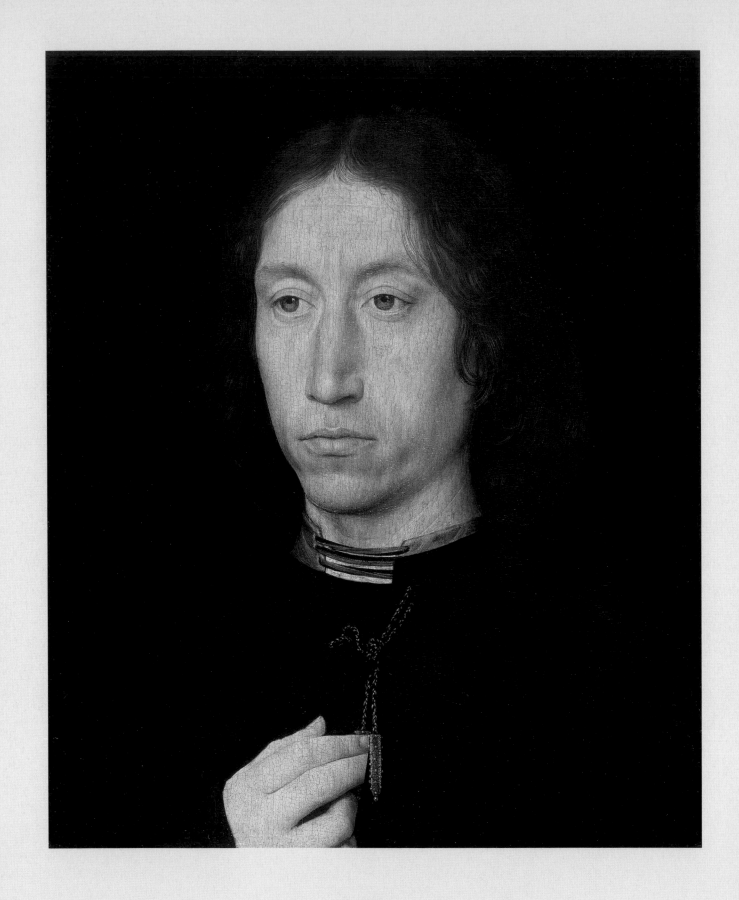

pl. 13
Portrait of a Man with a Gold Cord
*c.* 1475–80
Panel, 31.8 x 27.1 cm
The Royal Collection © H. M. Queen Elizabeth II, inv. 3020
[cat. 12]

pl. 14
**Portrait of a Man with an Arrow**
*c.* 1475–80
Panel, 31.9 x 25.8 cm
Washington, National Gallery of Art, Andrew W. Mellon Collection,
inv. 1937.1.42
[cat. 13]

pl. 15a–b
## Two Donor Fragments from an Altarpiece with the Virgin and Child
*c.* 1475–80
Panel, 44.7 x 32.4 cm and 44.5 x 32 cm
Sibiu, Museum Sammlung Samuel Brukenthal
[cat. 14]

pl. 16
## Portrait of a Young Man
*c.* 1475–80
Panel, 39.9 x 28.3 cm
New York, The Metropolitan Museum of Art, Robert Lehman Collection,
inv. 1975.1.112
[cat. 15]

pl. 17
**Portrait of a Young Man before a Landscape**
*c.* 1475–80
Panel, 26 x 20 cm
Venice, Galleria dell'Accademia, inv. 586
[cat. 16]

pl. 18
**Portrait of a Young Woman ('Sibyl')**
Dated 1480
Panel, 46.5 x 35.2 cm
Bruges, Stedelijke Musea, Memlingmuseum – Sint-Janshospitaal, inv. OSJ 174.1
[cat. 17]

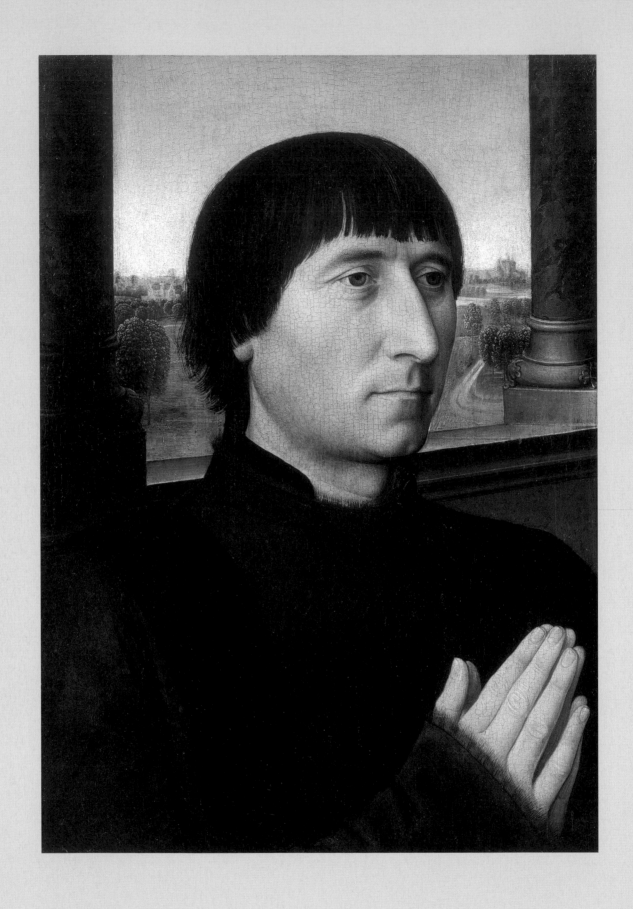

pl. 19a–b
## Two Wings with the Portraits of Willem Moreel and Barbara van Vlaenderberch
*c.* 1480
Panel, 39.4 x 29 cm and 39.3 x 29.5 cm
Brussels, Musées Royaux des Beaux-Arts de Belgique, inv. 1451–1452
[cat. 18]

pl. 20
**Portrait of a Young Man**
*c.* 1480 or later?
Panel, 33.4 x 22.8 cm
The Montreal Museum of Fine Arts, Horsley & Annie Townsend Bequest
and William Gilman Cheney Bequest, inv. 56.1129
[cat. 19]

pl. 21
**Portrait of a Young Man**
*c.* 1480–85
Panel, 26.7 x 19.8 cm
Zurich, Kunsthaus, Stiftung Betty and David M. Koetser

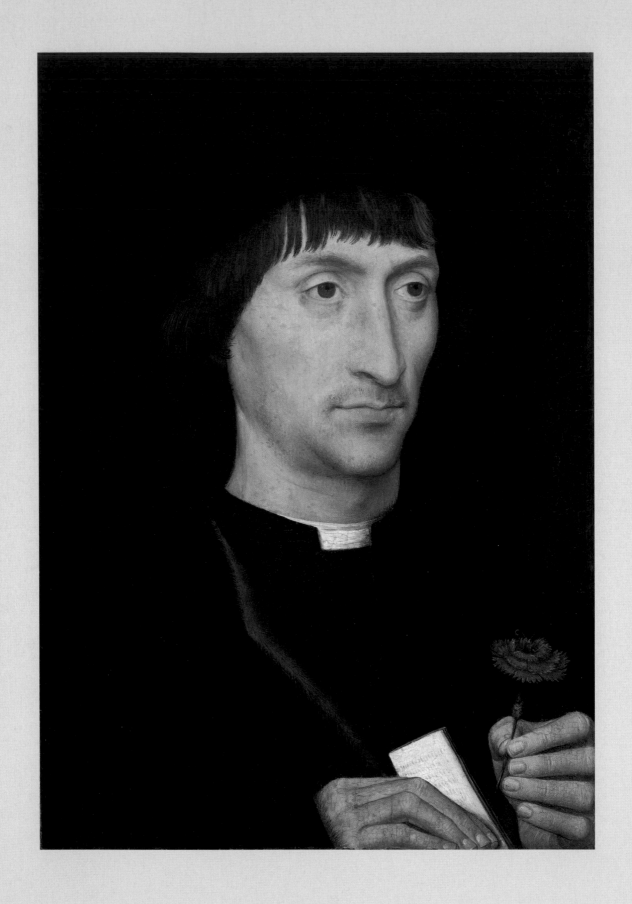

pl. 22

**Portrait of a Man with a Pink**
*c.* 1480–85
Panel, 39.5 x 28.4 cm
New York, The Pierpont Morgan Library
[cat. 20]

pl. 23
**Portrait of a Man at Prayer before a Landscape (Charles de Visen?)**
*c.* 1480–85
Panel, 30 x 22 cm
The Hague, Mauritshuis, inv. 595
[cat. 21]

pl. 24
**Triptych with Saints Christopher, Giles and Maurus**
**(Moreel Triptych)**
Dated 1484
Panel, 141 x 87 cm, 141 x 174 cm and 141 x 86.8 cm
Bruges, Stedelijke Musea, Groeningemuseum, inv. OGRO0091–95.1
[cat. 22]

pl. 25
**Diptych of Maarten van Nieuwenhove**
Dated 1487
Panel, each 52 x 41.5 cm
Bruges, Stedelijke Musea, Memlingmuseum – Sint-Janshospitaal, inv. OSJ178.1
[cat. 23]

pl. 26

**Portrait of a Young Man at Prayer**
*c.* 1475–80
Panel, 39 x 25.5 cm
London, National Gallery, inv. 2594

pl. 27
**The Virgin and Child with a Donor**
On the reverse of the donor wing: St Anthony of Padua
*c.* 1485–90
Panel, 34.5 x 26.5 cm and 34.7 x 26.5 cm
The Art Institute of Chicago, Mr & Mrs Martin A. Ryerson Collection
and Gift of Arthur Sachs, inv. 1933.1050 and 1953.467

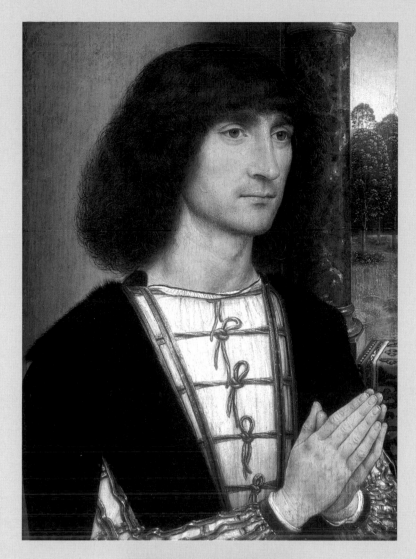

pl. 28

**Portrait of a Young Man at Prayer**
On the reverse: Flower Still Life
*c.* 1485–94
Panel, 29.2 x 22.5 cm
Madrid, Museo Thyssen-Bornemisza, inv. 1938.1
[cat. 25]

pl. 29
**Portrait of a Man (Folco Portinari?)**
1487 or later?
Panel, 35 x 25 cm
Florence, Galleria degli Uffizi, inv. 1101
[cat. 24]

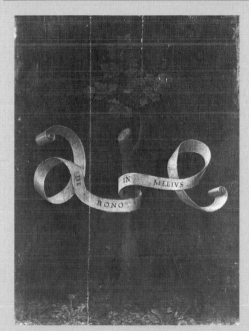

pl. 30
### Triptych of Benedetto Portinari
Dated 1487
Panel, 45.5 x 34.5 cm, 41.5 x 31.5 cm and 45 x 34 cm
Staatliche Museen zu Berlin, Preussischer Kulturbesitz, Gemäldegalerie, inv. 528B (centre panel)
Florence, Galleria degli Uffizi, inv. 1100 and 1090 (wings)

pl. 31

**Portrait of a Man**

*c.* 1485–90

Panel, 16 x 12 cm

Banbury, Upton House, Bearsted Collection (The National Trust), inv. 298

[cat. 26]

pl. 32
**Portrait of a Man Holding a String of Beads**
*c.* 1490–94
Canvas (transferred from panel), 43.5 x 31.5 cm
Copenhagen, Statens Museum for Kunst, inv. Sp. 738

pl. 33
**Fragment of a Portrait of a Man with a Pink**
*c.* 1490?
Panel, 40 x 25 cm
Vicenza, Museo Civico, inv. 298
[cat. 27]

**pl. 34**
Antwerp School?
**Portrait of Jacob (?) Obrecht**
Dated 1496
Panel, 50.8 x 36.1 cm
Fort Worth, The Kimbell Art Museum, inv. KAM 1993.02
[cat. 28]

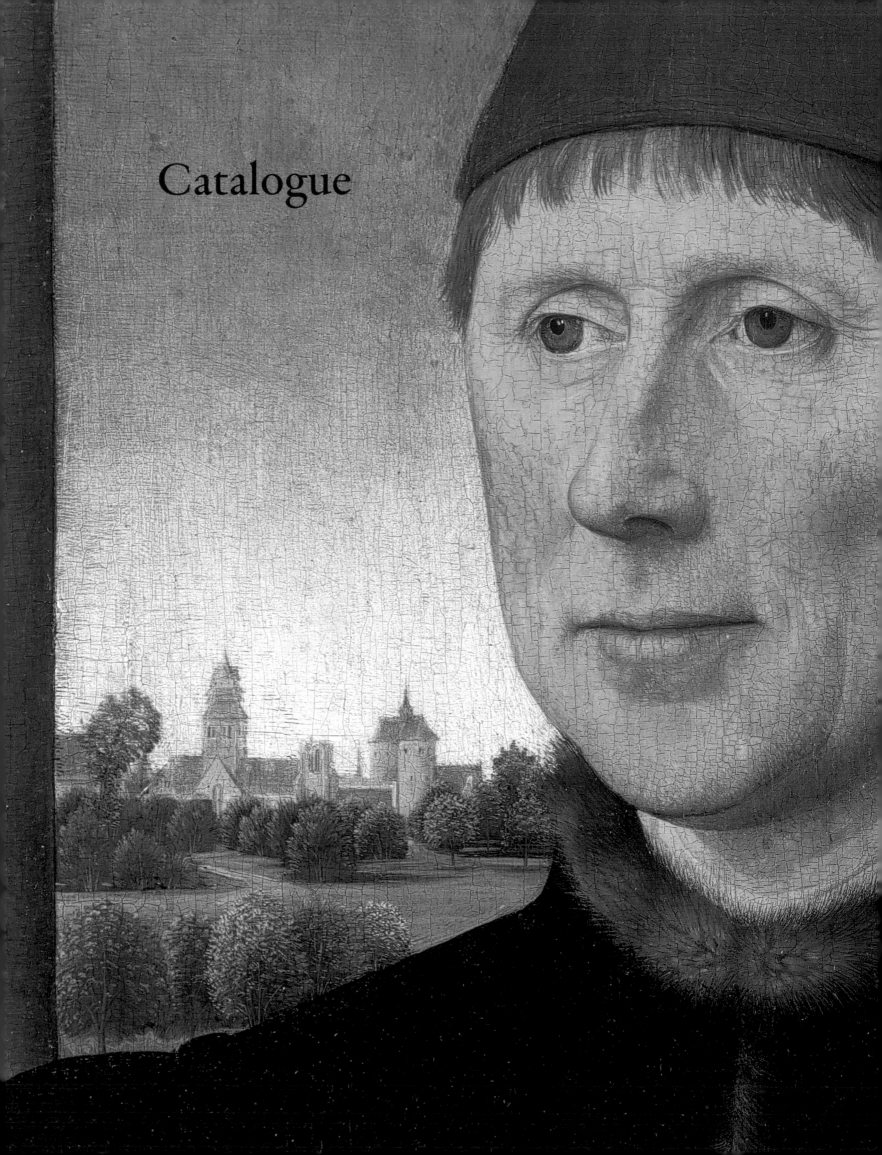

Catalogue

# 1  Portrait of a Man in a Red Hat

*c.* 1465–70
Panel (oak), 41.8 x 30.6 cm
Frankfurt, Städelsches Kunstinstitut und Städtische Galerie, inv. 945

PROVENANCE

28 April 1823 purchased by L. J. Nieuwen-huys and sold to Prince William of Orange (Brussels); 1850 bought by the Städelsches Kunstinstitut at the sale of William II of Orange (no. 20), The Hague.

EXHIBITION

Frankfurt 1995, no. 16.

BIBLIOGRAPHY

Passavant 1833, 351; Passavant 1841, 34; Nieuwenhuys 1843, no. 18; Förster 1853, 121; Crowe and Cavalcaselle 1875, 327; Wauters 1893, 101, 106; Kaemmerer 1899, 24; Bock 1900, vii–viii; Weale 1901, 68, 103; Voll 1906, 189–90; Fierens-Gevaert 1909, 216–17; Voll 1909, 173; Wurzbach 1910, 141; Ring 1913, 139; Friedländer 1916, 178; Conway 1921, 240; Winkler 1924, 128; Hulin de Loo 1927, 106; Friedländer 1928 (1971), no. 73; Baldass 1942, 27–8, 41; Panofsky 1953, 349; Pope-Hennessy 1966, 60 n. 85; Faggin 1969, no. 108; Davidson 1971, 381–4; Lane 1980, no. 26; Hinterding and Horsch 1989, 10, 17, 60–61; Sander 1989, 123–35; Sander 1993, 296–305; De Vos 1994, no. 7; Sander 1995, 45–6; Stroo *et al.* 1999, 184, 186–7.

Not only is the *Portrait of a Man in a Red Hat* one of Memling's earliest portraits with a landscape background, it is one of his earliest portraits *per se*, executed shortly after his arrival in Bruges. Dendrochronological evidence establishes 1457 as the most likely felling date of the wood used for the panel, suggesting the mid-1460s for the execution of the painting, a date consistent with Memling's early stylistic development. The man, of mature age, is shown head and shoulders in three-quarters view to the left. His dress consists of a black doublet with a narrow collar over which is placed a black, tightly buttoned tunic. The latter is lined with brown fur which is visible at the edges of the neck, sleeves and down the front. The man wears a tall red hat over straight brown hair. His hands, of which only the left is adorned with rings, rest on a ledge which coincided with the original frame (now lost). This illusionistic device of combining pictorial space with that of the viewer, is one Memling used in a schematic manner in many later portraits.

For the Frankfurt as well as for later portraits, Memling chose a pose in which the sitter's upper body and arms are cut off by the picture frame, thus imbuing him with a sense of monumentality. In this respect, the artist followed the convention established by Jan van Eyck (see fig. 7) and Rogier van der Weyden and continued in Bruges by Petrus Christus (see fig. 51). What is new, indeed spectacular, is the landscape which covers almost the entire background as well as the simulated stone frame before which the sitter is posed. Whereas the combination of frame and landscape can be seen as a logical development of the 'portrait with view through a window' type, commonly believed to have been introduced by Dieric Bouts in 1462 (see fig. 54), in the Frankfurt panel Memling goes considerably farther. The stone frame carries a double function: on the one hand, it serves as a kind of window frame through which we see a low, wooded landscape with a distant town; on the other, it acts in *trompe-l'œil* fashion as a frame for the actual painting. This pictorial device, testifying to Memling's confrontation with the art of Jan van Eyck, creates the illusion of moving the sitter from the picture plane into the real space of the viewer. The effect is intensified by the red hat, part of which overlaps the upper edge of the stone frame.

It is noteworthy that Memling tried to improve on his ambitious composition during its execution, specifically as it relates to the simulated stone frame and the cap. The underdrawing, executed with the brush and primarily indicating contours, reveals that originally the frame was wider and the cap smaller. During the painting process, the frame was made narrower in favour of the landscape and the cap broadened, apparently for greater illusionistic effect (Sander 1993).

Two further early portraits by Memling show strong compositional correspondences: the Frick *Portrait of a Man* (cat. 2) and the portraits of Tommaso Portinari and his wife, Maria Baroncelli (see pl. 2). The former, which has been cut down

on the left and right sides, shows a similarly fictive frame separating the background landscape from the sitter, who projects out of the picture into the viewer's space; there too the frame was made narrower during the process of painting in favour of the landscape (see Maryan Ainsworth's essay).

*Trompe-l'œil* frames are also to be found in the Portinari portraits. The couple married in 1469 and lived in Bruges from 1470 onwards. Their portraits are fragments of a devotional triptych which the couple apparently commissioned from Memling soon after. Although the fictive stone frames in the Portinari portraits are introduced purely for visual effect, they are similar in concept and execution to the one in the Frankfurt panel. The veil of Maria Baroncelli's hennin covers the frame, which was enlarged during the painting process, enhancing the spatial illusion of both portraits.

Compared to the *Portrait of Gilles Joye*, dated 1472 (cat. 3), both the *Portrait of a Man in a Red Hat* and the portraits of Tommaso Portinari and Maria Baroncelli appear more accomplished, even though they were probably painted a couple of years earlier. Apparently, Memling experimented with different portrait types at this time. This is witnessed, for example, by the Brussels portrait (cat. 7) showing the male sitter before a landscape without illusionistic framing devices, which was executed only a little later, at the beginning of the 1470s.

## 2  Portrait of a Man

*c.* 1470–75
Panel (oak), 33.5 x 23 cm
New York, The Frick Collection, inv. 67.1.169

PROVENANCE
Northern Italy; Baron Van der Elst, Vienna
(1937); Baron Van der Elst, Oostkerke
(Damme); 1968 acquired by The Frick
Collection.

EXHIBITIONS
New York 1942; Bruges 1953, no. 13;
Brussels 1955, no. 13.

BIBLIOGRAPHY
Friedländer 1937 (1971), Suppl. 231;
Baldass 1942, 28, no. 53; Faggin 1969,
no. 110; Davidson 1971; Lane 1980, no. 25;
Campbell 1990, 109, 120, 233; Sander 1993,
301–303; De Vos 1994, no. 12; Stroo *et al.*
1999, 184, 186, 187 n. 26, 213 n. 16.

The bust-length portrait of a man, shown in three-quarters view to the left, is placed before a fictive stone frame opening onto a low, forested summer landscape with distant hills at the horizon. The man wears a dark coat. His curly-haired head is bare; in his right hand he holds the strap of his headdress. The light falls from the left onto the man's face which displays composure and calmness; the gesture of his hand, however, implies decisiveness. The castle in the right background might contain a reference to the sitter whose identity, however, is unknown.

The fictive stone moulding separating the sitter from the landscape functions at the same time, in *trompe-l'œil* fashion, as a frame for the picture, which appears to project the sitter into the spectator's space. Undoubtedly the illusionistic effect was stronger before the panel was cut at both sides, as the reflections still visible on remnants of the fictive frame would suggest. Such frames can also be seen in the early *Portrait of a Man in a Red Hat* (cat. 1) and the two Portinari portraits (see pl. 2). It should be noted, however, that Memling, while painting the present portrait, narrowed the fictive frame, and with it the illusionistic effect, in favour of the landscape.

The Frick *Portrait of a Man* is one of the most impressive portraits with landscape background in Memling's oeuvre. Apparently having been in a north Italian collection (Bruges 1953), it was discovered late. When Friedländer (1937) published it as a work by the Flemish master, it was in the possession of the Belgian diplomat and publicist Baron Joseph van der Elst in Vienna. Van der Elst left Austria in 1938 and settled in Oostkerke near Bruges where he moved his collection.

Based on the freedom in the conception and execution of the Frick portrait, Ludwig von Baldass (1942) dated it, alongside that from the Corsini collection (cat. 11), immediately after Memling's early portraits. Davidson (1971) placed the painting (which had entered The Frick Collection in 1968 via the art dealer Duveen) at the beginning of the artist's series of portraits with landscapes, since in the present work the landscape is not fully integrated. Lane (1980) and Campbell (1990) dated it to about 1470, while De Vos (1994), pointing out similarities with the *Portrait of Gilles Joye*, dated 1472 on the frame (cat. 3), placed it between 1470 and 1472.

The generally held view that the Frick portrait is early is supported by dendrochronological findings which suggest that it was painted after 1453 (see Appendix, Peter Klein's report). But the precise chronological sequence of Memling's three portraits with fictive frames remains to be investigated further. The portraits of Tommaso Portinari and Maria Baroncelli almost certainly were painted around or shortly after 1470, the year of their marriage. The *Portrait of a Man in a Red Hat* (cat. 1) is probably the earliest, whereas the Frick *Portrait of a Man* is slightly later, not least because of Memling's use of aerial perspective which, despite a similarly constructed landscape, is absent in the Frankfurt painting. Stylistically, the present portrait

comes closest to the *Double Portrait of an Elderly Couple* (cat. 5), which seems to date from the beginning of the 1470s.

Notwithstanding the overall powerful impression conveyed by the present portrait, closer inspection reveals some paint losses on the surface. The collar of the man's white shirt is almost entirely lost, thus providing an indication of the abrasion suffered on the entire paint surface. This also becomes evident in the unevenly transparent sky, underneath which one detects the flesh-coloured *imprimatura*. However, the evenly and carefully applied paint layers modelling the man's face have been retained; they testify to the procedure applied by Memling in his early portraits. Maryan Ainsworth (see her essay) observes that the use of lead white in the present portrait is more advanced than in the Portinari portraits; she suggests a slightly later date for the Frick panel – about 1475.

# 3  Portrait of Gilles Joye

Dated 1472
Panel (oak), 37.3 x 29.2 cm (including original frame)
Williamstown (Mass.), Sterling and Francine Clark Art Institute, cat. no. 408

PROVENANCE
Sacristy St Donatian's Church, Bruges,
until 1799 when the building was
demolished; Sir Henry Michael Hawley,
5th Bart. of Leybourne Grange, Maidstone
(before 1919); his sale Christie's, London,
16 April 1919, no. 19; purchased 1920
by Sterling Clark through Colnaghi's,
London.

EXHIBITION
Bruges 1994, no. 6.

BIBLIOGRAPHY
Friedländer 1928 (1971), no. 72; Friedländer
1949, 31–2; Van Molle 1960; Eisler 1961,
66–70; Faggin 1969, no. 3; McFarlane
1971, 42 n. 54; Lane 1980, no. 15; Dewitte
1985, 156–7; Strohm 1985, 27–9; Dülberg
1990, 66 n. 370, and 220, no. 146; De Vos
1991, 203ff; Koch 1992, 76–7; De Vos 1994,
no. 18; Strohm 1994, 42–3; Verougstraete
and Van Schoute 1997, 279 81.

Inscribed with the year 1472 on the original frame, the painting was first attributed to Memling by Friedländer (1928). With the exception of McFarlane (1971), the attribution has been generally accepted. It is the first firmly dated portrait by Memling and thus functions as a starting point for dating other portraits from this period. At the same time, however, the work differs in character from other portraits by the master presumed to date early in his career. This is due on the one hand to the severely abraded paint surface, and on the other to the painting's pictorial conception, especially the sitter's position in relation to the picture plane, which is unusual in Memling's oeuvre. Comparison with the portraits of Agnolo Tani and Caterina Tanagli in the *Last Judgement* altarpiece of *c.* 1472–3 (see fig. 41) shows that the artist followed a more conventional and formalistic approach in the present panel. The portrait's unique position within Memling's oeuvre becomes even more apparent when we compare it to the portraits of Tommaso Portinari and his wife of about 1470 (pl. 2), which may serve as the best examples of Memling portraits with neutral backgrounds. There the artist was concerned with the representation of individual features while using light

for the modelling of physiognomies. Moreover, they typically demonstrate Memling's interest in pictorial space, which in many other likenesses is enhanced through the introduction of landscape backgrounds. In the present portrait the relationship between the sitter and his surroundings remains ambiguous, and less attention is paid to the modelling of the sitter's features. In the context of contemporary artistic production in Bruges, the work is an anachronism and as such relates to the portraits from the workshop of Rogier van der Weyden or by his immediate successors. Regardless of these discrepancies, Memling's authorship is in no doubt. Painterly technique, including the application of lead white, as well as the efficient manner of outlining contours, as seen in the underdrawing, is typical for the artist at this time (see Maryan Ainsworth's essay).

It is conceivable that the unusual composition reflects the picture's purpose or function, as determined by painter and patron. As first recognized by Van Molle (1960) on the basis of an old inscription on the back of the panel, the sitter is the famous Flemish composer Gilles Joye (1425–1483). Because the hands are clasped in prayer, Eisler (1961) and Dülberg (1990) assumed that the panel constituted the right wing of a devotional diptych, of which the left side held an image of the Virgin. This was rejected by De Vos (1994), who observed that there are no traces of hinges on the still-intact frame (though Eisler and Dülberg cited examples of diptych panels attached with leather bands or paper strips). De Vos suggested instead that the picture was conceived as an independent epitaph. A number of formal elements would seem to support this: the sitter's coat of arms as well as his emblem (a small gold chain linking the letters 'IOIE' and surrounding a coin press) are painted on the frame instead of the back of

the panel as commonly found. The inscriptions on the simulated marbled frame, which state the date of the painting and the age of the sitter, are composed in *trompe-l'œil* fashion of metal letters in relief, reminiscent of inscriptions on tomb slabs in bronze or brass. Such simulated relief letters can be found on the frame of Van Eyck's *Virgin and Child with Canon Van der Paele* (see fig. 18), also an epitaph, as well as his *Portrait of Jan de Leeuw* (see fig. 27), which may have functioned as one. Thus it is possible that the memorial aspect of Memling's *Portrait of Gilles Joye*, formalized in the inscriptions on the frame, determined its compositional format. It is precisely its old-fashioned appearance which imbues it with the timelessness suitable for memorial portraits.

As Van Molle (1960) pointed out, at the time of the execution of the portrait, the composer was ill, and, as was also the case with Canon Van der Paele, the commission may have been motivated by his illness. Joye's tomb remained in the sacristy of St Donatian's in Bruges until the church was demolished in 1799; Memling's portrait must have hung there too.

Apparently of illegitimate birth, Gilles Joye was canon at St Donatian's before he entered the service of Philip the Good, first as a clerk, then as ducal chaplain (1462–9). He also received a prebend from Our Lady in Cleves and a living from St Hippolytus's Church (today's Oude Kerk) in Delft. Gilles Joye, one of the most talented singers and composers of the time, spent most of his days in Bruges. Infamous for his life style, he spent enormous sums for the copying of music manuscripts which, despite managing the ducal donations, made him till the end of his life the most prominent debtor to copyists and book dealers in Bruges.

## 4 The Virgin and Child with St Anthony Abbot and a Donor

Dated 1472
Panel (oak), 92.7 x 53.6 cm
Ottawa, National Gallery of Canada, inv. 6191

PROVENANCE

Laetitia Bonaparte (?), Rome; 1829 acquired by John, Earl of Shrewsbury, Alton Towers, Staffs; sale Christie's, London, 9 July 1857, no. 347; collection Gsell, Vienna; sale collection Gsell, Vienna, 26 March 1872, no. 201; Prince of Liechtenstein, Vienna and Vaduz; Agnew's, London, 1954; acquired by the National Gallery of Canada.

EXHIBITIONS

Bruges 1902, no. 81; Lucerne 1948, no. 78.

BIBLIOGRAPHY

Waagen 1854, III, 386; Wauters 1883, 294; Wauters 1893, 92 n. 2; Bode 1895, 115; Kaemmerer 1899, 46; Bock 1900, 176; Weale 1901a, 71; Hulin de Loo 1902, no. 72; Hymans 1902, 287; Friedländer 1903, 83; Weale 1903, 35; Frimmel 1904, 185; Voll 1909, xx, 16, 171; Doehlemann 1911, 508; Conway 1921, 236; Glück 1923, 13; Voll 1923, 178; Winkler 1924, 132; Friedländer 1928 (1971), no. 64; Sjöblom 1928, 66–7; Baldass 1942, 39; Strohmer 1943, 95; Friedländer 1949, 22, 29–31; Faggin 1969, no. 2; McFarlane 1971, 13 n. 61; Lane 1980, no. 6; Laskin and Pantazzi 1987, 189–90; Johnston 1988, 323, 326; Ainsworth 1994; De Vos 1994, no. 19; Strohm 1994, 37; Faries 1997, 248–9, 251.

Assigned to Hugo van der Goes by Waagen (1854), the painting was first attributed to Memling by Wauters (1883). The panel, which is inscribed with the year 1472 on the back wall (to the right of the canopy), is crucial in our understanding of the stylistic development of the artist in the period between the Gdańsk *Last Judgement* (completed 1472–3) and the altarpieces for St John's Hospital in Bruges (the 'Triptych of the Two Saints John' and the 'Floreins Triptych', both Bruges, Memlingmuseum; figs. 17, 20–22), dated 1479. The artist had settled in Bruges in 1465. The Ottawa panel shows to what extent, in the early 1470s, he had absorbed and reshaped the artistic conventions established there by Jan van Eyck and Petrus Christus. Memling's composition of the standing Virgin and Child, with the patron saint interceding for the kneeling donor, is a type rarely seen outside of Bruges. We are reminded, above all, of Van Eyck's lost 'Maelbeke Madonna', known from drawn and painted copies, the 'Madonna of Jan Vos' (New York, The Frick Collection), completed by the Van Eyck workshop, as well as Petrus Christus's 'Exeter Madonna' (Berlin, Gemäldegalerie). However, Memling's panel is not a copy of these older images but a free adaptation, inspired by additional Eyckian models. The interior, for instance, is at least indirectly related to examples by Van Eyck and Christus. It is not without relevance that the light falling through a window at the right finds a remarkable parallel in Van Eyck's Arnolfini double portrait of 1434 (London, National Gallery), which may also have inspired Memling to date his painting on the back wall of the room instead of the frame. Even the pose of the Christ Child derives from an Eyckian model, as can be seen in the *Virgin and Child with Chancellor Rolin* (fig. 16). But Memling disguised his source by adapting his model to compositional necessities. Since his donor is situated at the right, he turned the Child accordingly and in so doing depicted it as it would have been seen by the donor in Van Eyck's painting (see figs. 15, 16).

These references to Van Eyck are assimilated into a new pictorial concept which may be seen as Memling's artistic contribution. Although of quite different size and scope, the present panel may be compared in this respect to the *Last Judgement* painted for Agnolo Tani. Among the artist's more ambitious innovations is the carefully designed asymmetry of the composition based on the perspective construction of the room (Doehlemann 1911; De Vos 1994). Memling divides the room into two halves, circumscribed at the right by the diagonally placed exterior wall with window and door opening, at the left by the bench placed before a fireplace under a brocaded baldachin, functioning as Mary's throne. Since Mary has left her throne to walk towards the donor and his patron saint following the converging orthogonals of the floor tiles, she is no longer at the centre of the axis formed by the bench but stands beside it.

# 5 Portrait of an Elderly Couple

c. 1470–75
Panel (oak), 36.1 x 29.4 cm
Berlin, Staatliche Museen zu
Berlin, Preussischer Kulturbesitz,
Gemäldegalerie, inv. 529c

c. 1470–75
Panel (oak), 35.4 x 29.3 cm
Paris, Musée du Louvre, inv. RF 1723

This composition of 1472 testifies to Memling's interest in spatially complex interiors which finds its culmination in the 'Diptych of Maarten van Nieuwenhove' (cat. 23).

In his full-length donor figures, as in his independent and half-length devotional portraits, Memling uses a limited repertoire of forms and motifs which he integrates into his compositions with ever-increasing mastery. The present donor portrait – similar to that of Agnolo Tani in the *Last Judgement* – is clearly composed of a separate torso and head, whereby the pose of the head and facial features were defined in the underdrawing executed in chalk (Faries 1997). Significantly, the painting style varies from the smooth, finely executed surfaces which we find in Memling's early half-length portraits. Designed to be seen up close, half-length images apparently required a more careful painterly treatment than the representative full-length donor portraits.

The original function of the *Virgin and Child with St Anthony Abbot and a Donor* continues to elude us. Neither formal nor compositional elements would suggest that it was once part of a diptych or triptych. It possibly served as an epitaph or ex-voto. Our ignorance about the original context of the panel might indicate that it held a unique position within the artistic tradition in Bruges at the end of the fifteenth century.

PROVENANCE

(Man) 1896 acquired from a Berlin art dealer for the Kaiser-Friedrich-Museum. (Woman) Sale Collection Maezza, Milan, 15 April 1884, no. 203; art dealer Warneck; 1896 acquired by the painter Léo Nardus (Paris); 1908 sold to the Louvre by Galerie Kleinberger.

EXHIBITIONS

Bruges 1902, no. 71 (Woman); Berlin 1906–8 (Woman); Bruges 1939, no. 13b (Woman); Brussels 1950, no. 69 (Man); Paris 1952–3, no. 49 (Woman); Paris 1995, no. VI.

BIBLIOGRAPHY

Bode 1896; Kaemmerer 1899, 21–4; Weale 1901, 67, 102; Hulin de Loo 1902, no. 71; Friedländer 1903, 82; Bode 1908, 154; Leprieur 1909; Voll 1909, 74–5; Durand-Gréville 1913, 426; Conway 1921, 240; Huisman 1923, 101–2; Winkler 1924, 128; Friedländer 1928 (1971), nos. 75–6; Fierens Gevaert 1929, 62; Bode 1930, 127–8; Michel 1953, 197–8; Panofsky 1953, 349; Arndt 1968, 9; Faggin 1969, nos. 91–2; Hinz 1974, 139–218; Grosshans 1975, 278; Campbell 1977, 187–9; Lane 1980, nos. 91–2; Wallen 1983, 47; Comblen-Sonkes 1988, 70; Campbell 1990, 54, 120; De Vos 1994, no. 14; Klein 1994, 103; Comblen-Sonkes and Lorentz 1995, 283–95; Lorentz 1995, 67–75; Martin and Ravaud 1995, 159; Klein 1997, 288–9; Stroo et al. 1999, 168, 185.

In 1521 the Venetian humanist Marcantonio Michiel saw in the collection of Cardinal Grimani '*li dui retratti pur a oglio del marito e moglie insieme alla Ponentina … del mano de l'istesso* [Zuan Memlino]' – 'the two portraits in oil of a man and wife together in the Western [Flemish?] manner by the same [Hans Memling]' (Morelli 1800, 79). Michel (1953) assumed that these two portraits are identical with those today in Berlin and Paris, respectively. Although the Italian provenance of the female portrait – the panel was in a private collection in Milan in the mid-nineteenth century – led some authors to accept the identification with the portraits in the Grimani collection (Faggin 1969; Grosshans 1975), Michiel's description is too vague to firmly establish this connection (Comblen-Sonkes and Lorentz 1995; see also Paula Nuttall's essay). It is interesting, however, that Michiel used the term '*insieme*' in connection with the phrase '*alla Ponentina*' (roughly 'in the manner of the West'), which apparently is meant to indicate a style different from that current in Venice. The fact that they were described as being together in Cardinal Grimani's collection is significant in terms of reconstructing the original panel.

Campbell (1977) was the first to show that the Berlin and Paris portraits which had been discussed as two independent entities in the older literature once formed a unit. The two panels were originally dowelled together, and while the panel with the woman's portrait has since been planed and cradled, the man's portrait still shows the original dowel holes (De Vos 1994).

As a double portrait, this elderly couple occupies a unique position in Memling's oeuvre as well as in early Netherlandish portrait painting. With the exception of Van Eyck's Arnolfini double portrait (London), which in neither function nor form can be considered Memling's model, the genre is practically unknown in fifteenth-century Netherlandish art, for although portraits of couples are common enough, they are either parts of devotional triptychs (see cat. 18) or pendants (see cat. 9).

On the other hand, double portraits were increasingly popular in the upper German regions during the last third of the fifteenth century. Yet, unlike Memling's portraits with landscape backgrounds, those of married couples are set against neutral backgrounds. With Israhel van Meckenem's engraved half-length portrait of *The Artist and his Wife Ida* of about 1497, the genre spread to the graphic arts (Lorentz 1995). It is unlikely, however, that Memling's German origin accounts for the

## 6  Fragment of a Male Portrait

*c.*1470–75
Panel (oak), oval, diameter 19/21.6 cm
Private collection

introduction of this portrait style into Bruges, as proposed by De Vos (1994). The genre only developed in Germany in the second half of the century, under both Netherlandish and Italian influence.

Most likely, Memling's *Double Portrait of an Elderly Couple* was an original invention combining Rogierian influences – such as the continuous landscape background in the 'Braque Triptych' (Paris, Louvre) – with the innovations of his own early portraits. The spatial ambivalence created by the *trompe-l'œil* frames in works such as *Portrait of a Man in a Red Hat* (cat. 1) and the *Portrait of a Man* in The Frick Collection (cat. 2) has been replaced by a clearly defined space. The two elderly people are shown before a gallery-like opening, framed by a red column on the left. In the panoramic landscape that stretches behind them, however, Memling does not use aerial perspective as he does in some of his landscape portraits from shortly before the mid-1470s. This would suggest a relatively early date for the present panels. Painterly technique, including the use of lead white for modelling and the smooth, finely painted surface, as well as dendrochronological findings (Klein 1994; 1997) point to a date shortly after 1470.

PROVENANCE
Sale Christie's, London, 30 January 1948, no. 61 (as Van Eyck); acquired through Colnaghi's, London, by Sir Thomas Barlow; B. S. Barlow.
EXHIBITIONS
London 1953–4, no. 25; Manchester 1957, no. 24; Manchester 1968, no. 2.
BIBLIOGRAPHY
Sutton 1954, 12; Faggin 1969, no. 102; Friedländer 1971, Add. 258; Lane 1980, no. 82; Campbell 1990, 64; De Vos 1994, no. 10.

This oval painting is a fragment of a larger panel. Though not unknown in the fifteenth century, oval portraits did not come into fashion until the sixteenth century, especially in courtly miniature portraits.

Overall, the fragment has the appearance of a sixteenth-century work, somewhat in the style of Holbein's English successors. It should be remembered though that the man is dressed in fifteenth-century costume. He wears a dark purple velvet jacket with a fur collar, as also seen in Memling's *Portrait of a Young Man* in the Lehman Collection (cat. 15), and a high cap, a style which went out of fashion in the Netherlands in the 1470s.

The man is shown head and shoulders, in three-quarters view to the right, placed before a green background. Such coloured backgrounds – now often darkened but originally mostly blue or green – are found in several of Memling's portraits. What is unusual, however, is the pronounced shadow cast on the background. While it is in fact the shadow that clarifies the distance between the sitter and his surroundings, Memling consciously leaves the viewer guessing. In Netherlandish portrait painting cast shadows do not appear until the early sixteenth century. De Vos (1994) therefore suspected that the shadow

in the present fragment was added later.

The original context of the fragment remains surprisingly problematic. The small size seems to indicate a religious composition; the neutral background, however, is unthinkable for such a subject. It is equally unlikely that the portrait fragment was cut from the wing of a diptych or triptych since the man would have looked out of the composition. Most probably, therefore, the present oval was cut from a rectangular portrait.

The exhibited painting was sold at auction in London in 1948, attributed to Van Eyck. Shortly after, it entered the collection of Sir Thomas Barlow, London. It was included in the 1953–4 Royal Academy exhibition 'Flemish Art 1300–1700' and published one year later by Denis Sutton as a work by Memling. Although the attribution has been generally accepted, scholars continue to disagree about the quality and date of the painting. Faggin (1969), who considered it to be of high quality, recognized in it Memling's late style and dated it to the last twenty years of the artist's life. Lane (1980), remaining on the side of caution, assigned the picture to the group of undatable fragments. On the basis of dress, Campbell (1990) suggested the beginning of the 1470s, and in this he was followed by De Vos (1994).

# 7 Portrait of a Man before a Landscape

*c.* 1470–75
Panel (oak), 35.4 x 25.8 cm
Brussels, Musées Royaux des Beaux-Arts de Belgique, inv. 1358

PROVENANCE
Steyaert-Vanden Bussche, Bruges; sale
Henri Le Roy Gallery, Brussels, 18 August
1856, no. 2 (as Memling).

EXHIBITIONS
Bruges 1939, no. 40; Bordeaux 1954, no. 49;
Schaffhausen 1955, no. 68; Brussels 1961,
no. 74.

BIBLIOGRAPHY
Fétis 1863, no. 23; Fétis 1889, no. 34;
Wauters 1893, 26, 101, 114; Kaemmerer
1899, 131; Weale 1901, 68, 99; Voll 1909,
20; Conway 1921, 238; Huisman 1923, 107;
Winkler 1924, 126; Friedländer 1928 (1971),
no. 84; Baldass 1942, 41; Panofsky 1953,
349 n. 10; Faggin 1969, no. 97; Lane 1980,
no. 29; De Vos 1991, 204–6; De Vos 1994,
no. 43; Stroo *et al.* 1999, 181–97.

This half-length portrait shows a man in three-quarters view to the right, set before a wooded landscape. He wears a black coat with a narrow fur collar and a black cap on his curly hair. His right hand rests on a ledge or balustrade situated beyond the pictorial plane; on the ring finger sits a gold ring. Old reproductions (see e.g. Kaemmerer 1899) show clearly that a green strip of cloth fell over the man's left shoulder, most likely attached to the cap; this has darkened considerably and is only recognizable in relief. It is not certain whether this band is original or the result of later overpainting (Stroo *et al.* 1999). Position and pose of the man indicate that the panel was not part of a devotional diptych; it could have functioned as one side of a marital portrait diptych or as an independent portrait.

The Brussels picture follows the format of the half-length portrait placed before a landscape, a compositional formula established by Memling with great success, especially among the local Italian merchant community. The portraits commissioned from the Bruges painter were brought to Italy when his patrons returned to their native cities. There they influenced Italian artists, above all in Florence and Venice, and revolutionized Renaissance portrait painting (see Paula Nuttall's essay).

However, Memling's innovative combination of bust portrait and landscape not only satisfied the tastes of his foreign clients but increasingly gained in popularity in the Burgundian Netherlands. The Brussels portrait was in a private collection in Bruges in the nineteenth century before it was sold to the Brussels museum in 1856. Although the identity of the sitter remains unknown (Weale's [1901] suggestion that he is Niccolò Strozzi is unfounded), the provenance of the panel suggests that he is a member of a family from Bruges or its surroundings. Nonetheless, the painting does indeed contain elements which are strongly reminiscent of the portraits painted by Memling for Italian merchants. De Vos (1994) observed similarities in dress and landscape to the *Portrait of a Young Man before a Landscape* from Venice (cat. 16). Here should also be mentioned the *Portrait of a Man with a Spotted Fur Collar* (Florence, Uffizi; cat. 8) depicting a member of the Florentine community in Bruges, which was executed shortly after the Gdańsk *Last Judgement*, in about 1475.

The landscape in all three portraits is devoid of any habitation. In the Brussels and Florence panels distance is achieved by horizontal layering, and both display a tree at the left edge. In terms of composition, the landscape background in the Venice portrait suggests a more advanced stage. For these reasons, a date shortly after 1470 and before 1475 for the Brussels picture seems plausible, although it should be pointed out that x-radiograph shows the landscape to have been partially overpainted (Stroo *et al.* 1999). Both the tree at the left and the bushes at the right were painted later, but since these constitute elements from Memling's repertoire, it is possible that the overpainting was done in his workshop. The original landscape (without tree or bushes) would have given the impression of greater distance between sitter and horizon, such as can be seen in Memling's earliest portraits with landscape backgrounds in Frankfurt and New York (cat. 1, 2). Thus the early date of about 1472 put forward (Stroo *et al.* 1999) on the basis of the dendrochronological data seems more convincing than the late date (after 1480) proposed by De Vos (1994). As suggested above, the most likely date for the Brussels panel is *c.* 1470–75 – around the date of the *Portrait of a Man with a Spotted Fur Collar*.

# 8 Portrait of a Man with a Spotted Fur Collar

*c.* 1475
Panel (oak), 38 x 27 cm
Florence, Galleria degli Uffizi, inv. 1102

PROVENANCE
Venetian art collector and dealer Abbot
Luigi Celotti (?); 1836 acquired for the
Uffizi (as Antonello da Messina).
EXHIBITION
Florence 1947, no. 7.
BIBLIOGRAPHY
Winkler 1924; Friedländer 1928 (1971),
no. 89; Panofsky 1953, 349 n. 10; Białostocki
1968; Faggin 1969, no. 106; Fahy 1969, 148;
Lane 1980, no. 30; Collobi-Ragghianti
1990, 63, no. 108; De Vos 1994, no. 28;
Nuttall 2004, 60, 69, 221.

The portrait was acquired for the Uffizi in 1836 as the work of Antonello da Messina. It belongs, together with other such works (see cat. 7, 10, 11, 15, 16), to that group of portraits which in all likelihood was executed by Memling for members of the Italian merchant communities – from Florence, Venice, Genoa and elsewhere – resident in Bruges.

The panel shows a young man in three-quarters view to the left, set before a landscape the horizon of which is placed level with the sitter's neckline, as in most of Memling's portraits. The man wears a black velvet tunic over a doublet with a red collar. The collar of the tunic and the edge of the sleeve are of light-brown fur with dark spots. The underdrawing shows that Memling intended the collar to be narrower. During the execution of the portrait he broadened it, especially upwards, thus largely covering the previously completed red collar of the doublet. Taking into account the preciousness of the fur, Memling may have decided to emphasize it in order to portray the elevated social status of his sitter. The man wears two gold rings set with precious stones on the fingers of his right hand, which rests on a narrow stone ledge. As in other

portraits by the artist, these rings are prominently displayed. They too are meant to be seen as an indication of the sitter's social rank.

By introducing a stone ledge separating the viewer's space from that of the sitter, Memling went back to a motif established in Bruges by Jan van Eyck and Petrus Christus, as well as in Venice, around 1470, by Antonello da Messina (fig. 66; see also Nuttall 2002, 201). As observed by De Vos (1994), such explicit use of the stone parapet is unusual for Memling. It can also be seen, albeit in more subtle form, in the Bruges *Portrait of a Young Woman* (cat. 17), dated 1480, and the *Portrait of a Man with a Letter* from the Corsini collection (cat. 11). In the latter portrait the ledge is suggested by a very narrow strip which appears to turn into the frame, thereby creating the illusion of a continuous space for sitter and viewer. In other autonomous portraits, including the Washington *Man with an Arrow* (cat. 13), the hand seems to rest directly on the frame (now lost).

Yet again Memling seems to have assembled his painting from various composite parts – head, hand, landscape. As the position of the hand can be seen in identical form, in mirror image, or with minor variations in several autonomous portraits by the artist and his workshop (see cat. 1, 13, 16, 19), the existence of a modelbook drawing is likely. Details of the landscape, such as the large tree at the right, can also be found in other works by Memling. The landscape distinguishes itself by the total absence of any buildings, roads or people. Only few other Memling portraits show a similarly sparse landscape (cat. 7, 16 and pl. 21), but the division into three horizontal planes – dark green hill, wide meadow, edge of a forest – is unique among his portraits.

The strict three-part division of the landscape may indicate an early date. De Vos noted stylistic parallels to the

*Portrait of a Man with an Arrow* (cat. 13), which, however, he dated *c.* 1478–80. It is likely that both paintings originated somewhat earlier, in about 1475. The early date finds support in the fact that the distinctive features of the man can be found among the blessed in the centre panel of the *Last Judgement*, which was completed in 1472–3 (fig. 14). The altarpiece was commissioned by Agnolo Tani, the manager of the Medici bank in Bruges (see Till Borchert's essay). Since Aby Warburg (1902), it has generally been acknowledged that the blessed are portraits of Florentine merchants in Bruges. Although Białostocki's hypothesis that the present portrait depicts the young Agnolo Tani is untenable, the inclusion of some of the motifs in Fra Bartolommeo's so-called *Portrait of Matteo Sassetti* (New York, Metropolitan Museum; Fahy 1969) suggests that the present painting was already in Florence at the end of the fifteenth century (Nuttall 2004).

# 9 Portrait of an Old Woman

*c.* 1475–80
Panel (oak), 26.5 x 17.8 cm
Houston, Museum of Fine Arts, The Edith A. and Percy S. Straus Collection,
inv. 44.530

PROVENANCE
Art market Paris (1910); von Hollitscher,
Berlin (1910–14); von Auspitz, Vienna
(untill 1931); art dealer Bachstitz, The
Hague (1931–4); Percy S. Straus, New
York; 1944 bequeathed to the Museum
of Fine Arts.
EXHIBITIONS
Bruges 1960, no. 42; Detroit 1960,
no. 37; New York 1973, no. 1; Paris, Kiev,
Leningrad, Moscow and Minsk 1976,
no. 4; New York 1998, no. 29.
BIBLIOGRAPHY
Bode and Friedländer 1912, 134; Friedländer
1928 (1971), no. 93; Faggin 1969, no. 120;
Lane 1980, no. 12; Houston 1981, no. 49;
Bauman 1986, 34; De Vos 1994, no. 60;
Klein 1994, 103; New York 1998, 169.

Although in generally good condition since its recent restoration, the *Portrait of an Old Woman* shows signs of damage due to excessive cleaning during an earlier conservation treatment. Memling's subtle flesh tones, which distinguish his best portraits (see pl. 2; cat. 1, 10, 13, 17, 18, 23), are almost entirely absent here as the surface glazes have disappeared. Highlights along the bridge of the nose give an idea of the artist's manner of modelling with light, and, in spite of the wear, it is possible to recognize Memling's hand in the plasticity of the head, achieved by the efficient and sparse application of lead white.

The painting brilliantly shows Memling's way of working with gradations of white. The woman's wimple, which covers her forehead and frames her face, is subtly transparent so that the flesh tones and dress edged in fur are revealed. The earlier hypothesis that the wimple was added later, has long been refuted (Bruges 1960; Detroit 1960). The woman's head as it appears now fills the entire panel, which was cut at all four sides. Originally, the composition must have been more balanced, and the contrast between the white wimple and green-blue background less severe

(the background has darkened considerably).

The *Portrait of an Old Woman* was first attributed to Memling by Bode and Friedländer (1912). This was followed more than seventy years later by the discovery that it is a pendant to the *Portrait of an Old Man* in the Metropolitan Museum (see pl. 10a; Bauman 1986, 64). The latter, first attributed to Memling by Hulin de Loo (1902) and Friedländer (1903), following the 1902 Bruges exhibition 'Les Primitifs flamands', was generally dated early, *c.*1470, on account of stylistic similarities with the Berlin–Paris panels of the *Double Portrait of an Elderly Couple* (cat. 5). Because of their almost identical sizes Jack Schrader suggested in 1970 to the museums in Houston and New York that their respective portraits were pendants. This has been confirmed by x-radiography of the Houston panel (fig. 91), which revealed a hand at the lower left corner, thus matching the man's hand in the lower right corner of the Metropolitan Museum portrait. The woman's hand was overpainted at a later date, probably when the two portraits were separated.

Bauman (1986), who discussed the reconstruction of the two portraits, pointed out their stylistic relationship to Memling's presumed master, Rogier van der Weyden, specifically his female portraits. He therefore dated them immediately after Memling's move to Bruges, about 1465–70. Bauman assumed that the two portraits formed pendants, whereas De Vos (1994) considered them to have been a continuous composition on one panel analogous to the *Double Portrait of an Elderly Couple* (cat. 5). Dendrochronological examination of the *Portrait of an Old Woman* (Klein 1994), which suggests that the panel was painted after 1480, convinced De Vos that the alleged double portrait was painted in the last decade of Memling's life. This date was upheld in the New York exhibition 'From Van Eyck to

Bruegel' (New York 1998) where, however, the portraits are discussed as separately framed pendants.

In the last analysis, it is no longer possible to determine whether the Houston and New York portraits originally formed one or two separate panels, since both are cut at all sides. In light of the painterly technique, which shows similarities with Memling's portraits of the early 1470s, Maryan Ainsworth questions the late dating of the portraits (see her essay). Taking the earliest felling date and shortest possible storage time of the wood into consideration, a date of shortly after 1472 for the two portraits seems possible.

# 10 Portrait of a Man with a Coin of the Emperor Nero (Bernardo Bembo?)

1473–4?
Panel (oak), 31 x 23.2 cm
Antwerp, Koninklijk Museum voor Schone Kunsten, inv. 5

PROVENANCE
Acquired by Vivant Denon in Lyon as a work by Antonello da Messina; 1828 purchased by Florent van Ertborn (Antwerp) at the sale of the Denon collection; 1841 bequeathed to the city of Antwerp.

EXHIBITIONS
London 1892, no. 20; Bruges 1902, no. 55; Paris 1923, no. 21; London 1927, no. 53; Antwerp 1930, no. 193; Paris 1935, no. 66; Bruges 1939, no. 37; Amsterdam–Rotterdam 1946, no. 47; Paris 1952–53, no. 53; London 1953–4; Bruges 1994, no. 19; Bruges 1998, no. 5; Bruges 2002, no. 48.

BIBLIOGRAPHY
Weale 1871, 60; Wauters 1893, 5, 98–102; Kaemmerer 1899, 15; Weale 1901, 13–14, 96; Hulin de Loo 1902, no. 55; Friedländer 1903, 81; Voll 1909, xxi–xxii, 19, 172; Conway 1921, 238; Huisman 1923, 19; Bode 1924, 389; Winkler 1924, 128; Hulin de Loo 1927; Friedländer 1928 (1971), no. 71; Fierens-Gevaert 1929, 61; Lavalleye 1939, 37; Baldass 1942, 41; Panofsky 1953, 349; Cahn 1962, 66–8; Pope-Hennessy 1966, 60; Białostocki 1968, 108; Faggin 1969, no. 96; McFarlane 1971, 14–15 n. 69; Trzeciak 1977, no. 8; Lane 1980, no. 34; Fletcher 1981; Castelfranchi Vegas 1983, 187; Silver 1984, 163; Vandenbroeck 1985, 135–8; Fletcher 1989; De Vos 1991, 202–3; Lightbown 1992, 231; Schneider 1992, 44; Belting and Kruse 1994, 262–3; De Vos 1994, no. 42; Madou 1994, 51; Rohlmann 1994, 85–6; Borchert 1995, 171; Kathke 1997, 188, 311–12; Lane 1999, 245 n. 9; Venice 1999, 192; Stroo et al. 1999, 183; Nuttall 2004, 221, 224.

Previously attributed to Antonello da Messina, the portrait was first attributed to Memling by Weale (1871). Its provenance can be traced back to around 1800 when Baron Vivant Denon, who organized the transport of works of art for Napoleon, acquired it in Lyon for his private collection as a work by the Italian master. Presumably the painting had reached Lyon from an Italian collection during the turmoil of the Napoleonic wars.

The sitter, a man of mature age, is shown head and shoulders in 'seven-eighths' view to the right (see Lorne Campbell's essay; see also cat. 11, 12), before a landscape. Light falls onto his face from the left. He wears a black tunic tied at the neck below the white shirt collar. A black cap sits on his dark brown, curly hair. In his left hand he holds a Roman coin with the profile of Emperor Nero and the inscription 'Nero Claud[ius] Caesar Aug[ustus] Germ[anicus] Tr[ibucinia] p[otestate] Imper[ator]'. Cahn (1962) identified the coin as a sestertius which, according to McFarlane (1971), was struck in Lyons, the capital of the Roman province of Gallia Lugdunensis. The landscape background consists of forested hills with mountains in the far distance. On the right is a lake with two swans, a palm tree on its near shore and a rider beyond.

The painting is the only one in Memling's surviving portrait oeuvre in which accessories may have emblematic functions. Besides the coin, which undoubtedly contains a reference to the sitter, laurel leaves appear at the lower edge. Similarly unusual is the motif of the man looking at the viewer; this compositional device, known to Memling from portraits by Jan van Eyck (see figs. 27, 36, 37), can be seen in only one other of his works, the Portrait of a Man with a Letter (cat. 11).

The coin persuaded earlier authors to recognize the man as a medallist. Wauters (1893) identified him with Niccolò di Forzore Spinelli, who died in Lyon in 1499; Bode (1924) and Hulin de Loo (1927) believed him to be Giovanni di Candida, who worked for the Burgundian court between 1472 and 1480. Friedländer (1928) observed that anyone producing modern medals is unlikely to have chosen an antique coin as his attribute and suggested instead that the man might have been a humanistically educated collector. McFarlane (1971) was the first to link the coin and the palm tree with the possible name of the sitter. He was followed by De Vos (1994), who remarked on the popularity of emblematic pictograms in Italian humanist circles. The emblem of the Venetian Bernardo Bembo, for example, consists of a laurel and palm branch, but De Vos was primarily thinking of names such as Palma, Allori or Neroni, whereby the latter, a Florentine family, had ties to Flanders, as pointed out by Rohlmann (1994). Reconsidering Bernardo Bembo (see Fletcher 1981), Lobelle (Bruges 1998) suggested that the Antwerp portrait does indeed depict the Venetian humanist.

Bernardo Bembo (1433–1519) was a member of the humanist circle around the Venetian historiographer Marcantonio Michiel. His rich collection of paintings, among them a diptych by Memling (Munich, Alte Pinakothek, and Washington, National Gallery of Art; see De Vos 1994, no. 50), included antique coins. In 1473 Bembo resided as Venetian envoy at the court of Charles the Bold in Flanders before being called to Florence as ambassador in 1475. References to Memling's portrait in Florentine art can only be explained by its presence in the city. As Lightbown (1992) observed, it directly inspired Botticelli's Portrait of a Man with a Medal of Cosimo de' Medici, generally dated around 1475 (fig. 69; Florence 2004, no. 34), as well as the landscape background in Leonardo's Portrait of Ginevra de' Benci (fig. 70; see Paula Nuttall's essay). Significantly, the latter was intended for Ginevra's admirer, Bernardo Bembo, whose emblem is on the reverse (fig. 70b).

Finally, the identification of the Antwerp man with the Venetian humanist would explain the facial similarities between him and the man portrayed by Giovanni Bellini in the Royal Collection Portrait of a Man of c. 1505, which has been generally recognized as that of Bernardo's son Pietro (fig. 60). Besides the similar physiognomies, the prominent use of a landscape background could have been inspired by Memling (this was discussed by Barbara Lane during the Van Eyck Symposium in Bruges, 2002).

Memling's Antwerp portrait was executed most likely during Bembo's stay in Flanders, i.e. around 1473–4, for, as we have seen, the composition was known to Botticelli in Florence as early as 1475. The early date corresponds with that suggested in the older literature, whereas De Vos's (1994) late date of after 1480 seems hardly tenable.

## 11   Portrait of a Man with a Letter

*c.* 1475
Panel (oak), 35 x 26 cm
Florence, Galleria degli Uffizi, inv. 9970

PROVENANCE
Tommaso Corsini, Florence (Palazzo
Corsini, no. 209); 1910 acquired by the
Ministero della Pubblica Istruzione; 1989
acquired by the Galleria degli Uffizi.

EXHIBITIONS
Rome 1950, no. 4; Florence 1952, no. 15;
Venice 1999, no. 5.

BIBLIOGRAPHY
Wauters 1893, 33, 131; Bode 1896, 3
(as Antonello da Messina); Kaemmerer
1899, 131; Weale 1901, 67–8, 101; Voll 1909,
xxi–xxiii (as Italian follower of Memling);
Conway 1921, 238; Friedländer 1928 (1971),
no. 86; Panofsky 1953, 349 n. 10; Pope-
Hennessy 1966, 58; Faggin 1969, no. 103;
Lane 1980, no. 31; Campbell 1990, 120–21;
Collobi-Ragghianti 1990, 63–4, no. 109;
De Vos 1994, no. 44; Lane 1997, *passim*;
Nuttall 2002; Nuttall 2004, 143, 210–11.

COPY
Petworth House (Italian, beginning
16th century).

The bust portrait of a man in a black
coat and cap is placed before the
broad expanse of a hilly landscape
with a road at the left and a lake and
distant castle at the right. His face
is strikingly set off against the light
background. Instead of the traditional
three-quarters view, Memling chose
the almost frontal 'seven-eighths' view
to portray this unidentified man (see
also cat. 10, 12). Besides the Antwerp
*Man with a Coin* (cat. 10), this is the
only surviving portrait by the artist
in which the sitter looks directly out
of the picture. On account of this,
both panels are considered to be
independent portraits carrying no
other function.

Unlike the slightly smaller Antwerp
painting in which the sitter is placed
immediately at the picture's edge,
the Uffizi man is separated from the
viewer's space by a narrow ledge.
His left hand rests on the ledge which
originally must have formed a visual
unity with the frame, now lost (see
cat. 17). Despite *pentimenti* visible to
the naked eye, which suggest that
Memling experimented with the
position of the hand, it is no more
than a variant, in mirror image, of
a gesture that appears repeatedly in
the artist's portraits. With his thumb
and forefinger the man holds a folded

piece of paper, presumably a letter,
which functions as an attribute or
accessory. The barely decipherable
letters reveal no meaning beyond
creating the illusion of a written
document.

Placing the work within the
chronology of Memling's oeuvre
poses certain difficulties. Stylistically
as well as pictorially it is most
closely related to the Antwerp
portrait (cat. 10), likewise undated.
Noticeable is the calligraphic manner
of rendering the clouds that both
paintings have in common. Although
most authors date both works
early, De Vos (1994) suggested for
the present portrait a date after
1480, based on the man's dress.
His argument is unconvincing,
since similar fashion can be seen
in Antonello da Messina's portraits
of *c.* 1475. In line with the Antwerp
portrait of Bernardo Bembo, the
present portrait would be datable to
around 1475.

An early sixteenth-century Italian
copy of the Uffizi portrait (Petworth
House, Sussex; Campbell 1990;
Nuttall 2004; fig. 63) testifies to
the presence of the latter in Italy
shortly after its completion around
1475. It is therefore entirely possible
that the sitter is an Italian merchant
temporarily resident in Bruges, as
has been suggested by De Vos (1994)
among others. It remains uncertain if
the man was a Florentine or Venetian
– both cities were prominently
represented in Bruges – since
elements of Memling's portrait can
be found in Tuscany as well as Venice
before 1500.

Contrary to the view expressed
in the older literature (Panofsky 1953;
Pope-Hennessy 1966) that Memling's
landscape backgrounds were
influenced by Italian Renaissance
portraits, more recent research has
shown that exactly the opposite is
true, and that in this respect, too,
Italian portraiture is indebted to early
Netherlandish painting (see Lane 1997
and Nuttall 2002; 2004). It is hard

to overestimate the role played by
Memling's *Man with a Letter* in the
development of Giovanni Bellini as
well as Perugino as portrait painters
(see Campbell 1990; Venice 1999).
The latter's *Portrait of Francesco delle
Opere* of 1494 (fig. 76) is particularly
instructive in this context.

## 12 Portrait of a Man with a Gold Cord

*c.* 1475–80
Panel (oak), 31.8 x 27.1 cm
The Royal Collection © H. M. Queen Elizabeth II, inv. 3020

PROVENANCE
Documented in the English Royal Collection from the eighteenth century (as Quentin Massys).

EXHIBITIONS
Manchester 1857, no. 392; London 1946–7, no. 157; London 1953–4, no. 29; London 1962, no. 11; Bruges 1994, no. 12.

BIBLIOGRAPHY
Kaemmerer 1899, 17; Friedländer 1928 (1971), no. 91; Faggin 1969, no. 115; Lane 1980, no. 18; Campbell 1985, 85–6; De Vos 1994, no. 30.

The sitter is set against a neutral blue-green background which must have been lighter originally, comparable to the Washington portrait of approximately the same date (cat. 13). Against this lighter background, the flesh colour, the nearly shoulder-length brown hair and the dress of the man would have stood out more clearly. Using the head-and-shoulders format, Memling followed the convention established in the Netherlands by Van Eyck, Campin and Van der Weyden, but by showing the sitter in 'seven-eighths' view, he adopted a more frontal pose than the traditional three-quarters view (cf. cat. 10, 11).

The dress of the man – a plain black jacket over a white shirt – does not give any clear indication of his social rank. The collar of his doublet is tied across the neck with a cord. A gold cord attached to a button on the left of the jacket ends in two leather strips decorated with pearls. The tips of the middle finger and forefinger of the man's right hand – which was only revealed in 1953, after removal of old overpainting – are pushed beneath the left jacket lapel, level with the ends of the cord. The gold cord as well as the gesture are unique in Memling's oeuvre. Campbell (1985) speculated that the cord carried emblematic meaning, whereas De Vos (1994) was reminded of saintly attributes.

As the gesture does indeed recall Christ's blessing or, alternatively, the swearing of an oath, it might be worth considering that the portrait was executed in connection with an oath, for example its commemoration or confirmation. In all probability the painting is an independent portrait whose precise origin and function, however, remain unclear. The likelihood that it once had a female pendant can be ruled out since the man would be on the woman's left (see cat. 5, 9, 18), and the same goes for the hypothesis that it once formed part of a devotional diptych or triptych since the man is not shown with the appropriate gesture of adoration (see e.g. cat. 23).

The identity of the man remains obscure. We do not know the early provenance of the panel, nor is there a coat of arms or any other identifying mark. The fact that the panel was in the English Royal Collection in the eighteenth century under the name of Massys might indicate that it reached England via the Netherlandish art market and thus might not have left the Netherlands before then.

When it comes to dating the portrait, we have to rely on stylistic criteria since there are no securely dated comparable works by Memling. While the picture is dated early in the older literature, De Vos (1994) suggested a slightly later date, *c.* 1478–80, based on hairstyle and dress. Campbell (see his essay) puts forward a date of *c.* 1475. On grounds of technique and compositional devices, it seems convincing to place the panel between the completion of the Gdańsk *Last Judgement* (1472–3) and the work on the Bruges 'Triptych of the Two Saints John' (1479). Compared to the *Portrait of Gilles Joye* (cat. 3), dated 1472 on the frame, the painterly quality is more fluid and accomplished, though the area of nose, mouth and eyes is conceived in a similarly schematic manner. The contours of the face, determined in the underdrawing, were corrected during the execution of the painting, as can be seen around the chin, where the underdrawing is visible with the naked eye underneath the partly transparent flesh tones. Especially noticeable are the mismatched proportions of face, upper body and hand. Evidently Memling used different patterns from a modelbook which he did not yet unify successfully as he did in his portraits of the 1480s (see cat. 19, 21).

# 13 Portrait of a Man with an Arrow

*c.* 1475–80
Panel (oak), 31.9 x 25.8 cm
Washington, DC, National Gallery of Art, Andrew W. Mellon Collection,
inv. 1937.1.42

PROVENANCE

English private collection (until 1895); art dealer Bourgeois, Cologne (1895); Oppenheim, Cologne (until 1912); Kleinberger and Co., New York (until 1916); Michael Dreicer, New York (until 1921); Dreicer Bequest, The Metropolitan Museum of Art, New York, acc. 22.60.45 (until 1933); Mrs Dreicer Whyte, New York (until 1935); M. Knoedler and Co., New York (1936); February 1936 acquired by the Andrew W. Mellon Educational and Charitable Trust, Pittsburgh; 1937 donated to The National Gallery of Art, Washington, DC.

EXHIBITIONS

Bruges 1902, no. 70; Brussels 1912, no. 2031; Bruges 1994, no. 11.

BIBLIOGRAPHY

Kaemmerer 1899, 19–21; Hulin de Loo 1902, no. 70; Friedländer 1903, 82; Weale 1903, 336; Molinier 1904, 10; Voll 1906, 188–9, 225; Fierens-Gevaert 1909, 126; Voll 1909, xxi–xxii, 21; Fierens-Gevaert 1912, 195; Friedländer 1916, 179; Friedländer 1920, 107–8; Huisman 1923, 126–7; Stein 1926, 30–31; Friedländer 1928 (1971), no. 85; Fierens-Gevaert 1929, 62, 72; Bazin 1939, 20; Kantorowicz 1939–40, 178; De Tolnay 1941, 186, 200; Buttin 1954, 59; Nickel 1968, 78; Faggin 1969, no. III; Wuyts 1969, 82; Lane 1980, no. 23; Hand and Wolff 1986, 188–93; De Vos 1994, no. 29; Stroo and Syfer-d'Olne 1996, 118; Wilson 1998, 59.

The head-and-shoulders portrait of a man in three-quarters view to the left is posed before a dark background originally bright blue-green in colour. The pictorial surface is extremely polished and the brushwork all but imperceptible in the face, which is lit from the right. By contrast, the hair and eyebrows are drawn with thin brushstrokes in an almost calligraphic manner. The man's clothing is painted with similar care. He wears a brown tunic open at the front so that the white shirt and the collar of his black doublet are visible. His black cap barely contrasts with the background, which has darkened over time. On the upturned brim is pinned a small badge of the Virgin and Child on a crescent moon, probably the insignia of a religious confraternity (Hand and Wolff 1986). The most striking feature, however, is the arrow in the man's right hand. An arrow is also the attribute of Antoine, the 'Grand Bâtard' of Burgundy in Rogier van der Weyden's famous portrait (where it refers to his honourable function as assessor at tournaments and was used to designate the winner). In Memling's portrait, the arrow might have similar meanings, or denote membership of a confraternity devoted to St Sebastian.

It may be significant that the arrow was added when the portrait was already completed, probably in Memling's workshop (pigment analysis shows that it was painted in the fifteenth century; Hand and Wolff 1986), or, alternatively, was intended from the start but painted during the last phase of execution (De Vos 1994). If the former, it might signify an important event in the sitter's life that happened shortly after the portrait was completed and thus might help in identifying him. De Vos's interpretation is supported by the fact that Memling apparently composed his portraits using a repertoire of forms and motifs. Once he had painted the face, rudimentarily set down in the underdrawing and filled out using individual physiognomic studies, he relied on a rather limited number of gestures which he incorporated into his compositions again and again. The position of the hand in the present portrait corresponds to that in several other works (cat. 1, 8, 11, 16, 19), even though a *pentimento* visible in the underdrawing indicates that some experimentation took place. Building up a composition from such ready-made building blocks would almost certainly require that attributes, such as the arrow, were added at the last stage of the painting process (though may have been intended all along).

Recent restoration revealed a fly at the lower edge of the picture, in the area between the man's thumb and his white shirt. Originally, the fly appeared to sit on the frame of the painting, an illusionistic device going back to Classical Antiquity. In the nineteenth century the panel was expanded at all sides and the edges painted over. At this time, the fingertips, which originally were cut off by the frame, were completed (Hand and Wolff 1986).

*Trompe l'œil* images of flies belong to those classical motifs with which painters showed off their skill. Pliny the Elder's anecdotes about the great painters of Antiquity competing with each other in illusionistic effects were well known in Bruges's humanist circles. Petrus Christus painted a *trompe-l'œil* fly perched just above the artist's signature on the fictive frame of his *Portrait of a Carthusian* of 1446 (fig. 51), and the Antwerp Master of Frankfurt added a fly momentarily settled on his wife's wimple in the *Self-Portrait with his Wife*, dated 1496 (fig. 49).

Memling's *Portrait of a Man with an Arrow* is yet another example of the portrait with *trompe-l'œil* features, a genre apparently not unknown in the Netherlands. In the Washington picture the illusion is doubled, so to speak, as it is in Christus's painting. Originally, the fly would have appeared to perch on the frame, thus giving the impression of being in front of it, i.e. outside the pictorial space. Similarly, the man's thumb appears to project out of the picture. It is possible that the fingertips, which originally were cut off by the frame, were actually completed on the frame, as they are in the *Portrait of a Young Woman* in Bruges (cat. 17). Memling's interest in *trompe l'œil*, as demonstrated in the Washington painting, helps to place it in the period between his early portraits (cat. 1–5) and those of his middle period, such as the Bruges female portrait, dated 1480. This is supported by other stylistic criteria which similarly suggest that the *Man with an Arrow* was painted around the same time as the *Man with a Gold Cord* of *c.* 1475–80 (cat. 12), a work most closely related to it. This is the time Memling worked on the large 'Triptych of the Two Saints John' in Bruges (see figs. 17, 20).

# 14  Two Donor Fragments from an Altarpiece with the Virgin and Child

*c.* 1475–80
Panel (oak), 44.7 x 32.4 cm (Man); 44.5 x 32 cm (Woman)
Sibiu, Museum Sammlung Samuel Brukenthal

PROVENANCE
Archduke Leopold Wilhelm, Brussels
(before 1656); before 1676 sent by Gilliam
Forchondt (Antwerp) to the Vienna branch
of Forchondt (arrived Vienna 14 January
1676); 3 February 1676 purchased by Prince
Karl of Liechtenstein, Vienna. In the
eighteenth century the panels made their
way into the collection of Baron Samuel
von Brukenthal in Sibiu; since 1817 in the
Muzeul Brukenthal; 1948 transferred to
the Muzeul National in Bucharest.
EXHIBITIONS
Bruges 1902, nos. 74–5; Bruges 1994, no. 37.
BIBLIOGRAPHY
Kaemmerer 1899, 122; Hulin de Loo 1902,
nos. 74–5; Hymans 1902, 59; Friedländer
1903, 82; Weale 1903, 336; Csaki 1909, 219;
Voll 1909, 56–7; Friedländer 1928 (1971),
no. 20; Winkler 1928; Denucé 1931, 147,
180; Baldass 1942, 45; Panofsky 1953, 347
n. 8; Faggin 1969, no. 84; Răchiteanu 1975,
nos. 286–7; Teodosiu 1977, 42–62; Lane
1980, no. 83a–b; Schneeman 1991, 40, 45;
De Vos 1994, no. 85; Madou 1994, 51;
Goethgebeur 1997; Matache 1999, 184–5.

The two donor panels of husband and
wife are fragments from an originally
much larger composition which was
dismembered in the seventeenth
century. Both fragments, together
with a third showing the Virgin
and Child, were in Brussels in the
collection of Archduke Leopold
Wilhelm, whose seal is on the reverses.
Leopold Wilhelm left Brussels for
Vienna in 1656; to all appearances,
however, the three panels were not
shipped to Vienna with the rest of his
collection for they are not listed in
the inventory compiled there in 1659.
De Vos (1994) has shown that they
apparently went on the art market
instead. The accounts of the Antwerp
dealer Gilliam Forchondt reveal that
they were sent to the Vienna branch
of the house in 1676, from which they
were sold as early as February of that
year to Prince Karl of Liechtenstein
('*no. 8 3 Stucken een marienbelt met twee
conterfeytsels van Memmelinck voor de 3
stuckxkens Ryxd.* 90'; Denucé 1931, 180).

De Vos (1994) recognized that the
*Virgin and Child* (private collection),
formerly in the Liechtenstein
Collection, must be the same as
the '*marienbelt*' (image of [the Virgin]
Mary) mentioned in the Forchondt
documents. This is supported by the
scientific examination of the panel
(Goethgebeur 1997). Although the

*Virgin and Child* (first attributed to
Memling by Waagen 1867) and the
two donor fragments (first attributed
to Memling by Kaemmerer 1899)
have long been known to Memling
scholars, the connection between
them remained obscure. This is
surprising considering that all three
panels carry the seal of Leopold
Wilhelm (with the year 1656) as well
as the inscription '*vom Memlinck*'.
The old attribution is of special
significance because it suggests that
the panels might have been signed on
the original frame. This hypothesis is
further corroborated by the spelling
'Memlinck' – in the Forchondt
documents he is spelled 'Memmelinck'
twice – which seems to be based on
Van Mander's *Schilderboeck* (1604) and
thus to reflect contemporary practice.

The landscapes in the two donors'
portraits are partly painted on boards
that were added later. Originally the
donors were accompanied by their
patron saints, as for example in the
'Moreel Triptych' of 1484 (cat. 22);
remnants of the female saint's
garment are still visible on the right
wing. The two donors originally knelt
before the Virgin who stands between
two columns with historiated capitals
before a brocaded cloth of honour.
The two scenes represented on the
capitals, the Adoration of the Magi

and Presentation in the Temple refer
to Christ's infancy. De Vos (1994)
further suggested that the painting
was produced to honour the couple's
wedding. He pointed out that the
child behind the male donor is
marked with a small cross referring to
its early death; this figure – clearly not
a portrait – was probably added at a
later date by Memling's workshop.

The original composition most
likely resembled Memling's *Virgin
and Child with Saint Anthony Abbot
and a Donor* (cat. 4), dated 1472.
Conversely, the symmetrical
composition is reminiscent of
the so-called 'Altarpiece of Jacob
Floreins' (fig. 25) which is thought
to be late. The dating of the donor
fragments is problematic. Whereas
the older literature generally has
assigned an early date to the
*Virgin and Child* and a late date to
the two donors, De Vos (1994)
suggested a date of about 1490 for
all three panels. On the other hand,
dendrochronological examination
of the panels determined an
earliest felling date around 1446
(Goethgebeur 1997). While it is
possible that Memling used a panel
made from almost fifty-year-old
wood, the donors' dress, similar to
that of Tommaso Portinari and Maria
Baroncelli (pl. 2) or that in the *Portrait
of an Elderly Couple* (cat. 5), would
suggest the period between 1475
and 1480 for the fragments under
discussion.

## 15  Portrait of a Young Man

*c.* 1475–80
Panel (oak), 39.9 x 28.3 cm (excluding a 7 cm wide addition at the right)
New York, The Metropolitan Museum of Art, Robert Lehman Collection, inv. 1975.1.112

PROVENANCE
Francis, 9th Earl of Wemyss, Gosford
House, Longniddry, Scotland (died 1889);
Francis Richard, 10th Earl of Wemyss,
Gosford House, until 1912; J. H. Dunn,
London (1913); Knoedler, New York (1914);
Philip Lehman, New York (1915); Robert
Lehman, New York (1975); bequeathed to
the Metropolitan Museum of Art.

EXHIBITIONS
Manchester 1857, no. 398; Colorado
Springs 1951–2; Paris 1957, no. 41; New
York 1998, no. 28; Bruges 2002, no. 49.

BIBLIOGRAPHY
Waagen 1854, III, 440; Wauters 1893, 83
n. 1; Bode 1896, 4; Kaemmerer 1899, 21;
Conway 1921, 239; Friedländer 1928 (1971),
no. 74; Panofsky 1953, 349; Heinrich 1954,
220, 227; Sterling 1957, 35; Pope-Hennessy
1966, 60; Faggin 1969, no. 113; Lane 1980,
no. 53; Campbell 1983; Bauman 1986, 42–3;
Ames-Lewis 1989, 112; De Vos 1994, no. 48;
Klein 1994, 103; Baetjer 1995, no. 251;
Lorentz 1995, 70; Wolff 1998, no. 13;
Nuttall 2002, 202; Nuttall 2004, 64–70,
153, 217, 233.

First attributed to Memling by Waagen in 1854, the painting was exhibited under that name three years later in Manchester. At this time the subject was thought to be St Sebastian because the man held an arrow between his hands and had a halo. This later overpainting was removed in 1912 when the panel was restored (Campbell 1983).

The sitter, young and clean-shaven, is shown head and shoulders in three-quarters view to the left. His dark purple tunic, decorated with a brocade pattern and edged in fur, is worn over a dark doublet with a high collar. On his right ring finger are two gold rings set with rubies. As in most of Memling's portraits, the fictive balustrade – a motif ultimately derived from Jan van Eyck – is at the height of the man's chest, i.e. too high to rest his arms on it.

From the elevated viewpoint we may infer that the setting is a tower-like room. At the left, our eyes are led past porphyry columns to a distant landscape whose horizon rests at the height of the man's mouth. The columns, framing a loggia or window opening, add an aristocratic air to the setting. Although the pictorial conception is unusual for Memling's independent portraits, Pope-Hennessy's (1966)

assumption that the Flemish master was inspired by Italian models has been disproven: the loggia motif is reminiscent of Petrus Christus's *Portrait of a Young Man* of *c.* 1450 (fig. 53), whereas the landscape view through a window appears for the first time in Netherlandish portrait painting in Dieric Bouts's *Portrait of a Man (Jan van Winckele?)*, dated 1462 (fig. 54). On the contrary, Memling's portrait served as model to Florentine painters, specifically from the workshop of Verrocchio. Campbell (1983) recognized that a member of Verrocchio's studio used the motif of a landscape seen through columns in the *Virgin and Child* in the Louvre (fig. 67). Moreover, Perugino's *Self-Portrait* (fig. 64) was inspired by Memling's composition (Campbell 1983; Nuttall 2002; Nuttall 2004, 153; see also Paula Nuttall's essay). From these observations, Campbell concluded that Memling's portrait reached Italy as early as the 1470s.

More recently, the Louvre *Virgin and Child* has been attributed to Domenico Ghirlandaio; for stylistic reasons it cannot be dated later than 1482 (see New York 1998). Thus the Louvre painting offers a most persuasive *terminus ante quem* for Memling's portrait. Dendrochronological examination of the panel determined an earliest felling date of 1474. Taking account of a minimum seasoning and storage time of two years (see Klein 2003), Memling could have used the panel in 1476 at the earliest. In light of both the dendrochronological results and the arguments proposed by Maryan Ainsworth (see her essay), the date of 1475–80 suggested by Wolff (1998) seems plausible. In any event, the painting must have reached Florence shortly after its completion. It is therefore most likely that it was commissioned by one of Memling's Italian patrons in Bruges.

# 16 Portrait of a Young Man before a Landscape

c. 1475–80
Panel (oak), 26 x 20 cm
Venice, Galleria dell'Accademia, inv. 586

PROVENANCE
Collection Manfrin, Venice; 1856 acquired
by Emperor Francis Joseph of Austria for
the Kunsthistorisches Museum in Vienna;
later transferred to Venice.

EXHIBITIONS
Venice 1946; Florence 1947, no. 8; Bruges
1951, no. 15; Venice and Rome 1951, no. 12;
London 1953–4, no. 28; Schaffhausen 1955,
no. 67; Bruges 1994, no. 20; Venice 1999,
no. 6.

BIBLIOGRAPHY
Burckhardt 1879, 615; Bode 1896, 4;
Kaemmerer 1899, 18–19; Weale 1901, 106;
Stein 1909, 44; Voll 1909, 23; Conway
1921, 239; Friedländer 1928 (1971), no. 77;
Baldass 1942, 41; Van Gelder 1951, 327;
Moschini Marconi 1955, 183–4; Faggin 1969,
no. 107; Lane 1980, no. 28; Castelfranchi
Vegas 1983 (1984), 160; Nepi Scirè and
Valcanover 1985, 138; Collobi-Ragghianti
1990, 62–3, no. 107; De Vos 1994, no. 49;
Pächt 1994, 243.

The *Portrait of a Young Man before a Landscape*, despite its small size, is one of the most impressive examples of Memling's work in this genre. The new portrait type which places the sitter before a landscape, to all appearances an invention of the artist, is here formulated in an exemplary manner, combining the sitter shown in close proximity with the distant landscape. At the same time, the portrait's plasticity liberates it from the background, which acts as a foil. The new pictorial invention seems to have appealed above all to the Italian merchants resident in Bruges who regularly supplied Memling with commissions, as they had Jan van Eyck and Petrus Christus before him. It was Memling's portraits, however, more than those of his predecessors, which fundamentally influenced the development of Italian portrait painting, especially in Venice, Florence and central Italy (see Paula Nuttall's essay).

After the recent removal of the old varnish that hampered a full appreciation of the panel (see reproduction of the old state in De Vos 1994, 203), its true qualities have been revealed: the refined modelling of the man's face, stressed by the subtle use of light; the technical mastery in the handling of the landscape. Stylistically, the panel belongs to a number of portraits grouped around the Antwerp *Man with a Coin* (cat. 10), which in the recent literature (see De Vos 1994) has been dated to the years around 1480 but was probably painted between *c*. 1475 and *c*. 1480.

First documented in Italy in the nineteenth century, the present portrait depicts a man in traditional three-quarters view to the left, placed before a landscape. His right hand originally rested on the frame, which thus functioned as a ledge – a pictorial device used by Memling on several occasions (cat. 1, 8, 11) and still visible in the *Portrait of a Young Woman* in Bruges (cat. 17) where the original frame is preserved. The position of the hand – the fingers of which are ringless – follows a pattern established in other portraits by Memling (cat. 7, 13), probably derived from a common patternbook model.

The young man wears a black jacket over a white shirt, the collar of which is visible at the neck. A black cap sits on his brown hair which falls in gentle waves over his ears. Dress and hairstyle are the same as those in some other portraits by Memling thought to be of Italian merchants. It is a style also found in several male portraits by Antonello da Messina from the mid-1470s. But as they remained fashionable until the beginning of the sixteenth century, above all in Venice, as witnessed by Giovanni Bellini's *Portrait of a Man (Pietro Bembo?)* (fig. 60), dated 1504, the man's costume and hairstyle are of only limited help in dating Memling's portrait.

Strikingly, the landscape in the present portrait is devoid of people or buildings. As in the apparently slightly earlier *Man with a Spotted Fur Collar* (cat. 8), the background consists of no more than a green meadow at the edge of a forest, arranged in overlapping layers. The group of three trees at the left, leading the eye into the distance, can also be found on the St John's panel of Memling's 'Bembo Diptych' (Washington, National Gallery of Art, and Munich, Alte Pinakothek), which is documented in Venice at the beginning of the sixteenth century. This motif was variously taken up by Umbrian painters.

The Venice portrait was not part of a devotional diptych or triptych. Although the possibility that it may have had a pendant – a portrait of a relative, for example (cf. cat. 24) – cannot be excluded, it was most likely meant as a secular, autonomous work.

# 17 Portrait of a Young Woman ('Sibyl')

Dated 1480
Panel (oak), 46.5 x 35.2 cm
Bruges, Stedelijke Musea, Memlingmuseum – Sint-Janshospitaal, inv. OSJ 174.1

PROVENANCE
Sint-Juliaansgasthuis, Bruges; 1815 transferred to Sint-Janshospitaal.

EXHIBITIONS
Bruges 1902, no. 62; Paris 1935, no. 69; Bruges 1939, no. 32; Paris 1952–3, no. 50; Madrid 1958–9, no. 8; Bruges 1960, no. 41; Bruges 1976, no. 54; Bruges 1994, no. 16; Bruges 1998, no. 4.

BIBLIOGRAPHY
Keverberg 1818, 145, 232; Michiels 1845, 319–75; De Brou 1860, 108; Everaert 1864, no. 5; Weale 1864–5, 190–91; Weale 1871, 49–50; Crowe and Cavalcaselle 1875, 304; Wauters 1893, 20 n. 2; Kaemmerer 1899, 110; Weale 1901, 28, 41–2, 97; Hulin de Loo 1902, no. 62; Friedländer 1903, 81; Voll 1909, 60, 173; Fierens-Gevaert 1922, 30; Huisman 1923, 98–100; Winkler 1924; Friedländer 1928 (1971), no. 94; Fierens-Gevaert 1929, 66; Marlier 1934, 48–58; Lavalleye 1939, 20; Baldass 1942, 42; Panofsky 1953, 294; Faggin 1969, no. 10; Lane 1980, no. 24; Hull 1981, 226–7; Harbison 1985, 94; Lobelle 1985, 80; Verougstraete-Marcq and Van Schoute 1989, 146–7; Campbell 1990, 73–4; Lobelle 1991; De Vos 1991; Belting and Kruse 1994, 263; De Vos 1994, no. 36; Madou 1994, 51; Lane 1997, 61; Verougstraete and Van Schoute 1997, 280, 282, 284–95; Janssens 2003, 99–100.

The portrait, inscribed on the frame with the year 1480, is the only independent female portrait by Memling to have survived. The woman is shown at half length, turned in three-quarters view to the left, before a dark background which originally was blue green. Her delicately drawn hands, one placed on top of the other, rest on the marbled brown frame, preserved in its original state. The fingertips of the right hand are painted on the frame. This *trompe-l'œil* motif, probably inspired by portraits by Jan van Eyck, creates the illusion of projecting the sitter into the space of the viewer. But in the present portrait Memling's approach in combining the pictorial with the real world differs from the one he adopted in his early portraits (see cat. 1, 2; pl. 2).

Judging by her clothes and jewellery, the woman is from a well-to-do Bruges family. She wears a purple dress with a white fur collar, a dark red stomacher and a broad, green belt. Her swept-back hair is hidden beneath her headdress from which a transparent veil falls onto her shoulders. A gold chain with a crucifix of precious stones and pearls (cf. cat. 21) and no less than seven rings adorn her otherwise severe appearance and testify to her wealth (Madou 1994).

The Bruges *Young Woman* comes closer to Van der Weyden's portraits than Memling's earlier efforts in the genre, such as the *Portrait of Maria Baroncelli* (pl. 2), the woman in the *Portrait of an Elderly Couple* (cat. 5), or the *Portrait of Barbara van Vlaenderbech* (cat. 18). Rogier's (or his workshop's) female portraits in London and Washington (fig. 61) are Memling's inspiration, down to the subdued palette. Memling's development as a portraitist in the period between the *Maria Baroncelli* of a decade earlier and the Bruges *Young Woman* is surprising. A comparison of the flesh tones is particularly instructive: the smooth, polished surface of the Baroncelli portrait has given way to surface texture in which nuances are achieved by different means. The modelling of the face is undertaken at all stages of the painting process, i.e. during the underpainting, the application of *imprimatura* and finally the thin white glazes. Whereas the veil of Maria Baroncelli's hennin shows its materiality – and Memling's skill at rendering visual surface qualities such as tactile values – that of the woman in the present portrait is used to conduct light.

Neither the function of the portrait (attributed to Memling as early as the eighteenth and early nineteenth centuries; Keverberg 1818) nor the identity of the young woman is known. Indeed, her name was already forgotten in the late sixteenth century when a cartouche in the upper left corner and a banderole with an inscription on the frame were added, which inform us that the woman is the Persian Sibyl. De Vos (1994) identified the painter of these additions with the Bruges artist Pieter Claeissens the Younger (for the inscriptions, see De Vos 1994). Weale (1864–5) believed the woman to be Maria Moreel, second daughter of Willem Moreel and Barbara van Vlaenderberch (see cat. 18), but this identification does not correspond

with Maria's age, as already observed by Kaemmerer (1899). Moreover, though the *Portrait of a Young Woman* possibly could have formed the right wing of a marital diptych, this is unlikely since there are no hinge-marks on the still extant frame. The possibility that the picture served as an epitaph may find support in the manner it is inscribed, with the year 1480 formed of fictive metal numbers. Such an inscription can also be seen on the *Portrait of Gilles Joye* (cat. 3), documented as having hung above the composer's tomb. This manner of inscribing portraits is found on Van Eyck's epitaphs, which obviously served as Memling's source.

## 18 Two Wings with the Portraits of Willem Moreel and Barbara van Vlaenderberch

*c.*1480
Panel (oak), 39.4 x 29 cm; 39.3 x 29.5 cm
Brussels, Musées Royaux des Beaux-Arts de Belgique, inv. 1451–1452

PROVENANCE

Sale Désiré Van den Schrieck, Leuven, 8–10 April 1861, nos. 49–50.

EXHIBITIONS

Bruges 1902, nos. 64–5; Bern 1926, nos. 9–10; London 1927, nos. 56, 59; Paris 1935, nos. 67–8; Bruges 1939, nos. 35–6; Amsterdam and Rotterdam 1946, nos. 48–9; Paris 1947, nos. 71–2; Amsterdam and Brussels 1951, nos. 25–6; Dijon 1951, nos. 24–5; Brussels 1961, nos. 72–3; Bruges 1994, no. 7.

BIBLIOGRAPHY

Passavant 1841, 34; Crowe and Cavalcaselle 1857 (1878), 304; Weale 1864–5, 179–96 (189–90); Weale 1871, 57; Crowe and Cavalcaselle 1875, 304; Wauters 1893, 20, 31, 66, 84, 101, 113; Kaemmerer 1899, 110–16; Weale 1901, 40, 98–9; Hulin de Loo 1902, nos. 64–5; Friedländer 1903, 81; Voll 1909, 58–9; Conway 1921, 240; Huisman 1923, 96–8; Winkler 1924, 128; Hulin de Loo 1927, 106; Friedländer 1928 (1971), nos. 67–8; Fierens-Gevaert 1929, 65; Baldass 1942, 42; Panofsky 1953, 294, 349, 479 n. 16; Schouteet 1955, 83; Faggin 1969, nos. 89–90; Trzeciak 1977, no.16; Lane 1980, nos. 56–7; Collobi-Ragghianti 1990, 65–6; Dülberg 1990, 85 and 178, nos. 9–10; Ainsworth 1994, 86; De Vos 1994, no. 22; Madou 1994, 51; Martens 1994, 20; Périer-d'Ieteren 1994, 67, 71; Campbell 1995, 254; Lorentz 1995, 71–4; Martens 1995, 358–9; Campbell 1998, 359–60; Wilson 1998, 53–4; Stroo *et al.* 1999, 202–14; Janssens 2003, 66–110.

COPY

Copy of the portrait of Barbara van Vlaenderberch supposedly formerly in the collection Chiaramonte Bordonardo, Palermo (Collobi-Ragghianti 1990).

The portraits of Willem Moreel and his wife Barbara van Vlaenderberch originally formed the wings of a devotional triptych (see Dülberg 1990). As with the portraits of Tommaso Portinari and Maria Baroncelli (pl. 2), the centre panel most likely featured an image of the Virgin and Child, probably at half length, as in the 'Triptych of Benedetto Portinari', dated 1487 (pl. 30). The portraits differ considerably from the other two surviving marital portraits by Memling (cat. 5, 9). Husband and wife are placed in a loggia looking onto a landscape. Opening the wings at an angle of about 45 degrees would have redressed the diagonal perspective of the loggia, in a way similar to the 'Diptych of Maarten van Nieuwenhove' (cat. 23). The backs of the panels show the coats of arms of the couple in reversed position – the man's on the reverse of the woman's portrait and vice versa. This led Campbell (1998) to assume that the wings were fixed. Consequently, even on the reverse Moreel's escutcheon was situated to the 'heraldic right', the more important side, of the religious image, thus preserving heraldic decorum. While the hypothesis of a fixed triptych offers a better explanation for the

arrangement of the coats of arms on the reverse than the traditional format of the folding triptych (cf. Dülberg 1990), it implies at the same time that the work was placed in a prominent, publicly accessible location.

The panels were first attributed to Memling by Passavant (1841). Crowe and Cavalcaselle (1857) identified the sitters through the coats of arms and inscriptions on the reverses: '*Arma / Guillermi Moreel*', on the woman's portrait; '*Arma Domicelle / Barbare de Vlaenderberch / Alias de Hertsvelde / Uxoris Guillermi*', on the man's. Weale (1864–5) first reconstructed the couple's biographies, using the available sources in the Bruges city archives.

Willem Moreel (died 1501) was a member of one of the most affluent and influential families in Bruges whose wealth depended on property holdings and the spice trade. While he himself bore the title of Burgrave of Roeselare, he inherited that of Lord of Oostcleyhem from his father. Besides his activities as spice merchant and banker for the Banco di Roma, he occupied various political offices in Bruges, starting in 1472: first as *schepen* or alderman (1472, 1475), then burgomaster (1478, 1483), bailiff (1488), and finally treasurer

(1489). From October 1481 to March 1482 he was jailed because he opposed the politics of the future emperor Maximilian I of Austria. In 1490 he was one of the forty wealthiest citizens of Bruges (Janssens 2003).

In 1464 Willem Moreel married Barbara van Vlaenderberch, also known as Hertsvelde (died 1499), who bore him five sons and thirteen daughters. In 1484 (1485 'new style', i.e. according to today's calendar) the couple was granted permission to set up an altar dedicated to St Maurus and St Egidius in St James's Church and to be buried there. On that occasion they commissioned Memling to paint a large altarpiece, the 'Moreel Triptych' (cat. 22), which carries the date 1484 on the frame. The donor portraits on the wings provide a reference point for the dating of the Brussels portraits, though it remains unknown whether 1484 is the date of the donation or the completion of the triptych (see also under cat. 22). Although most authors suggest a date of around 1480 for the Brussels portraits, De Vos (1994) pointed out the difference in painting styles between the 'Moreel Triptych' and the Brussels panels. Indeed, the smooth and finely executed portraits, typical for Memling's early works, contrast with the coarser style of the triptych. Moreover, De Vos believed Willem Moreel to be younger in the present portrait than in the triptych, therefore suggesting a date of about 1472–5 for the former.

De Vos's arguments do not stand up upon closer inspection. It has since been observed (Stroo *et al.* 1999) that the different dimensions and functions of the two works restrict a comparison of their painting styles and thus do not allow for dating based on stylistic criteria. The Brussels panels, meant to be seen up close, required a more careful handling of surface textures than the monumental altarpiece. It is also difficult to detect the age difference between the two representations of

## 19 Portrait of a Young Man

*c.* 1480 or later?
Panel (oak), 33.4 x 22.8 cm
The Montreal Museum of Fine Arts, Horsley & Annie Townsend Bequest;
William Gilman Cheney Bequest, inv. 56.1129

Willem Moreel that De Vos believed to recognize, since both portraits – and this applies to Barbara van Vlaenderberch as well – go back to the same model, probably a drawing.

Dendrochronological analysis gives an estimated earliest felling date of 1466 for the wood used for the portrait of Moreel, and 1472 for that of Van Vlaenderberch. Considering the normal storage time of wood, the date for the Brussels panels would be at the earliest some time after 1474, more likely after 1482.

No connection can be shown between the commission of the Brussels portraits and Willem Moreel's release from prison in 1482. The prominently displayed coats of arms on the reverse of the panels, familiar from portraits of Burgundian courtiers and officials, would seem to indicate that the portraits (as part of the entire triptych) were commissioned to mark high social rank or political office (Wilson 1998). It may indeed be worth considering whether the commission was connected to Moreel's political career, specifically his election to burgomaster of Bruges in 1483.

PROVENANCE
Sale John Edward Taylor, Christie's, London, July 1912, no. 39; art dealer Julius Böhler, Munich; John N. Willys, Toledo (OH), 1925; Sale Parke-Bernet, New York, 21 October 1945; A. and R. Ball (1945); Schaeffer Galleries, New York (1948); 1956 acquired by the museum.

EXHIBITIONS
New York 1929, no. 20; Chicago 1933, no. 51; New York 1939, no. 255; Bruges 1960, no. 44; Detroit 1960, no. 36; New York 1961, no. 6.

BIBLIOGRAPHY
Friedländer 1920, 103, 108; Conway 1921, 239; Flint 1925, 363–7; Friedländer 1928 (1971), no. 80; Faggin 1969, no. 100; De Vos 1994, no. 46; Rohlmann 1994; Stroo *et al.* 1999, 187 n. 8.

Somewhat ignored in the older literature, the picture was first published as a Memling portrait by Friedländer (1920). Hairstyle and dress of the young man indicate that he may have been a member of the Italian merchant community in Bruges, as already suggested by Conway (1921). This was accepted by Ninane (Bruges 1960) and most recently Rohlmann (1994), though the provenance of the painting gives no indication of an Italian origin.

The pose of the man, shown head and shoulders in three-quarters view before a landscape, is typical for Memling, who may be credited with its invention. Similarities exist with a series of portraits of Italian merchants which the artist executed in the mid-1470s, including the portrait from the Corsini collection (cat. 11) or the *Man with a Coin* in Antwerp (cat. 10). The hand and its position is yet another motif repeatedly found in Memling's portraits. Interesting is the parchment or paper scroll. With the exception of the two previously mentioned portraits, the artist generally refrained from introducing such attributes.

De Vos (1994) already referred to the problematic condition of the painting. Evidently the hair and flesh tones suffered during restoration.

The thin glazes with which Memling modelled his flesh tones so brilliantly have disappeared completely, thus no longer enabling us to separate the work of the master from that of his workshop. However, other elements remain which throw doubt on Memling's authorship. Lorne Campbell (see his essay) rightly noted the unusual proportion of the head, 'which is more distorted than anything by Memling'. Equally unfamiliar is the high viewpoint of the landscape, the horizon of which runs along the height of the man's forehead instead of the neck as common with Memling. Despite the fact that the condition of the panel does not allow a definitive verdict, the arguments cited above would seem to be sufficiently valid to reconsider the question whether the work was executed by Memling, his workshop, or rather by a Bruges contemporary or successor.

# 20  Portrait of a Man with a Pink

*c.* 1480–85
Panel (oak), 39.5 x 28.4 cm
New York, The Pierpont Morgan Library

PROVENANCE
  Charles du Bourg, Perreaux (France);
  Rudolphe Kann, Paris; before 1920
  acquired by J. Pierpont Morgan.
EXHIBITIONS
  Paris 1904, no. 59; New York 1935, no. 11;
  London 1935, no. 12; Princeton 1937, no. 1;
  New York 1939, no. 254; Worcester and
  Philadelphia 1939, no. 20; New York 1942,
  44–5.
BIBLIOGRAPHY
  Bode 1907, no. 106; Friedländer 1920, 108;
  Conway 1921, 238; Friedländer 1928 (1971),
  no. 83; Faggin 1969, no. 99; Lane 1980,
  no. 22; Silver 1984, 168; De Vos 1994, no. 26.

Alongside the portraits with landscape backgrounds, Memling regularly produced conventional portraits with neutral settings, following the convention established by Jan van Eyck and Rogier van der Weyden. The *Portrait of a Man with a Pink* is a typical example of this category. The sitter, shown at bust length in three-quarters view to the right, is placed before a background which was originally bright blue-green but which has darkened over time. He wears a black doublet over a white shirt; a brown, fur-lined coat is placed on top. A black cap sits on his straight, brown hair which forms a fringe across his forehead. He holds a pink in his left hand and a folded piece of paper in his right. The right hand rests on the edge of the picture which functions as a ledge.

Traditionally a symbol of love and fidelity, the pink in the man's hand suggests that we are probably dealing with an engagement portrait. Thus the piece of paper in his other hand might be a love letter or, on a more prosaic level, a marriage contract. Engagement portraits were commonly used, especially among the nobility but also by members of the merchant class, to present absentee brides-to-be with an impression of their future husbands. However, it is more likely that the *Portrait of a Man with a Pink* formed a diptych together with a portrait of a woman. A possible candidate, at least as far as concerns size, would be the Bruges *Portrait of a Young Woman* of 1480 (cat. 17), but for formal and stylistic reasons such reconstruction is highly unlikely.

The present painting, formerly in a private collection in Perreaux, was included in the 1904 Paris exhibition 'Les Primitifs français' as a work of a French master from the Loire region. Friedländer (1920) was the first to attribute the portrait, which by then had entered the collection of J. Pierpont Morgan, to Memling. Conway (1921) included it among Memling's early portraits of Italian merchants, suggesting a date between 1467 and 1472, parallel to the *Last Judgement* altarpiece for Agnolo Tani. Friedländer (1928) concurred with the early dating, *c.* 1475, pointing out similarities with the *Portrait of a Man with an Arrow* (cat. 13). A date in the second half of the 1470s was suggested by Lane (1980) and De Vos (1994).

Dendrochronology suggests 1454 as the earliest felling date for the wood used for the Morgan panel; statistically more probable, however, is a date around 1460 or later. Taking into account the minimum two-year seasoning and drying time for the wood, Memling could have painted the portrait as early as 1456; a ten-year storage period would push the date to around 1470 or later. Be that as it may, dendrochronology seems to support the traditional early dating. However, since the recent cleaning of the portrait, the criteria applied to establish its date may be expanded to include analysis of style and painting technique. As Maryan Ainsworth demonstrates (see her essay), the supple, virtuoso brushwork and more painterly approach contrast strongly with the polished and finely painted surfaces of Memling's early portraits (cat. 1, 2, 12; pl. 2). Therefore a later date – *c.* 1480–85 – for the present portrait seems likely.

## 21 Portrait of a Man at Prayer before a Landscape (Charles de Visen?)

*c.* 1480–85
Panel (oak), 30 x 22 cm
The Hague, Mauritshuis, inv. 595

PROVENANCE
Andrew Fountaine, Harfold Hall, Norfolk (before 1850); purchased by the Vereniging Rembrandt at the Fountaine sale, Christie's, London, 7 July 1894, no. 46; 1895 bequeathed to the state.

EXHIBITIONS
Bruges 1902, no. 73; Bruges 1939, no. 42; Amsterdam 1945, no. 58; The Hague 1945, no. 69; Paris 1952–3, no. 51; Schaffhausen 1955, no. 64; Bruges 1994, no. 18; The Hague 1997, no. 2.

BIBLIOGRAPHY
Bredius 1895, 229; Bode 1896, 3–4; Kaemmerer 1899, 19–20; Weale 1901, 66–7; Hulin de Loo 1902, no. 73; Friedländer 1903, 82; Weale 1903, 335; Voll 1909, 24, 172; Mauritshuis 1914, 203–4; Conway 1921, 241; Huisman 1923, 105–6; Friedländer 1928 (1971), no. 79; Fierens-Gevaert 1929, 76; Marlier 1934, 48–58; Martin 1935, 197–8; Schöne 1939, 28; Baldass 1942, 42; Friedländer 1949, 53; Panofsky 1953, 349; Bruyn 1961, 2a–b; Faggin 1969, no. 109; McFarlane 1971, 14 n. 64; Trzeciak 1977, no. 26; Lane 1980, no. 35; Hoetink 1985, 228–9; Broos 1987, 231–5; Dülberg 1990, 178–9, no. 11; De Vos 1994, no. 40; Klein 1994, 103; Madou 1994, 51; Pächt 1994, 243; Klein 1997, 289.

The picture shows a powerful man, with strong features and heavy jowl, whose magnetic presence, as in no other of Memling's portraits, fills almost the entire picture plane. The painting is in excellent condition; only the dark grey clouds were added later. The monumental effect is mainly due to the plasticity of the face, achieved through the sophisticated lighting (note the small reflections on the man's right cheek). This is enhanced by the low viewpoint of the landscape and the sharp contrast between the man's head and the blue sky.

The panel originally formed the right wing of a devotional diptych of which the left wing featured an image of the Virgin (see cat. 23), now lost. The motif of praying hands cut off – just below the tips of the thumbs – by the lower edge of the picture is unique in Memling's oeuvre. This unusual detail, however, was intended from the beginning. Contrary to the earlier assumption that the panel was cut at all sides (Dülberg 1990), it has only been trimmed at the right. Thus the picture's edge is just below the two rings set with precious stones, whose placement not only guarantees their visibility but draws our attention. The rings, together with the crucifix worn on a gold chain and the man's costly dress, especially the jacket lined with white fur flecked with brown, testify to the sitter's elevated status and wealth.

The man's high social rank is confirmed by the coat of arms on the reverse, identifying him as a member of the nobility. The crest of the escutcheon consists of a jousting helmet crowned with a white-gold chaplet from which falls a cloth with a fringe of stylized oak leaves. This is surmounted by a white hawk with spread wings (called a 'hawk displayed' in heraldry) to whose claws are attached round bells. The coat of arms is painted over another one the shape of which can be made out in relief under raking light. A reconstruction of it was published by Martin (1935) and most recently, with full discussion, by Van Suchtelen (The Hague 1997, 45 n. 2). It closely matches that of the L'Espinette family of Franche-Comté which, however, carried pear-shaped bells in their coat of arms instead of the round *grelots* (De Vos 1994).

The coat of arms of the L'Espinette family is almost identical to that of the de Visen family, also of Franche-Comté. This persuaded Lorne Campbell (see his essay) to identify the man in the Mauritshuis portrait with Charles de Visen (born in Dijon; died 1486), a courtier, *valet de chambre* and confidant to Duke Charles the Bold. Charles de Visen was the son of Jean de Visen (died 1460) who was *receveur général de Bourgogne* under Philip the Good. He married Jacqueline Le Tourneur in Brussels in 1457. She was the daughter of the *sommelier de corps* of Charles the Bold, in whose castle of Béthune the wedding took place on 9 August 1457, possibly in the presence of the duke and his wife, Isabella of Bourbon. In his capacity as *sommelier de corps* and *garde des menus joyaux* to Charles the Bold, Charles de Visen was a member of the ducal household. As his title implies, he was responsible for the ducal jewels, a duty which included the ordering of collars of the Order of the Golden Fleece from the goldsmith Gérard Loyet. Charles was an outstanding knight and warrior; for a while he held the position of captain of the castle of Châtillon-sur-Seine. Philippe de Commynes, who met Charles de Visen before the city of Liège in the entourage of Charles the Bold, referred to him as 'a man of honour, trusted by his master' (*Mémoires*, 11, 7).

The identification of the man in the Mauritshuis painting with Charles de Visen would favour a dating in the 1480s traditionally assigned to it for stylistic reasons. This is confirmed by dendrochronological analysis which established 1474 as the earliest felling date of the wood used for the panel. Painting would have taken place in 1476 or, more probably, after 1482. It is possible that the portrait served a memorial function; Charles de Visen died in 1486, not long after completion of his portrait.

On the reverse of the wings: John the Baptist and St George
Dated 1484
Panel (oak), 141 x 174 cm (centre panel); 141 x 87 cm (left wing); 141 x 86.8 cm (right wing), including original frame
Bruges, Stedelijke Musea, Groeningemuseum, inv. OGRO0091–95.1

PROVENANCE
Triptych for the altar of St Maurus
and St Giles, Sint-Jacobskerk, Bruges,
after 1484; 1699 documented in Sint-
Juliaansgasthuis; 1794 transferred to Paris
and exhibited in the Musée Napoléon;
1816 returned to Bruges and placed in
the Academy.
EXHIBITIONS
Bruges 1902, no. 66; Bruges 1939, no. 8;
Dijon 1951, no. 26; Amsterdam 1951, no. 39;
Brussels 1951, no. 27; Bruges 1953, no. 14;
Bruges 1960, no. 43; Bruges 1994, no. 25;
Bruges 2002, no. 53.
BIBLIOGRAPHY
Descamps 1769, 300–301; Schlegel 1802–4
(1959), 44–5; Passavant 1841, 34; Michiels
1845, 319–75; Weale 1861, nos. 4–8; Waagen
1862, I, 119–21; Weale 1864–5; Wauters 1893,
20 n. 2; Kaemmerer 1899, 116; Weale 1901,
II, 42, 96–7; Hulin de Loo 1902, no. 66;
Friedländer 1903, 82; Voll 1909, xxx–xxxi,
62–3; Fierens-Gevaert 1922, 31–2; Huisman
1923, 86–91; Winkler 1924, 126; Friedländer
1928 (1971), no. 12; Fierens-Gevaert 1929, 68;
Depoorter 1934–5, 5; Marlier 1934, 44–6;
Lavalleye 1939, 20; Baldass 1942, 20, 45;
Behling 1957, 67–8; Janssens de Bisthoven
1959, no. 12; Pauwels 1963, no. 11; Winkler
1964, 176; Sosson 1966; Lugt 1968, no. 38;
Blum 1969, 97–103; Faggin 1969, no. 12;
McFarlane 1971, 31; Evers 1972, 17–18;
Rotsaert 1974, 14–17; De Mirimonde 1974,
90–93; Geldhof 1975, 60–61, 95; Heller
1976, 112–18; Lane 1980, no. 55; De Vos
1982, 159–62; Janssens de Bisthoven 1983,
1–17; Dhanens 1984, 15; Martens and Van
Miegroet 1984, 70–71; Grams-Thieme 1988,
224–7; Van Miegroet 1990, 270; Haskell
1993, 434–5, 455–6; Belting and Kruse 1994,
255–7; De Vos 1994, no. 63; Madou 1994,
53–4; Martens 1994, 19–20; Van Biervliet
1994, 113–17; Borchert 1995, 152–4; Lorentz
1995, 36, 92–4; Martens 1995, 50; Martens
1995, 355–66; Miller 1995, 259–60; Borchert
1997, 134–35; Verougstraete and Van
Schoute 1997, 282–3; Wilson 1998, 52–4;
Stroo et al. 1999, 208, 211; Janssens 2003,
61–110 (76–99).

The monumental triptych with Saints
Christopher, Giles and Maurus
on the centre panel and the two
donors with their patron saints and
numerous children on the wings is
without doubt one of Memling's most
important works. His authorship
was known in eighteenth-century
art-historical writings, but it was
the German philosopher Friedrich
Schlegel's enthusiastic endorsement
of the triptych that initiated the
rediscovery and scholarship of early
Netherlandish painting. (Schlegel
had seen the work in Paris where
it had been moved during the
French occupation of the Austrian
Netherlands.)

From an art-historical viewpoint,
the altarpiece's greatest significance
lies in its representation of landscape,
where it takes its place alongside
the works of Jan van Eyck, Rogier
van der Weyden, Dieric Bouts and
Hugo van der Goes. In this artistic
chain, it provides a crucial link
in the development of landscape
as an independent genre, as first
practised by Joachim Patinir in the
early sixteenth century. Besides
its role in the development of
landscape, the triptych features
the earliest and most convincing
group portrait in the Southern
Netherlands. As a family portrait
it ranks next to Van der Goes's
slightly earlier 'Portinari Altarpiece'
(see fig. 62), but accommodating
Willem Moreel's and Barbara van
Vlaenderberch's numerous children
(they had five sons and thirteen
daughters) required a new pictorial
approach. Memling's innovative
solution stands at the beginning of a
development in Bruges that stretches
from his own so-called 'Altarpiece

of Jacob Floreins' (see fig. 25) or the
portraits of the guild members on
the 'Altarpiece of the Black Heads of
Reval' (Tallinn, Niguliste Muuseum;
see fig. 30), attributed to the Master of
the Legend of St Lucy, to the 'Van de
Velde Diptych' by Adriaen Isenbrant,
dated 1521 (Brussels, Musées Royaux
des Beaux-Arts de Belgique, and
Bruges, Church of Our Lady).

Weale (1864–5) first identified the
donors as Willem Moreel and Barbara
van Vlaenderberch, alias Hertsvelde,
based on their resemblance to
authenticated portraits of the couple
in Brussels (see cat. 18, with biography
of Willem Moreel). Moreover,
Weale discovered a document of
1484 (1485 new style) granting the
couple permission to set up an altar
dedicated to Saints Maurus and Giles
at Sint-Jacobskerk and to prepare their
tomb nearby. The year 1484 inscribed
on the original frame probably does
not refer to the completion but to
the commission of the altarpiece.
The execution of the work must
have taken several years during
which Barbara van Vlaenderberch
bore her husband more children
who had to be integrated into the
composition (Janssens de Bisthoven
1959; De Vos 1994). All five sons
of the couple and eleven of their
daughters are represented; six of
the daughters, however, were

painted over the already completed
landscape.

The saints in the centre panel
and on the outside wings are
closely associated with the donors.
St Christopher – the figure seems
to go back to a lost Eyckian
original – is venerated on the same
day (25 July) as St James, the patron
saint of the Moreel family church
(St James's Church). St Maurus and
St Giles, the patron saints of the
family altar, were probably selected
on the basis of the surnames Moreel
and Hertsvelde (De Vos 1982; 1994):
'Maurus' and 'Moreel' share the same
etymology (Moor); the deer (hert) of
St Giles can be linked to the name of
Hertsvelde. On the wings, the donors
are protected by their patron saints,
St William of Maleval and St Barbara,
respectively. The two saints on the
exterior wings, John the Baptist and
St George, may refer to two sons, Jan
and Joris (Martens 1994). In view of
this highly personalized iconography,
it seems likely that the buildings in
the background on the wings can be
identified with those owned by the
family. Willem Moreel held the title
of Burgrave of Roeselare and Lord of
Oostcleyhem. The impressive castles
as well as the costly clothes of the
donors testify to their wealth and
elevated social status.

# 23  Diptych of Maarten van Nieuwenhove

Dated 1487
Panel (oak), each 52 x 41.5 cm (including original frame)
Bruges, Stedelijke Musea, Memlingmuseum – Sint-Janshospitaal, inv. OSJ178.1

PROVENANCE

Sint-Juliaansgasthuis, Bruges (?);
1815 transferred to Sint-Janshospitaal.

EXHIBITIONS

Bruges 1902, no. 67; Paris 1923, no. 18;
London 1927, no. 61; Copenhagen 1931,
no. 53; Paris 1935, no. 70; Bruges 1939, no. 11;
Amsterdam and Rotterdam 1946, no. 51;
Bruges 1953, no. 15; Brussels 1953, no. 11;
Bruges 1960, no. 45; Dijon 1960, no. 11;
Bruges 1976, no. 55; Bruges 1994, no. 33;
Bruges 1998, no. 6.

BIBLIOGRAPHY

Keverberg 1818, 145, 232; Schnaase 1834,
360; Passavant 1841, 314; Michiels 1845,
319–75; Everaert 1864, no. 5; Weale 1871, 50;
Crowe and Cavalcaselle 1875, 310; Wauters
1893, 20 n. 20, 112; Kaemmerer 1899,
118–20; Weale 1901, 45–6, 98; Hulin de
Loo 1902, no. 66; Friedländer 1903, 82; Voll
1909, xxxi–xxxii, 68–9; Conway 1921, 241;
Fierens-Gevaert 1922, 32; Huisman 1923,
36–40; Winkler 1924, 128; Friedländer 1928
(1971), no. 14; Fierens-Gevaert 1929, 68–9;
Lavalleye 1939, 24; Schöne 1939, 291–9;
Baldass 1942, 46; Friedländer 1949, 42–4;
Panofsky 1953, 295, 349; Ringbom 1965,
46; Sosson 1965, 229; Faggin 1969, no. 13;
McFarlane 1971, 41; Sterling 1973, 80–93;
Geldhof 1975, 31, 33, 96; De Jongh 1975–6,
76; Lobelle 1976, 514; Białostocki 1977,
62–63; Trzeciak 1977, no. 6; Białostocki
1978, 42–3; Lane 1980, no. 73; Hollanders-
Favart 1981, 79–84; Silver 1984, 162–3;
Harbison 1985, 98–9; Lobelle 1985, 83;
Bauman 1986, 49–50; De Vos 1986, 165–70;
Hull 1988, 21–22, 226–8; Frodl-Kraft 1989,
166–86; Verougstraete-Marcq and Van
Schoute 1989, 149–51; Van Miegroet 1990,
270; Lobelle 1991; De Vos 1991, 203–8;
Ainsworth 1994, 87, Batári 1994, 63–6,
Belting and Kruse 1994, 257–8; De Vos
1994, no. 78; Madou 1994, 51; Martens 1994,
21; Périer-d'Ieteren 1994, 67–77; Ridderbos
1995, 106–11; Verougstraete and Van
Schoute 1997, 280, 282–3; Wilson 1998,
51–2; De Vos 2002, 181–8.

The 'Diptych of Maarten van Nieuwenhove' is without doubt one of the high points in Memling's oeuvre. The figures of the Virgin and the donor are set in an interior extending over both wings with windows on two walls. This is the only devotional diptych by Memling which survives with its original frames and hinges. The lower members of the frames are inscribed, on the Virgin's side, with the name of the donor and the date: 'HOC·OPUS·FIERI·FECIT·MARTINUS·DE·NEWENHOVEN·ANNO·D[O]M[INE]·1487:·' (Maarten van Nieuwenhove had this work made in AD 1487); on the donor's side, with the age of the donor: 'AN°·VERO·ETATIS·SUE:·23:·' (at the age of 23). Both inscriptions end in a stylized dragon, the meaning of which eludes us.

Maarten van Nieuwenhove (died 1500) whose patron saint, St Martin, is featured in the stained-glass window behind him, commissioned the diptych in 1487 when he was 23 years old. Born 11 November 1463, he came from a prominent Bruges family, several members of which held important civic posts or worked for the Burgundian court. When Maarten commissioned this diptych, primarily for private devotion, he undoubtedly looked forward to a

similar career; his elder brother Jan already held the post of city councillor. But historical events determined otherwise. On 15 February 1488, following the future emperor Maximilian I's defeat in Béthune and his subsequent detention in Bruges, Jan van Nieuwenhove, as a member of the supposedly pro-Habsburg city council, was publicly tortured and executed together with other members of the council. Undoubtedly, it was these events which prevented Maarten from entering public office until after Maximilian's victory over the Flemish separatists in 1492. He became a councillor and eventually burgomaster in 1497.

Memling's painting shows no signs of the traumatic events that were to befall the city and the Van Nieuwenhove family; on the contrary, the diptych is bursting with family pride and hope, even more than the roughly contemporary and stylistically closely related 'Triptych of Benedetto Portinari' (see pl. 30). Everything – commission, composition, content – indicates that Maarten van Nieuwenhove intended the diptych to fulfil representational as well as devotional functions. Firstly, he assigned the work at a relatively young age to the most prominent painter in Bruges; secondly, his

personal motto – 'il ya cause' (Not without reason) – and his coat of arms with helm and crest appear between four medallions in the stained-glass window behind the Virgin on the left. In a way, Memling's work anticipates the political role Van Nieuwenhove aspired to by displaying and at the same time legitimizing his portrait, his piety, his descent from a prominent family and his social rank (Wilson 1998).

Interestingly, the patron's request for a diptych combining private devotion with representational functions resulted in one of Memling's most sophisticated compositions. He achieved this without abandoning the usual economy of means characterizing his workshop practice. Here too we find the well-known repertoire of figures and motifs, with only minor variations. The figures of the Virgin and Child follow the same types as those in the 'Triptych of Benedetto Portinari'; only the upper body of the infant Christ, the gesture of the Virgin's left hand, her robe and the angle of her head vary slightly. In the triptych the Virgin is placed in an arcade before a landscape. In the present work she sits in a luxurious interior, the window at the rear of which also opens onto a wide landscape. The parapet on which the Virgin leans is covered with an oriental carpet on which lies a brocaded cushion, providing a seat for the Christ Child. The same motif is found on the centre panel of the 'Triptych of Benedetto Portinari'.

What distinguishes the 'Diptych of Maarten van Nieuwenhove', not only from other works by Memling but from those by early Netherlandish masters in general, is the spatial relationship between the donor and the Virgin. Memling drew a geometric grid on the donor's wing which is visible to the naked eye. De Vos (1994) has shown that this grid, rather than determining linear perspective as was common

## 24  Portrait of a Man (Folco Portinari?)

1487 or later?
Panel (oak), 35 x 25 cm
Florence, Galleria degli Uffizi, inv. 1101

in Florentine painting, reflects the artist's attempt to achieve spatial coherence between the two panels, which stood at an angle somewhere between 135 and 90 degrees from each other. A crucial element in this attempt is supplied by the convex mirror at the left of the Virgin. The image reflected in the mirror clarifies the spatial relationship between the Virgin and the donor (who would see her in profile), and between the Virgin and the viewer (who sees her full face) in that it supplements those details of the room which are outside the picture plane. It should be noted, however, that originally, Maarten was positioned in front of the Virgin, adoring the Child.

Unlike the smoothly painted surfaces of Memling's early paintings, the 'Diptych of Maarten van Nieuwenhove' has clearly visible brushstrokes in the flesh parts (which correspond to the modelling in the upper paint layers) and a style that tends to emphasize contours characteristic of his later works.

PROVENANCE
Venetian art collector and dealer Abbot Luigi Celotti (?); 1836 (?) acquired by the Galleria degli Uffizi; first recorded in the 1863 Uffizi catalogue.
EXHIBITION
Florence 1947, no. 10.
BIBLIOGRAPHY
Warburg 1902, 263–4; Friedländer 1928 (1971), no. 88; Held 1936, 179; Ragghianti 1948, 141; Faggin 1969, no. 104; *Gli Uffizi* 1979, 380; Lane 1980, no. 20; Warburg 1980, 119–20; Collobi-Ragghianti 1990, 63, no. 108; Dülberg 1990, 226, no. 160; Bruges 1994, 202; De Vos 1994, no. 56; Rohlmann 1994, 86–9; Nuttall 2004, 70.

The Uffizi *Portrait of a Man* is most likely the pendant to another male portrait, formerly also in the Uffizi, but lost since 1944. Both men wear similar garments fashionable at the same period, while their portraits also correspond in size, composition and background. The two men turn towards each other; their hands are placed close to the picture plane, one folded over the other. Dülberg (1990) suggested that they originally formed a diptych.

The provenance of the now-lost picture can be traced back to the Venetian abbot-cum-art dealer Luigi Celotti from whom it was purchased by the Uffizi in 1836 together with other paintings (see cat. 8). Although the present portrait is first recorded in the Uffizi catalogue of 1863 (where it is attributed to a German master), it is likely that it came to Florence from the Celotti collection in 1836 together with its presumed pendant.

Aby Warburg (1902) discovered on the back of the lost panel, painted on a dark background, an emblem consisting of the trunk of an oak tree sprouting a new branch, the whole encircled by a banderole inscribed in French: '*De bien en mieuls*' (from good to better). The combination of emblem and personal motto is

often found on the back of portraits of members of the Burgundian-Netherlandish aristocracy whose *vivre noblement* was imitated by the numerous Italian merchants in Flanders. Warburg recognized the same emblem with the same motto, this time in Latin – '*De bono in melius*' – on the back of another Memling portrait, dated 1487, which is also in the Uffizi. This portrait originally formed the right wing of a devotional triptych (De Vos 1994, no. 79) with the Virgin and Child in the centre (now Berlin, Gemäldegalerie) and St Benedict on the left wing.

The two wings came to the Uffizi from the hospital of Santa Maria Nuova, founded by the Portinari family. The correspondence of the two mottos on the lost Uffizi portrait and the right wing of the devotional triptych led Warburg to identify the man as Benedetto Portinari. Moreover, he succeeded in establishing the presence in Bruges of one Benedetto Portinari, who was the youngest son of Pigello Portinari (died 1468), head of the Medici banking branch in Milan. In 1487, the date of the devotional triptych, Benedetto was 21 years old. Pigello was the brother of Tommaso Portinari, who represented Medici interests in Bruges and who supplied Memling and Hugo van der Goes with important commissions (see pl. 2 and fig. 62). After the early death of his father, Benedetto, together with his older brothers Ludovico and Folco, acted on behalf of their uncle Accerito Portinari for the Milan Medici branch, but when in 1496 their uncle retired to Florence, Benedetto and his four-year older brother Folco took over Tommaso's business in Bruges.

De Vos (1994, no. 57) and Rohlmann (1994) rightly proposed that the identical emblems and mottos on the back of the two panels prove that the sitter is one and the same person: Benedetto di Pigello Portinari. Rohlmann (1994) further pointed out that the tree trunk

On the reverse: Flower Still Life
*c.*1485–94
Panel (oak), 29.2 x 22.5 cm
Madrid, Museo Thyssen-Bornemisza, inv. 1938.1

probably alludes to the prematurely deceased father, whereas the sprouting branch signifies the son who continues the family tradition.

The *Portrait of Ludovico Portinari* by the Master of the St Ursula Legend (fig. 9) demonstrates that the exhibited portrait cannot represent Benedetto's eldest brother. Thus De Vos (1994) assumed that the man in the present portrait must be the other brother, Folco. If we take account of Benedetto's and Folco's biographies, the pendant portraits must be placed relatively late in Memling's career. It is possible that Tommaso commissioned the portraits of his nephews before he handed over his business in Bruges to them. They may have sat to Memling on a visit to the city (albeit undocumented) during which Benedetto would have commissioned his devotional triptych. Whereas the latter is entirely consistent with the artist's technique, the present portrait displays stylistic and technical discrepancies, specifically the pastose application of the highlights on the forehead, bridge of the nose and shirt. However, it is possible that these inconsistencies are the result of a later restoration. This is especially evident in the right background, as can be seen from the sharp contour of the man's left shoulder.

PROVENANCE
1822 documented in the collection of William Beckford, Fonthill Abbey, Wiltshire; entered the collection of the Dukes of Hamilton through marriage; 6th Duke of Montrose; Duchess of Montrose, Brodick Castle, Isle of Arran, Scotland (since 1906); 1938 purchased by Baron Heinrich Thyssen.
EXHIBITIONS
New York 1955–6; London 1961, no. 79; Washington *et al.* 1979, no. 25; London 1988, no. 35; Stuttgart 1988–9; Bruges 1994, no. 30.

BIBLIOGRAPHY
Friedländer 1937 (1971), Suppl. 232; Kay 1939, 156–60; Friedländer 1946, 117; Pächt 1948, 54; Friedländer 1949, 59; Fritz 1952, 103–4; Bergström 1956, 13, 296; Sterling 1959, 27; Castelfranchi Vegas 1966, 64; Faggin 1969, no. 101; Castagnola 1971, no. 214; McFarlane 1971, 42 n. 53; Strauss 1972, no. 4; Langemeyer and Peters 1979, 220; Lane 1980, nos. 34–5; Eisler 1989, 106–15; Périer-d'Ieteren 1989, 8–9; Dülberg 1990, 163, 260; De Ridder 1990–91, 65; Batári 1994, 63–6; Belting and Kruse 1994, 263; De Vos 1994, no. 72; De Moor 1995, 2–3; Falkenburg 1997, 149–61; Verougstraete and Van Schoute 1997, 280.

The portrait shows a young man with long, dark hair at prayer, who is depicted at half length, turned to the right. He wears a magnificent white shirt embroidered with gold bands and tied with gold ribbons, over which is placed a black fur cloak with slits for the arms. His finely drawn face is lit from the left, as a thin line of reflected light along the bridge of his nose indicates. The man sits before a diagonally receding wall. An idyllic wooded landscape is glimpsed through an opening on the right, bordered by a red marble column and a low balustrade over which is hung an oriental carpet.

On the reverse of the panel stands in a niche on yet another oriental carpet a maiolica jug, probably from Valencia (generally identified as Italian in previous literature). It holds a bouquet of columbines, irises and lilies, symbolizing Mary's joys and sorrows including the birth and death of Christ. The vase bears Christ's monogram IHS. Pächt (1948) already recognized the importance of the exquisite still life which, although anchored in medieval symbolism, is the precursor of the independent flower still life as it developed in Flanders in the course of the sixteenth century.

The *Portrait of a Young Man at Prayer* is one of Memling's best-preserved

portraits. The work began to receive scholarly attention as late as the mid-1930s, after the overpainting on the reverse had been removed (1933). In 1937 Friedländer published it on the basis of photographs as a work by Memling. Baron Heinrich Thyssen acquired it in 1938.

Friedländer and Pächt (1948) wrongly considered it to be the left wing of a devotional diptych whose right wing would have featured an image of the Virgin. As part of a diptych, the man would have been situated on the 'heraldic right' (i.e. the viewer's left), which would probably have offended fifteenth-century rules of decorum, if indeed not amounted to blasphemy. Devotional diptychs, such as that of Maarten van Nieuwenhove (cat. 23) or the one with the *Virgin and Child with a Donor* in Chicago (pl. 27), show the donor on the (viewer's) right of the Virgin. On the other hand, the man is commonly shown on the heraldic right in marital diptychs (see cat. 5, 9, 22). This also applies to devotional triptychs which feature husband and wife on the wings. In these instances, the man would be on the heraldic right and the woman on the left of the holy image in the centre, as in the portraits of Tommaso Portinari and Maria Baroncelli (pl. 2) and Willem Moreel

and Barbara van Vlaenderberch
(cat. 18). Thus the Thyssen painting
originally must have formed part of
a triptych of which the centre panel
with an image of the Virgin and Child
and the wing with the portrait of the
man's wife are lost (Washington 1979;
Eisler 1989; Dülberg 1990).

Originally, the landscape view on
the right of the Thyssen portrait most
likely extended to the centre panel
and the right wing. From a formal
point of view, the reconstructed
triptych comes closest to the
'Triptych of Benedetto Portinari',
dated 1487 (see pl. 30). For this
reason as well as stylistic similarities
with the 'Moreel Triptych' (cat. 22)
and the 'Diptych of Maarten van
Nieuwenhove' (cat. 23), also dated
1487, De Vos's (1994) suggested date
of c. 1485–90 for the Thyssen panel
is most convincing. The brilliant
technique, efficient application and
confident brushwork are typical of
the artist's late years (see Maryan
Ainsworth's essay).

The identity of the man remains
unknown. Eisler (1989) assumed him
to be Spanish on the basis of an old
inscription, De Vos Italian on the
basis of his costume. In fact, the dress
is not recorded in Italy but rather in
Spain (see the so-called 'Self-Portrait
of Pedro Berruguete' [Madrid, Museo
Lázaro Galdiano]; portrait by the
Master of Sopetrán [Prado]). Judging
by the prominent display of oriental
rugs on both sides of the panel, it is
at least possible that the sitter was
connected with the Spanish wool
and textile industry which became
increasingly prominent in Bruges
at the end of the fifteenth century.

## 26   Portrait of a Man

*c.* 1485–90
Panel (oak), 16 x 12 cm
Banbury, Upton House, Bearsted
Collection (The National Trust), inv. 298

PROVENANCE
Vienna?; art dealer De Burlet, Berlin
(after 1918); Colnaghi, London (1921);
1922 acquired through Knoedler's by
Lord Bearsted.
EXHIBITIONS
London 1924, no. 2; London 1927, no. 50;
Bruges 1939, no. 41; London 1948, no. 30;
London 1953–4, no. 30; London 1955,
no. 70; Bruges 1994, no. 34.
BIBLIOGRAPHY
Friedländer 1927, 212; Friedländer 1928
(1971), no. 87; Friedländer 1939, 132; Faggin
1969, no. 112; Lane 1980, no. 16; De Vos
1994, no. 80; Upton House (Warwickshire)
1995, 55.

The tiny size and unusual shape
of this portrait – first ascribed to
Memling by Friedländer in 1927
– give it a special place in the artist's
work. The paint surface is in excellent
condition: it has perfectly preserved
the rapid yet highly effective way
in which Memling laid down his
colours in thin layers through which
the underdrawing can be made out
with the naked eye. The brilliance
of handling and execution and the
impressive virtuosity displayed in
the rendering of individual elements,
such as the two different types of
fur, leave no room for doubt as to the
accuracy of Friedländer's attribution.

The panel, which undoubtedly
served as the right wing of a
devotional diptych, reveals Memling
to be a master portraitist, able to
create a monumental likeness even
in the tightest of spaces. Among his
portraits, it is closest stylistically
to the 'Diptych of Maarten van
Nieuwenhove' (cat. 23).

De Vos (1994) interpreted the
rounded top of the panel as evidence
of a late date, on the grounds that
portraits of this shape did not
become common in Netherlandish
and German painting until the
sixteenth century. For devotional
works, however, the type had been

*c.* 1490?
Panel (oak), 40 x 25 cm
Vicenza, Museo Civico, inv. 298

introduced substantially earlier.
De Vos's reference to a small portrait
diptych of 1486 attributed to the
Master of the St Ursula Legend
(Antwerp, Koninklijk Museum
voor Schone Kunsten) points up
the historico-cultural context of
Memling's portrait, suggesting that
the shape of the panel being discussed
here was not unusual in Bruges in the
1480s. A point which is overlooked
in De Vos's argument, however, is
that numerous illustrations of altar
worship in illuminated manuscripts
demonstrate that the format was
above all popular in the context
of portable devotional images.
Furthermore, Van Eyck had already
painted several small panels with
rounded tops: his *Virgin and Child
in a Church* (Berlin, Gemäldegalerie)
and 'Maelbeke Madonna' (now
known only from copies) both
confirm that there was a long-
standing tradition in Bruges of small
devotional panels with this shape.

PROVENANCE
    Carlo Vicentini del Giglio (Vicenza);
    1835 bequeathed to the Pinacoteca Civica,
    Vicenza.
BIBLIOGRAPHY
    Burckhardt 1901, III, 738; Arslan 1934, 35;
    Collobi-Ragghianti 1990, no. 114; Barbieri
    1995, 43; Rigoni 1997, 151 n. 130; Avagnina,
    Binotto and Villa 2003, 145–6, no. 23.

Bequeathed to the Pinacoteca Civica
in Vicenza by the Italian porcelain
manufacturer and art patron Carlo
Vicentini del Giglio, this fragment of
a man with a pink has received little
attention in the literature. Although
Jacob Burckhardt (1901) already
mentioned Memling's name in
connection with the fragment, albeit
hesitantly, it was rarely discussed,
even by Italian art historians, and
then mostly as a copy after the
Flemish master (Arslan 1934; Collobi-
Ragghianti 1990). Memling scholars
ignored the painting completely.

The condition of the panel, which
is cut at all sides, is too poor to
allow an attribution to Memling
or his workshop based on stylistic
criteria; nor is such an attribution
meaningful. The heavily abraded
surface is covered with innumerable
retouchings, especially on the
man's clothing. Conversely, the
composition, the man's demeanour,
the conception of the face as well
as the landscape background are
so typical of Memling that it is
worth discussing the fragment in

the context of his workshop. The
most significant evidence pointing to
Memling's workshop is provided by the
underdrawing, which was examined
using infra-red reflectography in
1994 by Molly Faries and myself and
which has since been fully discussed
in the most recent museum catalogue
(Avagnina, Binotto and Villa 2003).
The underdrawing in chalk shows
the same stylistic characteristics as
put forward for Memling by, among
others, Taubert (1975), Ainsworth
(1994), Borchert (1995) and Faries (1997).
The face is delineated in a cursory
manner; the outlines of eyes, the bridge
of the nose, the areas of mouth, chin
and neck are hesitantly defined. With
a few confident lines, some of which
show corrections already at this early
stage, the artist indicates the position
of shoulders, arms and hand as well as
the man's costume. Corrections are
particularly evident in the position of
the right arm and hand. The sketchy
and confident manner of drawing
is closely related to Memling's style.
Moreover, the underdrawing occupies
the same place in the painting process
as it does in Memling's work. Details
drawn on paper or parchment are
copied onto the panel where they may
undergo changes until the final stages
of painting.

It is, however, not possible to
determine whether the present
fragment is by Memling or an
anonymous workshop assistant, nor
is it possible to assign a date to it.
Equally unknown is the fragment's
original pictorial context. Possibly a
wing of a triptych, it could also be
a fragment of a larger single panel.
Collobi-Ragghianti (1990) observed
formal parallels to the allegorical
representation of a young woman in
the Metropolitan Museum (see De Vos
1994, no. 73), which, however, is at
best a product of Memling's workshop
(see Lorne Campbell's essay). Any
connection between the Vicenza
fragment and the Metropolitan
Museum picture can be ruled out
because of their different sizes.

# 28  Portrait of Jacob (?) Obrecht

Dated 1496
Panel (oak), 50.8 x 36.1 cm (including original frame)
Fort Worth, The Kimbell Art Museum, inv. KAM 1993.02

PROVENANCE
Private collection; sale Sotheby's,
New York, 15 January 1993, no. 139;
purchased by The Kimbell Art Museum,
Fort Worth.
EXHIBITION
Bruges 1994, no. 40.
BIBLIOGRAPHY
De Vos 1991, 192–209; Wegman 1991;
Wegman 1993; De Vos 1994, no. 93; Strohm
1994, 43–4; Wegman 1994; Verougstraete
and Van Schoute 1997, 279–80, 283.

The portrait shows the half-length figure of a praying man, turned to the right, set against a blue-green background. He wears a transparent surplice over a light-brown robe with a dark green collar and black lining. The collar is folded under the surplice on one side, revealing the black collar of the laced-up waistcoat beneath. This in turn is worn over a white shirt. A grey fur almuce is placed over the man's left arm, the standard attribute of a canon of a chapter church. The man has straight, brown hair and is not tonsured. His name is written in calligraphic letters in gold leaf on either side of his head: *Ja· Hobrecht*. The frame, which is original, is inscribed with the date of the portrait, 1496, and the age of the sitter, 38. Another inscription on the frame reads *No.·8·J[?]·F·*. This is probably a sixteenth-century inventory number. The frame is marbled in brown-red and shows hinge-marks on the right side.

The sitter was identified by De Vos (1991) as the famous composer Jacob Obrecht (died 1505). De Vos further speculated that the portrait was left unfinished at Memling's death (1494) and completed by his workshop. He proposed that the year on the frame does not refer to the execution of the painting but rather its installation in the context of a diptych, or more likely triptych.

Although the name Obrecht or Hobrecht was not especially common at the time, it was not unique either. Besides the famous composer who was active in Bergen op Zoom (1480–84), Cambrai (1484), Ferrara (1487 and 1504–5), Antwerp (1492–6), and Bruges (1485–91 and 1498–1504), we know of a priest by the same name who studied theology in Leuven in 1470 and died before 1494 (see Wegman 1993).

Against De Vos's identification speaks above all the age of the sitter as given on the frame, which indicates that he must have been born in 1458 or 1459. According to Wegman (1991), the composer Jacob Obrecht was the son of the Ghent city trumpeter Willem Hobrecht (died 1488). After studying theology – his academic degree is documented in 1484 – Jacob Obrecht was active at the church of St Gertrude (Gertrautis) in Bergen op Zoom from 1479/80 to 1484 when he was appointed *succentor* (subcantor) at Cambrai Cathedral. Shortly after that he was given the corresponding post at St Donatian's Church in Bruges. He celebrated his first mass in 1480, suggesting that he must have been ordained shortly before. This did not generally take place until the novice's thirtieth birthday, unless he obtained a dispensation which allowed him to be ordained five years earlier. In the event that Obrecht received such dispensation, he would still have been born in 1454 or 1455, which would have made him 41 or 42 (and not 38, as the inscription says) in 1496, when the portrait was painted. In order to retain the identification of the Fort Worth portrait with the composer, Strohm (1994) proposed the unlikely hypothesis that the painting was commissioned in 1489 on the occasion of Obrecht's appointment to chaplain at St Donatian's and that the age was added to the painting in 1491. He attributed the date 1496 on the frame to the completion of other, secondary tasks connected with the commission and not necessarily with that of the painting itself. According to Strohm, these incongruities were the result of Obrecht's absence from Bruges (he was at Our Lady's in Antwerp between 1492 and 1496 and only returned to Bruges in 1498), of Memling's death and of financial problems. Taking all these inconsistencies into account, it might be worth considering that the man in the portrait is not the famous composer after all but a different man with the name Hobrecht.

Moreover, neither Memling's authorship of the painting nor Bruges as its place of origin is certain. In placing the portrait in Bruges, De Vos (1991) was influenced by his belief that the sitter is the Bruges cleric. Comparing the portrait with works securely attributed to Memling, he further concluded that it comes closer to Memling than to Gerard David, another Bruges painter (see fig. 28). Yet as Maryan Ainsworth observes in this catalogue, the style of the underdrawing, handling and execution does not correspond with Memling's late portraits. The painting, one of the most important recent discoveries in Netherlandish portrait painting of the late fifteenth century, should be assigned to an artist capable of extraordinary technical virtuosity who, however, remains anonymous for the time being. Lorne Campbell (see his essay) suggests a painter active in Antwerp, a proposal consistent with the grisaille figure of a standing female saint on the reverse, which De Vos attributed to a painter of the early sixteenth century associated with the circle of Quentin Massys.

| | Catalogue no./ plate no. | De Vos 1994 | Wood | Number of boards | Number of annual rings | Youngest ring in board | Earliest possible felling date* | Origin of the wood | Notes |
|---|---|---|---|---|---|---|---|---|---|
| *Man of Sorrow*<br>Melbourne, NG Victoria, 1335/3 | – | DDV 24 | oak | I | 164 | 1411 | 1420 | Baltic | |
| *Virgin and Child*<br>Berlin, Gemäldegalerie, 529D | – | DDV 54 | oak | I | 310 | 1417 | | Baltic | I, II = 1 tree |
| | | | | II | 256 | 1420 | 1429 | | |
| *Adam*<br>Vienna, Kunsthistorisches Museum, 637 | – | DDV 53 | oak | I | 142 | 1421 | 1430 | Baltic | I and I Vienna 638 = 1 tree |
| *Eve*<br>Vienna, Kunsthistorisches Museum, 638 | – | DDV 53 | oak | I | 137 | 1414 | 1430 | Baltic | I and I Vienna 637 = 1 tree |
| *Tommaso Portinari*<br>New York, Metropolitan, 14.40.626 | pl. 2 | DDV 9 | oak | I | 172 | 1411 | | Baltic | |
| | | | | II | 94 | 1423 | 1432 | | |
| *Virgin and Child*<br>Lisbon, Museu Nacional, 1065 | – | DDV 70 | oak | I | 198 | 1426 | 1435 | Baltic | |
| *Portrait of an Old Man*<br>Berlin, Gemäldegalerie, 529C | cat. 5 | DDV 14 | oak | I | 233 | 1430 | 1439 | Baltic | |
| *Portrait of a Man*<br>New York, Frick Collection, 1968.1.169 | cat. 2 | DDV 12 | oak | I | 123+6 | 1439 | 1442 | Baltic | 6 sapwood rings |
| *Presentation in the Temple*<br>Washington, National Gallery, 1961.9.28 | – | DDV B4/1 | oak | I | 175 | 1428 | | Baltic | |
| | | | | II | 183 | 1433 | 1442 | | |
| *Man in a Red Hat*<br>Frankfurt, Städel, 945 | cat. 1 | DDV 7 | oak | I | 228 | 1442 | 1451 | Baltic | |
| *Donor*<br>New York, Morgan Library | – | DDV 5 | oak | I | 76 | 1442 | 1451[1] | Baltic | Boards with the same exponent are from the same tree |
| *Angel of the Annunciation*<br>Bruges, Groeningemuseum, 1254.1 | – | DDV 5 | oak | I | 122 | 1438 | 1451[1] | | |
| *Virgin of the Annunciation*<br>Bruges, Groeningemuseum, 1255.1 | – | DDV 5 | oak | I | 132 | 1439 | 1451[1] | | |
| *Portrait of a Man*<br>Montreal Museum of Fine Arts, 56.1129 | cat. 19 | DDV 46 | oak | I | 133 | 1444 | 1453 | Baltic | |
| *Man with a Pink*<br>New York, Morgan Library | cat. 20 | DDV 26 | oak | I | 259 | 1445 | 1454 | Baltic | |

| | | | | | | | | | |
|---|---|---|---|---|---|---|---|---|---|
| *Maria Baroncelli*<br>New York, Metropolitan, 14.40.627 | pl. 2 | DDV 9 | oak | I<br>II | 169<br>31 | 1448<br>– | 1457 | Baltic | |
| *Virgin and Child*<br>Kansas City, Nelson-Atkins Museum, 44.43 | – | DDV 1 | oak | I<br>II | 197<br>85 | 1452<br>1441 | 1461 | Baltic | I, II = 1 tree |
| *Passion of Christ*<br>Turin, Galleria Sabauda, 8 | – | DDV 11 | oak | I<br>II | 144<br>151 | 1452<br>1452 | 1461 | Baltic | |
| *Virgin and Child with Saints and Angels*<br>New York, Metropolitan, 14.40.634 | – | DDV 35 | oak | I<br>II<br>III | 139<br>138<br>109 | 1437<br>1453<br>1427 | <br>1462 | Baltic | |
| *Virgin and Child*<br>Cleveland Museum of Art, 34.29 | – | DDV A7 | oak | I | 166 | 1453 | 1462 | Baltic | |
| *Crucifixion Triptych*<br>Budapest, Szépmüvészeti Múzeum, 124 | – | DDV A5 | oak | | | | | Baltic | |
| Centre panel | | | | I<br>II<br>III | 208<br>128<br>169 | 1431<br>1450<br>1430 | | | |
| Left wing<br>Right wing | | | | I<br>II | 178<br>247 | 1433<br>1456 | <br>1465 | | |
| *Veronica*<br>Washington, National Gallery, 1952.5.46 | – | DDV 50 | oak | I | 221 | 1458 | 1467 | Baltic | |
| *Virgin and Child*<br>Berlin, Gemäldegalerie, 529 | – | DDV 54 | oak | I<br>II | 142<br>226 | 1460<br>1453 | 1469 | Baltic | |
| *Portrait of an Old Woman*<br>Houston, Museum of Fine Arts, 44.530 | cat. 9 | DDV 60 | oak | I | 158 | 1461 | 1470 | Baltic | |
| *Portrait of a Young Man*<br>New York, Metropolitan, 1975.1.112 | cat. 15 | DDV 48 | oak | I | 250 | 1461 | 1470 | Baltic | |
| *Virgin and Child*<br>New York, Metropolitan,<br>Lehman Collection, 1975.1.111 | – | – | oak | I | 140 | 1462 | 1471 | Baltic | |
| *Woman with a Pink*<br>New York, Metropolitan, 49.7.23 | – | DDV 73 | oak | I | 147 | 1465 | 1474 | Baltic | I and I Rotterdam 2470<br>= 1 tree |
| *Two Horses*<br>Rotterdam, Boijmans-Van Beuningen, 2470 | | DDV 73 | oak | I | 131 | 1446 | (1474) | Baltic | I and I New York 49.7.23<br>= 1 tree |
| *Virgin and Child with Angels*<br>Washington, National Gallery, 1937.1.41 | – | DDV 77 | oak | I<br>II | 307<br>117 | 1465<br>1425 | 1474 | Baltic | |
| *Man at Prayer before a Landscape*<br>The Hague, Mauritshuis, 595 | cat. 21 | DDV 40 | oak | I | 167 | 1465 | 1474 | Baltic | |
| *Bathsheba*<br>Stuttgart, Staatsgalerie, 644 | – | DDV 76 | oak | I | 275 | 1469 | 1478 | Baltic | *Bathsheba* and *David* = 1 tree |
| *King David*<br>Stuttgart, Staatsgalerie, 644 | – | DDV 76 | oak | I | 120 | 1306 | (1478) | Baltic | *David* and *Bathsheba* = 1 tree |
| *Anthony, the 'Grand Bâtard' of Burgundy*<br>Dresden, Gemäldegalerie Alte Meister, 801 | – | DDV A6 | oak | I<br>II | 82<br>81 | –<br>– | – | | not datable; I, II = 1 tree |
| *Lamentation*<br>Rotterdam, Boijmans-Van Beuningen, 2471 | – | DDV 16 | | | | | – | | not measurable |

* Based on an average of nine sapwood rings.

**Ainsworth 1989**

M. W. Ainsworth, 'Northern Renaissance Drawings and Underdrawings: A Proposed Method of Study', *Master Drawings* 27 (1989), 5–38.

**Ainsworth 1994**

M. W. Ainsworth, 'Hans Memling as a draughtsman', in *Essays 1994*, 78–87.

**Ainsworth 1998**

M. W. Ainsworth, *Gerard David. Purity of Vision in an Age of Transition*, New York 1998.

**Ainsworth 2003**

M. W. Ainsworth, 'Review of Early Netherlandish Drawings from Jan van Eyck to Hieronymus Bosch', *Master Drawings* 43 (2003), 305–16.

**Ames-Lewis 1989**

F. Ames-Lewis, 'On Domenico Ghirlandaio's Responsiveness to North European Art', *Gazette des Beaux-Arts* 114 (1989), 111–12.

**Arndt 1968**

K. Arndt, *Altniederländische Malerei in der Gemäldegalerie Berlin*, Berlin 1968.

**Arslan 1934**

E. Arslan, *La Pinacoteca Civica di Vicenza*, Rome 1934.

**Avagnina, Binotto and Villa 2003**

M. E. Avagnina, M. Binotto and G. C. F. Villa (eds.), *Pinacoteca Civica di Vicenza. Dipinti dal XIV al XVI secolo*, Milan 2003.

**Baetjer 1995**

K. Baetjer, *European Paintings in The Metropolitan Museum of Art by Artists Born in or before 1865: A Summary Catalogue*, 3 vols., New York 1995.

**Baldass 1942**

L. von Baldass, *Hans Memling*, Vienna 1942.

**Barbieri 1995**

F. Barbieri, *Il Museo del Palazzo Chiericati*, Vicenza 1995.

**Batári 1994**

F. Batári, 'The "Memling Carpets"', in *Essays 1994*, 63–6.

**Bauman 1986**

G. C. Bauman, 'Early Flemish Portraits, 1425–1525', *Metropolitan Museum of Art Bulletin* 43, no. 4 (spring 1986).

**Bazin 1939**

G. Bazin, *Memling*, Paris 1939.

**Behling 1957**

L. Behling, *Die Pflanze in der Mittelalterliche Tafelmalerei*, Weimar 1957, 67–8.

**Belting and Eichberger 1983**

H. Belting and D. Eichberger, *Jan van Eyck als Erzähler. Frühe Tafelbilder im Umkreis der New Yorker Doppeltafel*, Worms 1983.

**Belting and Kruse 1994**

H. Belting and C. Kruse, *Die Erfindung des Gemäldes: Das erste Jahrhundert der niederländischen Malerei*, Munich 1994.

**Bergström 1956**

I. Bergström, *Dutch Still-Life Painting in the Seventeenth Century*, New York 1956.

**Białostocki 1966**

J. Białostocki, *Les Primitifs flamands. Les Musées de Pologne*, Brussels 1966.

**Białostocki 1968**

J. Białostocki, 'Memling et Angelo Tani: le portrait du Musée des Offices no. 1102', in *Miscellanea Jozef Duverger*, 1, Ghent 1968, 102–9.

**Białostocki 1977**

J. Białostocki, 'Man and Mirror in Painting: Reality and Transcience', in *Studies in Late Medieval and Renaissance Painting in Honor of Millard Meiss*, New York 1977, 1, 61–72.

**Białostocki 1978**

J. Białostocki, 'Bemerkungen zu zwei Werken Memlings im baltischen Raum', *Nordelbingen* 47 (1978), 39–45.

**Van Biervliet 1994**

L. Van Biervliet, 'De roem van Memling', in *Essays 1994*, 109–24.

**Blockmans 1995**

W. Blockmans, 'The Creative Environment: Incentives to and Functions of Bruges Art Production', in M. W. Ainsworth (ed.), *Petrus Christus in Renaissance Bruges*, Turnhout 1995, 11–20.

**Blockmans and Prevenier 1997**

W. Blockmans and W. Prevenier, *De Bourgondiërs. De Nederlanden op weg naar eenheid, 1384–1530*, Amsterdam/Leuven 1997.

**Blum 1969**

S. N. Blum, *Early Netherlandish Triptychs, a Study in Patronage*, Berkeley/Los Angeles 1969.

**Bock 1900**

F. Bock, *Memling Studien*, Düsseldorf 1900.

**Bode 1895**

W. Bode, 'Die Fürstlich Liechtenstein'sche Galerie in Wien: Die altniederländische und deutsche Schule', *Die Graphischen Künste* 13 (1895).

**Bode 1896**

W. Bode, 'Ein männliches Bildnis von Hans Memling in der Berliner Galerie', *Jahrbuch der Preussischen Kunstsammlungen* 17 (1896), 3–4.

**Bode 1907**

W. Bode, *The Rodolphe Kann Collection*, Paris 1907.

**Bode 1908**

W. Bode, 'Un ritratto del Memling al Louvre', *Rassegna d'arte* 8 (1908), 154.

**Bode 1924**

W. Bode, [Review of] G. Habich, *Die Medaillen der italienischen Renaissance*, Stuttgart/Berlin 1923, *Zeitschrift für Numismatik* 34 (1924), 380–94.

**Bode 1930**

W. Bode, *Mein Leben*, 2 vols., Berlin 1930.

**Bode and Friedländer 1912**

W. Bode and M. J. Friedländer, *Die Gemäldesammlung des Herrn Carl von Hollitscher in Berlin*, Berlin 1912.

**Borchert 1993**

T.-H. Borchert, 'Some Observations on the Lübeck Altarpiece by Hans Memling', in Van Schoute and Verougstraete-Marcq 1993, 91–100.

**Borchert 1994**

T.-H. Borchert, *Untersuchungen zum Frühwerk des Malers Hans Memling*, thesis, University of Bonn, 1994, 3–26.

**Borchert 1995**

T.-H. Borchert, 'De geschiedenis van het verzamelen van de Oudnederlandse schilderkunst in de negentiende eeuw', in Ridderbos 1995, 140–88.

**Borchert 1995a**

T.-H. Borchert, 'Memling's Antwerp "God the Father" with Music-Making Angels', in Van Schoute and Verougstraete 1995, 153–68.

**Borchert 1995b**

T.-H. Borchert, 'Le dessin sous-jacent chez Memling', in Lorentz 1995, 80–90.

**Borchert 1996**

T.-H. Borchert, Review of De Vos 1994, *Kunstchronik* 49 (1996), 17–28.

**Borchert 1997**

T.-H. Borchert, '"A moving expression of Most Sincere Devotion and Piety". Aspects of Memling's rediscovery in early 19th century Germany', in Verougstraete and Van Schoute 1997, 133–46.

**Borchert 1997a**

T.-H. Borchert, 'Large- and Small-Scale Paintings and their Underdrawing in the Memling Group', in Van Schoute and Verougstraete 1997, 211–22.

**Borchert 2002**

T.-H. Borchert, 'Handel en Wandel. Brugge en de Europese Kunst', in Vandewalle 2002, 137–48.

**Bousmanne 1997**

B. Bousmanne, '*Item a Guillaume Wyelant aussi enlumineur*'. *Willem Vrelant. Un aspect de l'enluminure dans les Pays-Bas méridionaux sous le mécénat des ducs de Bourgogne Philippe le Bon et Charles le Téméraire*, Turnhout 1997.

**Bredius 1895**

A. Bredius, *Musée royal de La Haye (Mauritshuis). Catalogue raisonné des tableaux et des sculptures*, The Hague 1895.

**Broos 1987**

B. Broos, *Meesterwerken in het Mauritshuis*, The Hague 1987.

**Brown 1998**

D. A. Brown, *Leonardo da Vinci. Origins of a genius*, New Haven/London 1998.

**Brown 2001**

D. A. Brown (ed.), *Virtue and Beauty. Leonardo's 'Ginevra de Benci' and Renaissance Portraits of Women* (exh. cat. National Gallery of Art), Washington 2001.

**De Brou 1860**

C. de Brou, 'Peintures erronément attribuées à Memling', *Revue universelle des arts* 11 (1860), 192–201.

**Bruges 1994**

D. De Vos (ed.), *Hans Memling* (exh. cat. Groeningemuseum), 2 vols., Bruges 1994.

**Bruges 1998**

M. Martens (ed.), *Bruges et la Renaissance. De Memling à Pourbus* (exh. cat. Groeningemuseum), 2 vols., Bruges 1998.

**Bruges 2002**

T.-H. Borchert (ed.), *The Age of Van Eyck. The Mediterranean World and Early Netherlandish Painting 1430–1530* (exh. cat. Stedelijke Musea, Bruges), Ghent/London 2002.

Bruyn 1961
J. Bruyn, 'Hans Memling (omstreeks 1433–1494). Mansportret', *Openbaar Kunstbezit* 5 (1961), 2a–b.

Buchner 1953
E. Buchner, *Das deutsche Bildnis der Spätgotik und der frühen Dürerzeit*, Berlin 1953.

Burckhardt 1879
J. Burckhardt, *Der Cicerone. Eine Anleitung zum Genuss der Kunstwerke Italiens*, 4. Auflage, unter Mitwirkung des Verfassers und anderer Fachgenossen bearbeitet von Dr. Wilhelm Bode, II, Leipzig 1879.

Burckhardt 1901
J. Burckhardt, *Der Cicerone. Eine Anleitung zum Genuss der Kunstwerke Italiens*, IV, Leipzig 1901.

Buttin 1954
C. Buttin, 'La flèche des juges du camp', *Armes anciennes* 1 (1954), 59.

Cadogan 2000
J. K. Cadogan, *Domenico Ghirlandaio*, New Haven/London 2000.

Cahn 1962
E. B. Cahn, 'Eine Münze und eine Medaille auf zwei Bildnisporträts des 15. Jahrhunderts', *Zeitschrift für schweizerische Archäologie und Kunstgeschichte* 22 (1962), 66–72.

Campbell 1977
L. Campbell, 'A Double Portrait by Memling', *Connoisseur* 194 (1977), no. 781, 186–9.

Campbell 1981
L. Campbell, 'Notes on Netherlandish pictures in the Veneto in the fifteenth and sixteenth centuries', *The Burlington Magazine* 123 (1981), 467–73.

Campbell 1983
L. Campbell, 'Memling and the followers of Verrocchio', *The Burlington Magazine* 125 (1983), 675–6.

Campbell 1985
L. Campbell, *The Early Flemish Pictures in the Collection of Her Majesty the Queen*, Cambridge 1985.

Campbell 1990
L. Campbell, *Renaissance Portraits. European Portrait Painting in the 14th, 15th and 16th Centuries*, New Haven/London 1990.

Campbell 1995
L. Campbell, 'Review of *Hans Memling. The Complete works*, by Dirk de Vos, London 1994', *The Burlington Magazine* 137 (1995), 253–4.

Campbell 1995b
L. Campbell, 'Memling's Creative Process as seen in his Paintings in the National Gallery, London', in Van Schoute and Verougstraete 1995, 149–52.

Campbell 1998
L. Campbell, *National Gallery Catalogues. The Fifteenth Century Netherlandish Schools*, London 1998.

Castagnola 1971
J. C. Ebbinge-Wubben, C. Salm, C. Sterling and R. Heinemann, *Sammlung Thyssen Bornemisza (Schloss Rohoncz, Castagnola)*, Zurich 1971.

Castelfranchi Vegas 1966
L. Castelfranchi Vegas, 'I rapporti Italia-Fiandra II', *Paragone* 201 (1966), 42–69.

Castelfranchi Vegas 1983
L. Castelfranchi Vegas, *Italia e Flandria nella pittura del Quattrocento*, Milan 1983.

Collobi-Ragghianti 1990
L. Collobi-Ragghianti, *Dipinti Fiamminghi in Italia 1420–1570*, Bologna 1990.

Comblen-Sonkes 1988
M. Comblen-Sonkes, with I. Vandevivere, *Les Primitifs flamands. Les Musées de l'Institut de France*, Brussels 1988.

Comblen-Sonkes and Lorentz 1995
M. Comblen-Sonkes and P. Lorentz, *Musée du Louvre, Paris*, II (Corpus de la Peinture des anciens Pays-Bas méridionaux et de la Principauté de Liège au XVe siècle, 17), Brussels 1995.

Conway 1921
M. Conway, *The Van Eycks and their followers*, London 1921.

Crowe and Cavalcaselle 1857 (1878)
J. A. Crowe and G. B. Cavalcaselle, *The Early Flemish Painters: Notices of their Lives and Works*, London 1857 (3rd edn. London 1878).

Crowe and Cavalcaselle 1875
J. A. Crowe and G. B. Cavalcaselle, *Geschichte der altniederländischen Malerei (bearbeitet von Anton Springer)*, Leipzig 1875.

Csaki 1909
M. Csaki, *Baron Brukenthalisches Museum in Hermannstadt. Führer durch die Gemäldegalerie*, Hermannstadt 1909.

Davidson 1971
B. Davidson, 'Tradition and Innovation: Gentile da Fabriano and Hans Memling', *Apollo* 93 (1971), 378–85.

Demus, Klauner and Schütz 1981
K. Demus, F. Klauner, F. and K. Schütz, *Katalog der Gemäldegalerie. Flämische Malerei von Jan van Eyck bis Pieter Bruegel d. Ä. Kunsthistorisches Museum*, Vienna 1981.

Denucé 1931
J. Denucé, *Kunstuitvoer in de 17de eeuw te Antwerpen. De firma Forchoudt*, Antwerp 1931.

Depoorter 1934–5
A. Depoorter, 'Brugsche Kunstenaars van voorheen', *Burgerwelzijn* (1934–5).

Descamps 1769
J. B. Descamps, *Voyage pittoresque de la Flandre et du Brabant*, Paris 1769.

Devliegher 1997
L. Devliegher, 'Une copie du Triptyque de la crucifixion de Memling pour l'abbé Jan Crabbe', in Verougstraete and Van Schoute 1997, 31–3.

Dewitte 1985
A. Dewitte, 'Muziekleven in Brugge in de 16e eeuw', *Vlaanderen* 34 (1985), no. 3, 156–9.

Dhanens 1984
E. Dhanens, 'Tussen de van Eycks en Hugo van der Goes', *Academiae Analecta. Mededelingen van de Koninklijke Academie voor Wetenschappen, Letteren en Schone Kunsten van België* 45 (1984) no. 1, 15.

Doehlemann 1911
K. Doehlemann, 'Die Entwicklung der Perspektive in der Altniederländische Kunst', *Repertorium für Kunstwissenschaft* 34 (1911), 392–422, 500–535.

Duclos 1913
A. Duclos, *Bruges. Histoire et souvenirs*, Bruges 1913.

Dülberg 1990
A. Dülberg, *Privatporträts*, Berlin 1990.

Durand-Gréville 1913
E. Durand-Gréville, 'Notes sur les Primitifs néerlandais du Louvre', *Gazette des Beaux-Arts* (1913), 415–30.

Dussart 1892
H. Dussart, *Fragments inédits de Romboudt de Doppere découverts dans un manuscrit de Jacques de Meyere. Chronique brugeoise de 1491 à 1498*, Bruges 1892.

Eisler 1961
C. T. Eisler, *Les Primitifs flamands. New England Museums*, Brussels 1961.

Eisler 1989
C. T. Eisler, *The Thyssen-Bornemisza Collection. Early Netherlandish Painting*, London 1989.

Ekserdjian and Stevens 1988
D. Ekserdjian and M. A. Stevens, *Old Master Paintings from the Thyssen-Bornemisza Collection* (exh. cat. Royal Academy of Arts, London), London/Milan 1988.

Essays 1994
D. De Vos (ed.), *Hans Memling. Essays* (exh. cat. Stedelijke Musea, Bruges, vol. 2), Ghent 1994.

Esther 1976
J. P. Esther, 'Monumentenbeschrijving en bouwgeschiedenis', in *Sint Janshospitaal Brugge. 1188/1976*, Bruges 1976, I, 259–337.

Everaert 1864
J. Everaert, *Inventaris Sint-Janshospitaal 1864* (OCMW-archief, karton 384, nos. 115–24).

Evers 1972
H. G. Evers, *Dürer bei Memling*, Munich 1972.

Faggin 1969
G. T. Faggin, *L'opera completa di Memling*, Milan 1969.

Fahy 1969
E. Fahy, 'The earliest works of Fra Bartolommeo', *The Art Bulletin* 51 (1969), 142–54.

Falkenburg 1997
R. Falkenburg, 'The Scent of Holyness: Notes on the Interpretation of Botanical Symbolism in Paintings by Hans Memling', in Verougstraete and Van Schoute 1997, 149–61.

Faries 1997
M. Faries, 'The Underdrawing of Memling's Last Judgment Altarpiece in Gdańsk', in Verougstraete and Van Schoute 1997, 243–59.

Fétis 1863
E. Fétis, 'Notice historique', in *Catalogue descriptif et historique du Musée royal de Belgique*, Brussels 1863.

Fétis 1889
E. Fétis, *Catalogue descriptif et historique des tableaux anciens. Musées royaux de Peinture et Sculpture de Belgique*, 6th rev. edn., Brussels 1889.

Fierens-Gevaert 1909
H. Fierens-Gevaert, *La peinture en Belgique. Les primitifs flamands*, II, Brussels 1909.

**Fierens-Gevaert 1912**
H. Fierens-Gevaert, 'Correspondance de Belgique: L'exposition de la miniature à Bruxelles', *Gazette des Beaux-Arts*, 4e sér., 7 (1912), 194–5.

**Fierens-Gevaert 1922**
H. Fierens-Gevaert, *La Peinture à Bruges. Guide historique et critique*, Brussels/Paris 1922.

**Fierens-Gevaert 1929**
H. Fierens-Gevaert, *Histoire de la peinture flamande*, III, Paris/Brussels 1929.

**Fletcher 1981**
J. Fletcher, 'Marcantonio Michiel: his friends and collection', *The Burlington Magazine* 123 (1981), 453–67, 602–8.

**Fletcher 1989**
J. Fletcher, 'Bernardo Bembo and Leonardo's portrait of Ginevra de' Benci', *The Burlington Magazine* (1989), 811–16.

**Flint 1925**
R. Flint, 'John N. Willys Collection', *International Studio* 80 (1925), 363–7.

**Förster 1853**
E. Förster, *Geschichte der deutschen Kunst*, 5 vols., Leipzig 1853.

**Friedländer 1903**
M. J. Friedländer, 'Die Brügger Leihausstellung von 1902', *Repertorium für Kunstwissenschaft* 26 (1903), 66–91, 147–75.

**Friedländer 1916**
M. J. Friedländer, 'The Altman Memlings in the Metropolitan Museum of Art', *Art in America* 4 (1916), 187–95.

**Friedländer 1920**
M. J. Friedländer, 'About Some of Hans Memling's Pictures in the United States', *Art in America* 8 (1920), 107–16.

**Friedländer 1928**
M. J. Friedländer, *Die altniederländische Malerei*. VI: *Memling und Gerard David*, Berlin 1928.

**Friedländer 1937 (1971)**
M. J. Friedländer, *Die altniederländische Malerei*, XIV: *Pieter Bruegel und Nachträge zu den früheren Bänden*, Leiden 1937.

**Friedländer 1946**
M. J. Friedländer, 'Noch etwas über das Verhältnis Roger van der Weyden zu Memling', *Oud Holland* 61 (1946), 11–19.

**Friedländer 1949**
M. J. Friedländer, *Hans Memling*, Amsterdam 1949.

**Friedländer 1971**
M. J. Friedländer, *Early Netherlandish Painting*. 6a–6b: *Hans Memling and Gerard David*, Leiden/Brussels 1971.

**Frimmel 1888**
T. Frimmel (ed.), *Der Anonimo Morelliano. Marcantonio Michiels 'Notizia d'opere del disegno'* (Quellschriften für Kunstgeschichte und Kunsttechnik, N.F.1), Vienna 1888.

**Frimmel 1904**
T. Frimmel, *Handbuch der Gemäldekunde*, Leipzig 1904.

**Fritz 1952**
R. Fritz, 'Aquilegia, die symbolische Bedeutung der Akelei', *Wallraf-Richartz-Jahrbuch* 14 (1952), 103–4.

**Frodl-Kraft 1989**
E. Frodl-Kraft, 'Das Bildfenster im Bild. Glasmalereien in den Interieurs der frühen Niederländer', in *Bau und Bildkunst im Spiegel internationaler Forschung*, Berlin 1989, 166–81.

**Galassi 1999**
M. C. Galassi, 'La Crucifixion de Hans Memling du Museo Civico de Vicence: Apports de l'examen en réflectographie dans l'infrarouge', *AHAA* 21 (1999), 7–24.

**Garrido 1997**
C. Garrido, 'Hans Memling. Le *Triptyque de l'Adoration des Mages* du Musée du Prado, Quelques considérations techniques', in Verougstraete and Van Schoute 1997, 221–33.

**Geirnaert 1987–9**
N. Geirnaert, 'Hans Memlings Kruisigingstriptiek voor Johannes Crabbe. Nieuwe gegevens over bestemming en datering', *Brugge Stedelijke Musea. Jaarboek 1987–1989*, 174–83.

**Geirnaert 1992**
N. Geirnaert, 'Bruges and European Intellectual Life in the Middle Ages', in V. Vermeersch (ed.), *Bruges and Europe*, Antwerp 1992, 225–51.

**Geirnaert 1997**
N. Geirnaert, 'Le *Triptyque de la Crucifixion* de Hans Memling pour Jean Crabbe, abbé de l'abbaye des Dunes (1457–1488). Témoignage des documents contemporains', in Verougstraete and Van Schoute 1997, 25–30.

**Van Gelder 1951**
J. G. van Gelder, '"Fiamminghi e Italia" at Bruges, Venice and Rome', *The Burlington Magazine* 93 (1951), 324–7.

**Geldhof 1975**
J. Geldhof, *Pelgrims, dulle lieden en vondelingen te Brugge 1275–1975*, Bruges 1975.

**Geldhof 1976**
J. Geldhof, 'De kloostergemeenschap van het Sint-Janshospitaal, 1459–1975', in *Sint-Janshospitaal Brugge. 1188/1976*, Bruges 1976, I, 169–93.

**Gli Uffizi 1979**
*Gli Uffizi. Catalogo Generale*, Florence 1979.

**Glück 1923**
G. Glück, *Die Fürstlich Liechtensteinsche Bildergalerie*, Vienna 1923.

**Gmelin 1996**
H. G. Gmelin, 'Rode, Hermen', in *The Dictionary of Art*, 34 vols., London 1996, XXVI, 506–7.

**Goethgebeur 1997**
N. Goethgebeur, 'Étude technique de trois tableaux de Memling', in Verougstraete and Van Schoute 1997, 261–8.

**Goetinck and Ryckaert 1976**
M. Goetinck and M. Ryckaert, 'Brugse archivalia betreffende Hans Memling', in *Sint-Janshospitaal Brugge 1188/1976* (exh. cat.), Bruges 1976, II, 495–501.

**Grams-Thieme 1988**
M. Grams-Thieme, *Lebendige Steine. Studien zur niederländischen Grisaillemalerei des 15. und frühen 16. Jahrhunderts* (Böhlau Diss. zur Kunstgeschichte 27), Cologne/Vienna 1988.

**Grosshans 1975**
R. Grosshans, in *Gemäldegalerie Staatliche Museen Preussischer Kulturbesitz Berlin. Katalog der ausgestellten Gemälde des 13.–18. Jahrhunderts*, Berlin 1975.

**Groten 1993**
M. Groten, 'Stefan Lochner in Kölner Quellen', in *Stefan Lochner. Werk und Wirkung* (exh. cat.), Cologne 1993, 12.

**Hand and Wolff 1986**
J. O. Hand and M. Wolff, *The Collections of the National Gallery of Art, Systematic Catalogue, Early Netherlandish Painting*, Washington 1986.

**Harbison 1985**
K. Harbison, 'Visions and Meditations in Early Flemish Painting', *Simiolus* 15 (1985), 87–118.

**Haskell 1993**
F. Haskell, *History and its Images: Art and the Interpretation of the Past*, New Haven/London 1993.

**Hasse 1975**
M. Hasse, *Hans Memlings Lübecker Altarschrein*, Lübeck 1975.

**Vanden Haute 1913**
C. vanden Haute, *La corporation des peintres de Bruges*, Kortrijk [1913].

**Heinrich 1954**
T. A. Heinrich, 'The Lehman Collection', *Metropolitan Museum of Art Bulletin* 12 (April 1954).

**Held 1936**
J. S. Held, 'A Diptych by Memling', *The Burlington Magazine* 68 (1936), 176–9.

**Heller 1976**
E. Heller, *Das altniederländische Stifterbild*, Munich 1976.

**Hepburn 1986**
F. Hepburn, *Portraits of the Later Plantagenets*, Woodbridge 1986.

**Hinterding and Horsch 1989**
E. Hinterding and F. Horsch, '"A small but choice collection": the art gallery of King Willem II of the Netherlands (1792–1849)', *Simiolus* 19 (1989).

**Hinz 1974**
B. Hinz, 'Studien zur Geschichte des Ehepaarbildnisses', *Marburger Jahrbuch für Kunstwissenschaft* 19 (1974), 139–214.

**Hoetink 1985**
H. R. Hoetink *et al.*, *The Royal Picture Gallery Mauritshuis* (Art Treasures of Holland), Amsterdam/New York 1985.

**Hollanders-Favart 1981**
D. Hollanders-Favart, 'Le dessin sous-jacent chez Memling: le diptyque dit de Martin van Nieuwenhove (1487). Apport de la photographie à l'infrarouge', in *Archivum Artis Lovaniense. Bijdragen tot de geschiedenis van de kunst der Nederlanden opgedragen aan Prof. Em. Dr. J. K. Steppe*, Leuven 1981, 79–84.

**Houston 1981**
P. C. Marzio (ed.), *A Permanent Legacy. 150 Works from the Collection of the Museum of Fine Arts, Houston*, Houston 1981.

**Huisman 1923**
G. Huisman, *Memlinc*, Paris 1923.

**Hulin de Loo 1902**
G. Hulin de Loo, *Bruges 1902. Exposition de Tableaux Flamands des XIVe, XVe et XVIe siècles. Catalogue critique*, Ghent 1902.

**Hulin de Loo 1927**
G. Hulin de Loo, 'Le portrait du médailleur par Hans Memlinc: Jean de Candida et non Niccolo Spinelli', in *Festschrift für Max J. Friedländer zum 60. Geburtstag*, Leipzig 1927, 103–8.

Hull 1981
V. J. Hull, *Hans Memling's Painting for the Hospital of Saint John in Bruges*, New York 1981.

Hull 1988
V. J. Hull, 'Devotional aspects of Hans Memlinc's paintings', *Southeastern College Art Conference Review* 11 (1988), 207–13.

Hymans 1902
H. Hymans, 'L'exposition des primitifs flamands à Bruges', *Gazette des Beaux-Arts* 44 (1902).

Jahn 1980
W. Jahn, *Der Maler Hans Memling aus Seligenstadt*, Michelstadt 1980.

Janssens 1997
A. Janssens, 'De schilder Hans Memling, als Brugs poorter financieel, sociaal en politiek doorgelicht', *Handelingen van het genootschap voor geschiedenis gesticht onder de naam 'Société d'Émulation' te Brugge* 134 (1997), 65–89.

Janssens 2003
A. Janssens, 'Willem Moreel en Hans Memling. Bijdrage tot het onderzoek naar de schilderijen van Memling in opdracht van de familie Moreel', *Handelingen van het genootschap voor geschiedenis gesticht onder de naam 'Société d'Émulation' te Brugge* 140 (2003), 66–110.

Janssens de Bisthoven 1959
A. Janssens de Bisthoven, *Les Primitifs flamands. Corpus de la Peinture des anciens Pays-Bas méridionaux au quinzième siècle. 1: Le Musée Communal des Beaux-Arts Bruges*, Antwerp 1959.

Janssens de Bisthoven 1981/1983
A. Janssens de Bisthoven, with M. Baes-Dondeyne and D. De Vos, *De Vlaamse Primitieven. Stedelijk Museum voor Schone Kunsten (Groeningemuseum) Brugge*, Brussels 1981. French edn. 1983.

Johnston 1988
C. Johnston, 'Paintings from the Liechtenstein Collection', *Apollo* 12/ (1988) 313, 319–27.

De Jongh 1975–6
E. de Jongh, 'Pearls of virtue and pearls of vice', *Simiolus* 8 (1975–6), 69–97.

Kaemmerer 1899
L. Kaemmerer, *Memling*, Bielefeld/Leipzig 1899.

Kantorowicz 1939–40
E. Kantorowicz, 'The Este Portrait by Roger van der Weyden', *Journal of the Warburg and Courtauld Institutes* 3 (1939–40), 165–80.

Kathke 1997
P. Kathke, *Porträt und Accessoire. Eine Bildnisform im 16. Jahrhundert*, Berlin 1997.

Kay 1939
A. Kay, *Treasure Trove in Art*, London/Leiden 1939.

Keverberg 1818
[Baron] de Keverberg de Kessel, *Ursula, Princesse britannique d'après la légende et les peintures d'Hemling*, Ghent 1818.

Klein 1994
P. Klein, 'Dendrochronological analysis of panels of Hans Memling', in *Essays* 1994, 101–3.

Klein 1997
P. Klein, 'Dendrochronological Analyses of Panels of Hans Memling and his Contemporaries', in Verougstraete and Van Schoute 1997, 287–95.

Klein 2003
P. Klein, 'Dendrochronological Analyses of Netherlandish Paintings', in M. Faries and R. Spronk (eds.), *Recent Developments in the Technical Examination of Early Netherlandish Painting: Methodology, Limitations, and Perspectives*, Cambridge (Mass.)/Turnhout 2003, 65–81.

Koch 1992
R. A. Koch, 'Hans Memling, Portrait of Gilles Joye …', in G. C. Bauman and W. A. Liedtke (eds.), *Flemish Paintings in America: a Survey of Early Netherlandish and Flemish Paintings in the Public Collections of North America* (Flandria extra muros), Antwerp 1992, 74–5.

Koreny 2002
F. Koreny et al., *Altniederländische Zeichnungen von Jan van Eyck bis Hieronymus Bosch* (exh. cat. Rubenshuis), Antwerp 2002.

Koreny 2003
F. Koreny, 'Drawings by Vrancke van der Stockt', *Master Drawings* 43 (2003), 266–92.

Koster 2002
M. L. Koster, 'Italy and the North. A Florentine Perspective', in Bruges 2002, 78–90.

Küther 1978
W. Kuther, 'Seligenstadt, Mainz und das Reich', *Archiv für mittelrheinische Kirchengeschichte* 30 (1978), 9–57

Lane 1980
B. G. Lane, *Hans Memling, Werkverzeichnis. Die grossen Meister der Malerei*, Frankfurt/Berlin/Vienna 1980.

Lane 1991
B. G. Lane, 'The Patron and the Pirate: The Mystery of Memling's Gdańsk *Last Judgement*', *The Art Bulletin* 73 (1991), 623–40.

Lane 1997
B. G. Lane, 'The Question of Memling's Training', in Verougstraete and Van Schoute 1997, 53–85.

Lane 1999
B. G. Lane, 'Memling and the workshop of Verrocchio', in Van Schoute and Verougstraete 1999, 243–50.

Langemeyer and Peters 1979
G. Langemeyer and H. A. Peters, *Das Stilleben in Europa*, Münster 1979.

Laskin and Pantazzi 1987
M. Laskin Jr. and M. Pantazzi, *European and American Painting, Sculpture, and Decorative Arts*, 1: 1300–1800, Ottawa 1987.

Lavalleye 1939
J. Lavalleye, *Hans Memling*, Bruges 1939.

Leprieur 1909
P. Leprieur, 'Portrait d'une vieille femme par Memlinc', *Revue de l'art ancien et moderne* 26 (1909), 241–50.

Lightbown 1978
R. Lightbown, *Sandro Botticelli*, 2 vols., London 1978.

Lightbown 1992
R. Lightbown, *Piero della Francesca*, London 1992.

Lobelle 1976
H. Lobelle, 'Hans Memling (ca. 1433–1494) en zijn werken bewaard in het hospitaal', in *Sint-Janshospitaal Brugge 1188/1976* (exh. cat.), Bruges 1976, II, 502–19.

Lobelle 1985
H. Lobelle-Caluwé, *Het Memlingmuseum in het Sint-Janshospitaal te Brugge*, Bruges 1985.

Lobelle 1987
H. Lobelle-Caluwé, *Memlingmuseum* (Musea Nostra), Brussels 1987.

Lobelle 1991
H. Lobelle-Caluwé, 'Beknopte historiek van de Brugse OCMW-collecties', *Brugge Stedelijke Musea. Jaarboek 1989–1990*, 265–84.

Lobelle 1997
H. Lobelle-Caluwé, 'Hans Memling: A Self-Portrait?', in Verougstraete and Van Schoute 1997, 43–52.

Lorentz 1995
P. Lorentz, 'Memling portraitiste: le Portrait d'une femme âgée', in *Hans Memling au Louvre* (Les dossiers du Musée du Louvre), Paris 1995, 67–74.

Lorentz 1995a
P. Lorentz, *Hans Memling au Louvre*, Paris 1995.

Lübbeke 1991
I. Lübbeke, *The Thyssen-Bornemisza Collection. Early German Painting 1350–1550*, London 1991.

Lugt 1968
F. Lugt, *Musée du Louvre. Inventaire général des dessins des écoles du Nord. Maîtres des anciens Pays-Bas nés avant 1550*, Paris 1968.

Madou 1994
M. Madou, 'Kleding en mode in het oeuvre van Memling', in *Essays* 1994, 50–62.

Marlier 1934
G. Marlier, *Memlinc*, Brussels 1934.

Martens 1992
D. Martens, 'Le triptyque de Bientina: motifs et sources', *Gazette des Beaux-Arts* 134 (1992), 149–64

Martens 1994
M. P. J. Martens, 'De opdrachtgevers van Hans Memling', in *Essays* 1994, 14–29.

Martens 1994b
M. P. J. Martens, 'Petrus Christus: A Cultural Biography', in *Petrus Christus. Renaissance Master of Bruges*, New York 1994, 15–23.

Martens 1995
M. P. J. Martens, 'Discussion', in M. W. Ainsworth (ed.), *Petrus Christus in Renaissance Bruges*, Turnhout 1995, 43–51.

Martens 1995b
M. P. J. Martens, 'Patronage and Politics: Hans Memling's Saint John Altarpiece and the "Process of Burgundization"', *Colloque 10*, Louvain-la-Neuve 1995, 109–76.

Martens 1997
M. P. J. Martens, 'Hans Memling and his patrons: a cliometrical approach', in Verougstraete and Van Schoute 1997, 35–41.

Martens 2000
D. Martens, 'Der Brügger Meister der Lucialegende. Bilanz der Forschungen und Neue Hypothesen', *Die Kunstbeziehungen Estlands mit den Niederlanden in den 15.–17. Jahrhunderten (Essti Kunstisidemed Madalmaadega 15.–17. Sjandil)*, Tallinn 2000, 59–82.

Martens and Van Miegroet 1984
M.P.J. Martens and H.J. van Miegroet, 'Nieuwe inzichten omtrent de omstreden du Cellier-diptiek, toegeschreven aan Hans Memling', *Gentse Bijdragen tot de Kunstgeschiedenis en Oudheidkunde* 26 (1981–4), 59–88.

Martin 1935
W. Martin, *Musée royal de tableaux Mauritshuis à La Haye. Catalogue raisonné des tableaux et sculptures*, The Hague 1935.

Martin and Ravaud 1995
E. Martin and E. Ravaud, 'La radiographie des peintures de chevalet', *Techne* 2 (1995), 158–64.

Matache 1999
M. Matache, 'Portrait of a young man reading', in *The National Museum of Art of Romania. Guide to the Collection*, Paris 1999, 184–5.

Mauritshuis 1914
*Musée Royal de La Haye. Catalogue raisonné des tableaux*, The Hague 1914. Rev. edn. of Bredius 1895.

McFarlane 1971
K.B. McFarlane, *Hans Memling*, Oxford 1971.

Michel 1953
E. Michel, *Musée national du Louvre. Catalogue Raisonné des Peintures du Moyen-Age, de la Renaissance et des Temps Modernes. Peintures flamandes du XVᵉ et du XVIᵉ siècle*, Paris 1953.

Michiels 1845
A. Michiels, *Histoire de la peinture flamande et hollandaise*, II, Brussels 1845, 288–375.

Van Miegroet 1989
H. van Miegroet, *Gerard David*, Antwerp 1989.

Van Miegroet 1990
H. van Miegroet, 'Nieuwe criteria voor datering van het œuvre van Hans Memling', in *Handelingen van het congres van de Federatie van Nederlandstalige Verenigingen voor Oudheidkunde en Geschiedenis van België te Hasselt 19–22 augustus 1982*, II, Mechelen 1990, 267–78.

Miller 1995
J.I. Miller, 'Miraculous Childbirth and the Portinari Altarpiece', *The Art Bulletin* 77 (1995), 249–61.

De Mirimonde 1974
A.P. de Mirimonde, 'Le symbolisme du rocher et de la source chez Joos van Cleve, Dirck Bouts, Memling, Patenier, C. van den Broeck (?), Sustris et Paul Bril', *Jaarboek Koninklijk Museum voor Schone Kunsten Antwerpen* (1974), 73–100.

Molinier 1904
E. Molinier, *Collection du Baron Albert Oppenheim. Tableaux et objets d'art*, Paris 1904.

Van Molle 1960
F. van Molle, *Identification d'un portrait de Gilles Joye attribué à Memlinc*, Brussels 1960.

De Moor 1995
A. de Moor, '"Oosterse" tapijten op de schilderijen van Hans Memling', *Gentse Bijdragen tot de Kunstgeschiedenis en Oudheidkunde* 30 (1995), 1–8.

Moschini Marconi 1955
S. Moschini Marconi, *Gallerie dell'Academia di Venezia. Opere d'Arte dei secoli XIV e XV*, 1955.

Nepi Scirè and Valcanover 1985
G. Nepi Scirè and F. Valcanover, *Gallerie dell'Accademia di Venezia*, Milan 1985.

New York 1998
M.W. Ainsworth and K. Christiansen (eds.), *From Van Eyck to Bruegel. Early Netherlandish Painting in The Metropolitan Museum of Art*, New York 1998.

Nickel 1968
H. Nickel, 'Ceremonial Arrowheads from Bohemia', *Journal of the Metropolitan Museum of Art* 1 (1968).

Nieuwenhuys 1843
C.J. Nieuwenhuys, *Description de la galerie de S.M. le Roi des Pays-Bas*, Brussels 1843.

Nuttall 1992
P. Nuttall, 'The Patrons of the Chapels at the Badia Fiesolana', *Studi di storia dell'arte* 3 (1992), 97–112.

Nuttall 2002
P. Nuttall, '"Lacking only breath". Italian Responses to Netherlandish Portraiture', in Bruges 2002, 198–211.

Nuttall 2004
P. Nuttall, *From Flanders to Florence. The Impact of Netherlandish Painting, 1400–1500*, New Haven/London 2004.

Pächt 1948
O. Pächt, *The Master of Mary of Burgundy*, London 1948.

Pächt 1994
O. Pächt, *Altniederländische Malerei: von Rogier van der Weyden bis Gerard David*, ed. M. Rosenauer, Munich 1994.

Panofsky 1953
E. Panofsky, *Early Netherlandish Painting: its Origins and Character*, Cambridge 1953.

Parmentier 1938
R.A. Parmentier, *Indices op de Brugsche Poorterboeken*, 2 vols., Bruges 1938.

Passavant 1833
J.P. Passavant, *Kunstreise durch England und Belgien*, Frankfurt 1833.

Passavant 1841
J.P. Passavant, 'Beiträge zur Kenntnisse der altniederländischen Malerschulen des 15ten und 16ten Jahrhunderts', *Kunstblatt* 22 (1841), 9–10, 14–16, 18–20, 33–5, 39–42, 46–7, 49–50.

Pauwels 1963
H. Pauwels, *Catalogue Musée Groeninge*, Bruges 1963.

Périer-D'Ieteren 1989
C. Périer-D'Ieteren, 'Un tableau inédit d'Adriaen Isenbrant: une Vierge et Enfant trônant et la copie interprétative', *Belgisch Tijdschrift voor Oudheidkunde en Kunstgeschiedenis* 58 (1989), 5–21.

Périer-D'Ieteren 1994
C. Périer-D'Ieteren, 'La technique de Memling et sa place dans l'évolution de la peinture flamande du XVᵉ siècle', in *Essays* 1994, 67–77.

Polli and Koppel 2004
K. Polli and G. Koppel, *Low Sky, Wide Horizon. Art of the Low Countries in Estonia*, Tallinn 2004.

Pope-Hennessy 1966
J. Pope-Hennessy, *The Portrait in the Renaissance*, Washington 1966.

Răchiteanu 1975
C. Răchiteanu, *Muzeul de artă al Republicii Socialiste Romania. Catalogul Galeriei de artă universala*, III: *Pictura Tarilor de Jos*, Bucharest 1975.

Ragghianti 1948
C.L. Ragghianti, *Arte fiamminga e olandese dei secoli XV e XVI* (exh. cat.), Florence 1948.

De Ridder 1990–91
J.H.A. de Ridder, 'Kijkend naar het "Lam Gods", Agla en Akelei', *Gentse Bijdragen tot de Kunstgeschiedenis en Oudheidkunde* 29 (1990–91), 57–68.

Ridderbos 1995
B. Ridderbos and H. van Veen, *"Om iets te weten van de oude meesters". De Vlaamse Primitieven – herontdekking, waardering en onderzoek*, Nijmegen 1995.

Rigoni 1997
C. Rigoni, 'Fiammingi a Vicenza', in C. Limentani Virdis, *La pittura fiamminga nel Veneto e nell'Emilia*, Verona 1997, 133–65.

Ring 1913
G. Ring, *Niederländische Bildnismalerei*, Leipzig 1913.

Ringbom 1965
S. Ringbom, *Icon to Narrative: The Rise of the Dramatic Close-Up in Fifteenth-Century Devotional Painting*, Åbo 1965.

Rohlmann 1994
M. Rohlmann, *Auftragskunst und Sammlerbild. Altniederländische Tafelmalerei im Florenz des Quattrocento*, Alfter 1994.

Rohlmann 1995
M. Rohlmann, 'Memling's Pagagnotti triptych', *The Burlington Magazine* 137 (1995), 438–45.

Rotsaert 1974
J. Rotsaert, 'Altaarmetamorphose', *Het Brugs Ommeland* 14 (1974), 12–21.

Ryckaert 1994
M. Ryckaert, 'Het huis van Memling in Brugge', in *Essays* 1994, 104–8.

Sander 1989
J. Sander, 'The acquisition of paintings and drawings at the Willem II auction by the Städel Kunstinstitut, Frankfurt', *Simiolus* 19 (1989), 123–35.

Sander 1993
J. Sander, *Niederländische Gemälde im Städel, 1400–1550*, Mainz 1993.

Sander 1995
J. Sander, *Die Entdeckung der Kunst. Niederländische Kunst des 15. und 16. Jahrhundert in Frankfurt (Städelsches Kunstinstitut und Städtische Galerie)*, Mainz 1995.

**Schlegel 1802–4 (1959)**
F.-W. Schlegel, *Ansichten und Ideen von der christlichen Kunst* [originally published in *Europa Gemälde-Beschreibungen aus Paris und den Niederländen in den Jahren 1802 bis 1804*], *Kritische Gesamtausgabe*, ed. H. Eichner, IV, Paderborn 1959.

**Schnaase 1834**
C. Schnaase, *Niederländische Briefe*, Stuttgart/Tübingen 1834.

**Schneeman 1991**
L. Schneeman, 'The Brukenthal Museum in Sibiu. The State of Research of its Flemish and Dutch Collection', *Belgisch Tijdschrift voor Oudheidkunde en Kunstgeschiedenis* 60 (1991), 39–54.

**Schneider 1992**
N. Schneider, *Porträtmalerei. Hauptwerke europäischer Bildniskunst 1420–1670*, Cologne 1992.

**Schöne 1939**
W. Schöne, 'Hans Memling. Zur Ausstellung seines Lebenswerkes in Brügge', *Pantheon* 12 (1939), 291–9.

**Van Schoute and Verougstraete 1993**
R. Van Schoute and H. Verougstraete, *Le dessin sous-jacent et la technologie dans la peinture, Colloque IX: Dessin sous-jacent et pratiques d'atelier*, Louvain-la-Neuve 1993.

**Van Schoute and Verougstraete 1995**
R. Van Schoute and H. Verougstraete, *Le dessin sous-jacent et la technologie dans la peinture, Colloque X: Le dessin sous-jacent dans le processus de création*, Louvain-la-Neuve 1995.

**Van Schoute and Verougstraete 1997**
R. Van Schoute and H. Verougstraete, *Le dessin sous-jacent et la technologie dans la peinture, Colloque XI: Perspectives*, Louvain-la-Neuve 1997.

**Van Schoute and Verougstraete 1999**
R. Van Schoute and H. Verougstraete, *Le dessin sous-jacent et la technologie dans la peinture, Colloque XII: La peinture dans les Pays-Bas au 16⁰ siècle*, Leuven 1999.

**Schouteet 1955**
A. Schouteet, 'Nieuwe teksten betreffende Hans Memling', *Belgisch Tijdschrift voor Oudheidkunde en Kunstgeschiedenis* 24 (1955), 81–4.

**Schouteet 1989**
A. Schouteet, *De Vlaamse Primitieven te Brugge. Bronnen voor de schilderkunst te Brugge tot de dood van Gerard David (A–K)* (Fontes Historiae Artis Neerlandicae, ser. 2, vol. 1), Brussels 1989.

**Shearman 1983**
J. Shearman, *The Early Italian Pictures in the Collection of Her Majesty the Queen*, Cambridge 1983.

**Silver 1984**
L. Silver, *The Paintings of Quentin Massys*, Oxford 1984.

**Sjöblom 1928**
A. Sjöblom, *Die koloristische Entwicklung in der Niederländischen Malerei des XV. und XVI. Jahrhunderts*, Berlin 1928.

**Smeyers 1997**
M. Smeyers, 'Analecta Memlingiana', in Verougstraete and Van Schoute 1997, 171–94.

**Sosson 1965**
J.-P. Sosson, 'Les Primitifs flamands de Bruges et les premiers albums de reproductions photographiques', *Bulletin IRPA/KIK* 8 (1965), 223–31.

**Sosson 1966**
J.-P. Sosson, *Les Primitifs flamands. Les Primitifs flamands de Bruges, apports des archives contemporaines (1815–1907)*, Brussels 1966.

**Spronk 1998**
R. Spronk, 'Jan Provoost', in Bruges 1998, I, 94–6.

**Stein 1909**
H. Stein, 'Antonello da Messina', *Gazette des Beaux-Arts* (4⁰ pér.) I (1909).

**Stein 1926**
W. Stein, 'Die Bildnisse von Roger van der Weyden', *Jahrbuch der Preussischen Kunstsammlungen* 47 (1926), 1–37.

**Sterling 1957**
C. Sterling, *Exposition de la collection Lehman de New York*, Paris 1957.

**Sterling 1959**
C. Sterling, *La Nature morte de l'antiquité à nos jours*, Paris 1959.

**Sterling 1973**
C. Sterling, 'Les émules des Primitifs', *Revue de l'Art* 21 (1973), 80–93.

**Sterling et al. 1998**
C. Sterling *et al.*, *The Robert Lehman Collection II: Fifteenth- to Eighteenth-Century European Paintings*, New York/Princeton 1998.

**Strasser 1961**
H. W. Strasser, 'Hans Memling te Seligenstadt', *Handelingen van het Genootschap voor geschiedenis 'Société d'Émulation' te Brugge* 98 (1961), 97–100.

**Strauss 1972**
K. Strauss, 'Keramikgefässe, insbesondere Fayencegefässe auf Tafelbildern der deutschen und niederländischen Schule des 15. und 16. Jahrhunderts', *Keramik-Freunde der Schweiz. Mitteilungsblatt* 84 (1972), 7.

**Strohm 1985**
R. Strohm, *Music in Late Medieval Bruges*, Oxford 1985.

**Strohm 1990**
R. Strohm, *Music in Late Medieval Bruges*, revised edn, Oxford 1990.

**Strohm 1994**
R. Strohm, 'Music, ritual and painting in fifteenth-century Bruges', in *Essays* 1994, 30–44.

**Strohmer 1943**
E. V. Strohmer, *Die Gemäldegalerie der Fürsten Liechtenstein in Wien*, Vienna 1943.

**Stroo and Syfer-d'Olne 1996**
C. Stroo and P. Syfer-d'Olne, *The Flemish Primitives. I: The Master of Flémalle and Rogier van der Weyden Groups. Catalogue of Early Netherlandish Painting in the Royal Museums of Fine Arts of Belgium*, Brussels 1996.

**Stroo et al. 1999**
C. Stroo, P. Syfer-d'Olne, A. Dubois and R. Slachmuylders, *Catalogue of Early Netherlandish Painting in the Royal Museums of Fine Arts of Belgium, The Flemish Primitives. II: The Dirk Bouts, Petrus Christus, Hans Memling and Hugo van der Goes Groups*, Brussels 1999.

**Sutton 1954**
D. Sutton, 'Flemish Paintings at the Royal Academy', *Les Arts Plastiques* 6 (1954), no. 6.

**Teodosiu 1977**
A. Teodosiu, 'Analiza fizica si chimica factor hotaritor in cercetarea si conservarea unei opere de arta', *Revista muzeelor si monumentelor* 3 (1977).

**Thiébaut 1993**
D. Thiébaut, *Le 'Christ à la colonne' d'Antonello da Messina* (Les dossiers du musée du Louvre), Paris 1993, 92–109.

**De Tolnay 1941**
C. de Tolnay, 'Flemish Paintings in the National Gallery of Art', *Magazine of Art* 34 (1941), 186, 200.

**Trizna 1976**
J. Trizna, *Michel Sittow peintre revalais de l'école brugeoise (1468–1525/26)* (Les Primitifs flamands, Corpus, 1), Brussels 1976.

**Trzeciak 1977**
P. Trzeciak, *Hans Memling*, Berlin/Warsaw 1977.

**Vandenbroeck 1985**
P. Vandenbroeck, *Koninklijk Museum voor Schone Kunsten Antwerpen. Catalogus schilderijen 14e en 15e eeuw*, Antwerp 1985.

**Van der Velden 1997**
H. Van der Velden, 'Petrus Christus's Our Lady of the Dry Tree', *Journal of the Warburg and Courtauld Institutes* 60 (1997), 89–110.

**Vandewalle 1997**
A. Vandewalle, 'À propos du lieu de naissance de Memling', in Verougstraete and Van Schoute 1997, 19–24.

**Vandewalle 2002**
A. Vandewalle (ed.), *Les marchands de la Hanse et la banque des Médicis. Bruges, marché d'échanges culturels en Europe* (exh. cat.), Bruges 2002.

**Vasari 1878–85**
G. Vasari, *Le Vite de' più eccellenti pittori, scultori ed architettori …*, ed. G. Milanesi, 9 vols., Florence 1878–85.

**Venice 1999**
B. Aikema and B. L. Brown (eds), *Renaissance Venice and the North. Crosscurrents in the Time of Bellini, Dürer and Titian* (exh. cat.), Venice 1999.

**Verougstraete and Van Schoute 1997**
H. Verougstraete-Marcq, R. Van Schoute and M. Smeyers (eds), *Memling Studies. Proceedings of the International Colloquium, Bruges, 10–12 November 1994*, Leuven 1997.

**Verougstraete-Marcq and Van Schoute 1989**
H. Verougstraete-Marcq and R. Van Schoute, *Cadres et supports dans la peinture flamande aux 15⁰ et 16⁰ siècles*, Heure-le-Romain 1989.

**Viaene 1963**
A. Viaene, 'Een Brugs Vademecum voor Rome- en Jeruzalemvaarders samengesteld door Rombout de Doppere 1491', *Handelingen van het Genootschap 'Société d'Émulation' te Brugge* 100 (1963), 304–6.

**Viaene 1976**
A. Viaene, 'Vijf eeuwen ontmoeting met het Sint-Janshospitaal', in *Sint-Janshospitaal Brugge 1188/1976* (exh. cat.), Bruges 1976, I, 225–46.

**Voll 1906**
K. Voll, *Die altniederländische Malerei von Jan van Eyck bis Memlinc*, Leipzig 1906.

**Voll 1909**
K. Voll, *Memling: Des Meisters Gemälde*, Stuttgart/
Leipzig 1909.

**Voll 1923**
K. Voll, *Die altniederländische Malerei von Jan van Eyck bis
Memling*, Leipzig 1923.

**De Vos 1982**
D. De Vos, 'Het verzamelaarsmerk van Peter Stevens
(1590–1668) en diens aantekeningen over 15de-eeuwse Brugse
meesters', *Jaarboek Brugge Stedelijke Musea* (1982), 253–63.

**De Vos 1986**
D. De Vos, 'De constructie van Memlings van Nieuwenhove-
portret, een probleem van interpretatie van de voorbereidende
tekening', *Oud Holland* 100 (1986), 165–70.

**De Vos 1991**
D. De Vos, 'Een belangrijk portret van Jacob Obrecht
ontdekt: een werk uit de nalatenschap van het atelier van
Hans Memling?', *Brugge Stedelijke Musea. Jaarboek 1989–1990*,
192–209.

**De Vos 1994**
D. De Vos, *Hans Memling. The Complete Works*, Ghent/
London/New York 1994.

**De Vos 1999**
D. De Vos, *Rogier van der Weyden. The Complete Works*,
Antwerp/London/New York 1999.

**De Vos 2002**
D. De Vos, *The Flemish Primitives. The Masterpieces*, Antwerp/
Amsterdam 2002.

**Waagen 1854**
G. F. Waagen, *Art Treasures in Great Britain, Being an Account of
the Chief Collections of Paintings, Drawings, Sculptures, Illuminated
Mss.*, 3 vols., London 1854.

**Waagen 1857**
G. F. Waagen, *Galleries and Cabinets of Art in Great Britain*,
London 1857.

**Waagen 1862**
G. F. Waagen, *Handbuch der Geschichte der Malerei.
I: Die deutschen und niederländischen Malerschulen*,
Stuttgart 1862.

**Waldman 2001**
L. A. Waldman, 'New Documents for Memling's Portinari
Portraits in the Metropolitan Museum of Art', *Apollo* 153
(February 2001), 28–33.

**Wallen 1983**
B. Wallen, *Jan van Hemessen*, Ann Arbor 1983.

**Warburg 1902**
A. Warburg, 'Flandrische Kunst und florentinische
Frührenaissance', *Jahrbuch der Königlich Preussischen
Kunstsammlungen* 23 (1902), 247–66.

**Warburg 1932**
A. Warburg, *Gesammelte Schriften*, Leipzig/Berlin 1932.

**Warburg 1980**
A. Warburg, *Ausgewählte Schriften und Würdigungen*, Baden-
Baden 1980.

**Ward 1971**
J. L. Ward, 'A proposed Reconstruction of an Altarpiece by
Rogier van der Weyden', *The Art Bulletin* 53 (1971), 27–35.

**Wauters 1883**
A. J. Wauters, 'Découverte d'un tableau de Memling daté de
1472', *Journal des Beaux-Arts et de la Littérature* 25 (1883), 172.

**Wauters 1893**
A. J. Wauters, *Sept études pour servir à l'histoire de Hans Memling*,
Brussels 1893.

**Weale 1861**
W. H. J. Weale, 'Documents authentiques concernant la vie,
la famille, et la position sociale de Jean Memlinc, découverts
à Bruges', *Journal des Beaux-Arts* 3 (1861), 20–28, 34–6, 45–9,
53–5.

**Weale 1864–5**
W. H. J. Weale, 'Généalogie de la famille Moreel', *Le Beffroi* 2
(1864–5), 179–96.

**Weale 1871**
W. H. J. Weale, *Hans Memlinc, zijn leven en zijne schilderwerken:
eene schets*, Bruges 1871.

**Weale 1901a**
W. H. J. Weale, *Hans Memling*, London 1901.

**Weale 1901b**
W. H. J. Weale, *Hans Memling: biographie, tableaux conservés
à Bruges*, Bruges 1901.

**Weale 1903**
W. H. J. Weale, 'The Early Pictures of the Netherlands as
Illustrated by the Bruges Exhibition of 1902', *The Burlington
Magazine* 1 (1903), 41–52, 202–17, 329–40; 2 (1903), 35–42,
326–32.

**Weale and Brockwell 1912**
W. H. J. Weale and M. Brockwell, *The Van Eycks and their Art*,
London 1912.

**Wegman 1991**
R. C. Wegman, 'Het "Jacob Hobrecht" portret: enkele
biografische observaties', *Musica antiqua* 8 (1991), 153–4.

**Wegman 1993**
R. C. Wegman, *Obrecht in Missa*, dissertation, Amsterdam
1993.

**Wegman 1994**
R. C. Wegman, *Born for the Muses, The Life and Masses of Jacob
Obrecht*, Oxford 1994.

**Wiesflecker 1971**
Hermann Wiesflecker, *Kaiser Maximilian I., Das Reich,
Österreich und Europa an der Wende zur Neuzeit. Band I. Jugend,
Burgundisches Erbe und Römisches Königtum bis zur Alleinherrschaft
1459–1493*, Vienna 1971.

**Wilson 1998**
J. Wilson, *Painting in Bruges at the Close of the Middle Ages:
Studies in Society and Visual Culture*, University Park (Pa.) 1998.

**Winkler 1924**
F. Winkler, *Die altniederländische Malerei*, Berlin 1924.

**Winkler 1928**
F. Winkler, 'An Unknown Portrait of a Woman by Memling',
*Apollo* 7 (1928), 9–12.

**Winkler 1964**
F. Winkler, *Das Werk des Hugo van der Goes*, Berlin 1964.

**Wolff 1998**
M. Wolff, 'The Southern Netherlands, Fifteenth and
Sixteenth Centuries', in C. Sterling *et al.* 1998, 61–124.

**Woods Marsden 1999**
J. Woods Marsden, *Renaissance Self-portraiture*, London/
New Haven 1999.

**Wurzbach 1910**
A. von Wurzbach, *Niederländisches Künstler-Lexikon*, II, Vienna
1910, 142.

**Wuyts 1969**
L. Wuyts, 'Aantekeningen bij een vermeend portret van Jan
Lefevre door Rogier van der Weyden', *Koninklijk Museum voor
Schone Kunsten Antwerpen. Jaarboek* (1969), 61–96.

# Exhibitions

Amsterdam 1945
  Weerzien der meesters.

Amsterdam and Brussels 1951
  Bourgondische Pracht / Le siècle de Bourgogne.

Amsterdam and Rotterdam 1946
  Van Jan van Eyck tot Rubens.

Antwerp 1930
  Exposition Universelle. Exposition d'Art flamand ancien.

Berlin 1906–8
  Semi-permanent display.

Bern 1926
  Exposition de l'art belge ancien et moderne au Musée des Beaux-Arts et à la Kunsthalle de Berne.

Bordeaux 1954
  Flandres, Espagne, Portugal.

Bruges 1902
  Exposition des Primitifs flamands et d'art ancien.

Bruges 1939
  Memling Exhibition.

Bruges 1953
  Het Portret in de Oude Nederlanden.

Bruges 1960
  Le siècle des Primitifs flamands.

Bruges 1969
  Primitifs flamands anonymes.

Bruges 1976
  Sint-Janshospitaal Brugge 1188/1976.

Bruges 1994
  Hans Memling. five centuries of fact and fiction.

Bruges 1998
  Bruges and the Renaissance. Memling to Pourbus.

Bruges 2002
  Jan van Eyck, de Vlaamse Primitieven en het Zuiden 1430–1530.

Bruges, Venice and Rome 1951
  I Fiamminghi e l'Italia.

Brussels 1912
  Exposition de la miniature.

Brussels 1950
  Chefs-d'Œuvre des Musées de Berlin.

Brussels 1951
  See Amsterdam and Brussels 1951.

Brussels 1961
  Les plus beaux portraits de nos musées.

Chicago 1933
  A Century of Progress. Exhibition of Paintings and Sculpture Lent from American Collections.

Colorado Springs 1951–2
  Paintings and Bronzes in the Collection of Mr. Robert Lehman.

Copenhagen 1931
  Udstilling naf Belgisk Kunst grd. xv.–xx. Aardhundrede.

Detroit 1960
  Flanders in the Fifteenth Century: Art and Civilization. Masterpieces of Flemish Art: Van Eyck to Bosch.

Dijon 1951
  Le grand siècle des Ducs de Bourgogne.

Dijon 1960
  La chartreuse de Champmol, foyer d'art au temps des ducs de Valois.

Florence 1947
  Mostra d'Arte fiammingha ed olandese dei secoli XV e XVI.

Florence 1952
  Seconda Mostra Nazionale delle opere d'arte recuperate.

Frankfurt 1995
  Die Entdeckung der Kunst. Niederländische Kunst des 15. und 16. Jahrhunderts in Frankfurt.

London 1892
  Exhibition of Pictures by Masters of the Netherlandish and Allied Schools.

London 1924
  Burlington Fine Arts Club.

London 1927
  Exhibition of Flemish and Belgian Art 1300–1900, organized by the Anglo-Belgian Union (Burlington House).

London 1946–7
  Exhibition of the King's Pictures.

London 1948
  Five Centuries of European Painting.

London 1953–4
  Flemish Art 1300–1700.

London 1954
  Marlborough Fine Art.

London 1955
  Whitechapel Art Gallery.

London 1962
  London, Treasures from the Royal Collection.

London 1988
  Old Master Paintings from the Thyssen-Bornemisza Collection (Royal Academy).

Lucerne 1948
  Meisterwerke aus den Sammlungen des Fürsten von Liechtenstein.

Madrid 1958–9
  Arte flamenco en las colecciones españolas.

Manchester 1857
  Art Treasures of the United Kingdom.

Manchester 1957
  European Old Masters.

Manchester 1968
  Exhibition of Paintings from Sir Thomas Barlow's Collection.

New York 1929
  Loan Exhibition of Flemish Primitives in Aid of the Free Milk Fund for Babies.

New York 1935
  Knoedler & Co.

New York 1939
  Masterpieces of Art. New York World's Fair.

New York 1942
  Flemish Primitives.

New York 1955–6
  Paintings Lent from the Castle Rohoncz Museum.

New York 1961
  Schaeffer Galleries. Twenty-fifth Anniversary (1936–1961).

New York 1973
  Dutch Couples: Pair Portraits by Rembrandt and his Contemporaries.

New York 1998
  From Van Eyck to Bruegel. Early Netherlandish Painting in the Metropolitan Museum of Art.

Paris 1904
  Exposition des Primitifs français au Palais du Louvre (Pavillon Marsan) et à la Bibliothèque Nationale.

Paris 1923
  Exposition de l'art belge ancien et moderne.

Paris 1935
  De van Eyck à Bruegel.

Paris 1947
  Les Primitifs flamands.

Paris 1952–3
  Le Portrait dans l'Art flamand de Memling à van Dyck.

Paris 1995
  Hans Memling au Louvre.

Paris, Kiev, Leningrad, Moscow and Minsk 1976
  Chefs-d'œuvre de musées des Etats-Unis de Giorgione à Picasso/West European and American Painting from the Museums of the USA.

Rome 1950
  Seconda Mostra Nazionale delle opere recuperate in Germania.

Schaffhausen 1955
  Meisterwerke flämischer Malerei. Hundert Gemälde aus der Blütezeit der Malerei in Flandern von van Eyck bis Rubens.

Stuttgart 1988–9
  Meisterwerke der Sammlung Thyssen-Bornemisza.

The Hague 1945
  Nederlandsche Kunst van de xvde en xvide eeuw.

The Hague 1997
  Art on Wings. Celebrating the Reunification of a Triptych by Gerard David.

Venice 1946
  I Capolavori dei Musei Veneti.

Venice 1999
  Renaissance Venice and the North. Crosscurrents in the Time of Bellini, Dürer and Titian.

Washington et al. 1979
  Old Master Paintings from the Collection of Baron Thyssen-Bornemisza.

Solario, Andrea 77, 81
Sonnenburg, Hubert von 100
Spinelli, Niccolò di Forzore 160
Stevens, Peter 51
Stockt, Vrancke van der 20
Strozzi, Filippo 22
Strozzi, Niccolò 157
Styrne, Luca 12
Summonte, Pietro 77

Tanagli, Caterina 22, 50, 51, 153
Tani, Agnolo 22, 25–6, 32, 50, 51, 52, 69, 158, 170
Tornabuoni, Giovanna 78
Traut, Hans 87, 89
Tucher, Hans and Elsbeth 89

Valckenaere, Konrad de 13
Varwere, Willem van 13
Verhanneman, Hannekin 14
Verrocchio, workshop of 77, 77, 165
Villa, Oberto 20
Visen, Charles de 54, 55, 57, 137, 171
Vlaenderberch, Barbara van (alias Van Hertsvelde) 35, 52, 58, 133, 139, 167, 168–9, 172
Vrelant, Willem 14, 16, 19, 41

Weyden, Rogier van der 12, 16, 19, 20, 26, 27, 28, 31, 33, 35, 42, 44, 47, 59, 60, 62, 64, 66, 67, 70, 73, 99, 151, 153, 156, 159, 163, 167
Willemszoon, Anne 20, 23, 51, 52, 66
Winckele, Jan van 65, 66, 74, 165
Winter, Willem de 20, 51, 52
Wolgemut, Michael 88, 89
Woodville, Elizabeth 55, 55–6

Photos are to be credited to the owners of the works of art except as indicated below. Any copyright-holders to whom inaccurate acknowledgement has been made are invited to contact the publisher.

Basle, Kunstmuseum Basel – Martin Bühler p. 56
Berlin, BpK p. 16
Berlin, BpK – Jörg P. Anders p. 43, 63, 70b, 112, 118, 145b, 155a
Bruges, Hugo Maertens p. 24, 25, 50, 138, 139, 172
Brussels, KIK/IRPA p. 105a
Brussels, Speltdoorn p. 22, 59, 121, 132, 133, 157, 168
Chicago, The Art Institute of Chicago 1993 p. 70d, 71, 142
Chicago, The Art Institute of Chicago – Gift of Arthur Sachs p. 71, 142b/c
Copenhagen, SMK Foto p. 147
Dresden, SKD Estel Klut 2004 p. 81b
Edinburgh, National Galleries of Scotland – Antonia Reeve p. 85
Florence, Index p. 97, 144, 174
Florence, Scala p. 75b, 84b
Florence, Scala – courtesy Ministero Beni e Attività Culturali 1990 p. 122, 158; 1991 p. 84a/b; 1992 p. 76a/b; 1994 p. 78
Florence, Soprintendenza per il Polo Museale Fiorentino p. 2c, 70a/c, 83a, 125, 145a/c/d, 161, 176
The Hague, Royal Cabinet of Paintings Mauritshuis p. 137, 171
Jacksonville (Fl), SuperStock Inc. p. 44a
London, Courtesy of Dickinson Ltd. p. 120, 156
London, The National Gallery Picture Library p. 14, 15, 17a/b, 46b, 48, 53, 64, 141
London, The National Trust Photo Library p. 146, 176; Christopher Hurst p. 75
London, The Royal Collection © 2004 H. M. Queen Elizabeth II – EZM p. 126, 162; SC p. 72b, 83b; Rodney Todd-White p. 55a
London, SCT Enterprises Ltd p. 45b
Montreal, MBAM/MMFA – Denis Farley p. 134, 169
New York, The Frick Collection cover, p. 1, 108, 115, 152
New York, The MET–IRR p. 98a, 99, 109a; XR p. 96a, 104a/b, 107, 110
New York, The MET © 1981 p. 68, 92, 96b, 100, 102, 104c, 114; © 1982 p. 106d, 129, 165; © 1985 Malcolm Varon p. 82a; © 1986 p. 2a, 94a, 106c, 123a; ©1992 p. 62; © 2000 p. 82b; © 1996 Schecter Lee p. 86b
Paris, Photo RMN p. 27b, 37
Paris, Photo RMN – Arnaudet, J. Scho p. 36; J. G. Berizzi p. 76c, 77a; Gérard Blot p. 2b, 119, 155b; G. Blot – C. Jean p. 61; Harry Bréjat p. 58; C. Jean p. 47; H. Lewandowski p. 77b; H. Lewandowski-LeMage p. 84c
Philadelphia, John G. Johnson Collection p. 19; © 2003 Joe Mikuliak p. 86a
Venice, Soprintendenza speciale per il Polo Museale Veneziano p. 130, 166

Vicenza, Fototechnica Ceretta-Carta-Lago p. 23b, 148, 177
Washington, Image © 2004 Board of Trustees National Gallery p. 79, 87
Washington, Image © 2004 Board of Trustees National Gallery – Bob Grove p. 73; Lorene Emerson p. 2d, 95, 127, 163; Lyle Peterzell p. 81a
Weilheim, Artothek p. 89b
Weilheim, Artothek – Joachim Blauel p. 20a, 35; Blauel/Gnamm p. 20b; Bayer & Mitko p. 89a; Ursula Edelmann p. 113, 150, 151
Zürich, Kunsthaus tous droits réservés p. 12, 135

DATE